Frommer's®

PORTABLE

Maui

5th Edition

by Jeanette Foster

Here's what critics say about Frommer's:

"Amazingly easy to use. Very portable, very complete."
—*Booklist*

"Detailed, accurate, and easy-to-read information for all price ranges."
—*Glamour Magazine*

Wiley Publishing, Inc.

Published by:

WILEY PUBLISHING, INC.

111 River St.
Hoboken, NJ 07030-5774

ISBN: 978-0-470-16548-5

Editor: Christine Ryan
Production Editor: Michael Brumitt
Cartographer: Roberta Stockwell
Photo Editor: Richard Fox
Anniversary Logo Design: Richard Pacifico
Production by Wiley Indianapolis Composition Services

For information on our other products and services or to obtain technical
support, please contact our Customer Care Department within the U.S. at
800/762-2974, outside the U.S. at 317/572-3993 or fax 317/572-4002.

Wiley also publishes its books in a variety of electronic formats. Some con-
tent that appears in print may not be available in electronic formats.

Manufactured in the United States of America

5   4   3   2   1

Contents

List of Maps

ABOUT THE AUTHOR

A resident of the Big Island, **Jeanette Foster** has skied the slopes of Mauna Kea—during a Fourth of July ski meet, no less—and gone scuba diving with manta rays off the Kona Coast. A prolific writer widely published in travel, sports, and adventure magazines, she's also a contributing editor to *Hawaii* magazine and the editor of *Zagat's Survey to Hawaii's Top Restaurants*. In addition to this guide, Jeanette is the author of *Frommer's Hawaii 2008*, *Frommer's Maui 2008*, *Frommer's Honolulu, Waikiki & Oahu*, *Frommer's Hawaii with Kids*, *Frommer's Maui Day by Day* and *Frommer's Honolulu & Oahu Day by Day*.

AN INVITATION TO THE READER

In researching this book, we discovered many wonderful places—hotels, restaurants, shops, and more. We're sure you'll find others. Please tell us about them, so we can share the information with your fellow travelers in upcoming editions. If you were disappointed with a recommendation, we'd love to know that, too. Please write to:

Frommer's Portable Maui, 5th Edition
Wiley Publishing, Inc. • 111 River St. • Hoboken, NJ 07030-5774

AN ADDITIONAL NOTE

Please be advised that travel information is subject to change at any time—and this is especially true of prices. We therefore suggest that you write or call ahead for confirmation when making your travel plans. The authors, editors, and publisher cannot be held responsible for the experiences of readers while traveling. Your safety is important to us, however, so we encourage you to stay alert and be aware of your surroundings. Keep a close eye on cameras, purses, and wallets, all favorite targets of thieves and pickpockets.

FROMMER'S STAR RATINGS, ICONS & ABBREVIATIONS

Every hotel, restaurant, and attraction listing in this guide has been ranked for quality, value, service, amenities, and special features using a **star-rating system.** In country, state, and regional guides, we also rate towns and regions to help you narrow down your choices and budget your time accordingly. Hotels and restaurants are rated on a scale of zero (recommended) to three stars (exceptional). Attractions, shopping, nightlife, towns, and regions are rated according to the following scale: zero stars (recommended), one star (highly recommended), two stars (very highly recommended), and three stars (must-see).

In addition to the star-rating system, we also use **seven feature icons** that point you to the great deals, in-the-know advice, and unique experiences that separate travelers from tourists. Throughout the book, look for:

Finds	Special finds—those places only insiders know about
Fun Fact	Fun facts—details that make travelers more informed and their trips more fun
Kids	Best bets for kids and advice for the whole family
Moments	Special moments—those experiences that memories are made of
Overrated	Places or experiences not worth your time or money
Tips	Insider tips—some great ways to save time and money
Value	Great values—where to get the best deals

The following **abbreviations** are used for credit cards:

AE	American Express	DISC	Discover	V	Visa
DC	Diners Club	MC	MasterCard		

FROMMERS.COM

Now that you have this guidebook to help you plan a great trip, visit our website at **www.frommers.com** for additional travel information on more than 3,600 destinations. We update features regularly to give you instant access to the most current trip-planning information available. At Frommers.com, you'll find scoops on the best airfares, lodging rates, and car rental bargains. You can even book your travel online through our reliable travel booking partners. Other popular features include:

- Online updates of our most popular guidebooks
- Vacation sweepstakes and contest giveaways
- Newsletters highlighting the hottest travel trends
- Online travel message boards with featured travel discussions

Maui, the Valley Isle

Maui, also called the Valley Isle, is just a small dot in the vast Pacific Ocean, but it has the potential to offer visitors unforgettable experiences: floating weightless through rainbows of tropical fish, standing atop a 10,000-foot volcano watching the sunrise color the sky, and listening to the raindrops in a bamboo forest.

Whether you want to experience the "real" Hawaii, go on a heart-pounding adventure, or simply relax on the beach, this book is designed to help you create the vacation of your dreams.

In this chapter, I've compiled everything you need to know to plan your ideal trip to Maui: information on airlines, seasons, a calendar of events, and more.

1 The Island in Brief

CENTRAL MAUI

Maui's main airport lies in this flat, often windy corridor between Maui's two volcanoes. It's also home to the majority of the island's population. You'll find good shopping and dining bargains here but very little in the way of accommodations.

KAHULUI This is "Dream City," home to thousands of former sugar-cane workers who dreamed of owning their own homes away from the plantations. A couple of small hotels near the airport are convenient for 1-night stays if you have a late arrival or early departure, but this is not a place to spend your vacation.

WAILUKU With its faded wooden storefronts, old plantation homes, and shops straight out of the 1940s, Wailuku is like a time capsule. Although most people race through on their way to see the natural beauty of **Iao Valley** ★, this quaint little town is worth a brief visit, if only to see a real place where real people actually appear to be working at something other than a tan. Beaches surrounding Wailuku are not great for swimming, but the old town has a spectacular view of Haleakala, a couple of hostels and an excellent historic B&B, great budget restaurants, some interesting bungalow

Maui

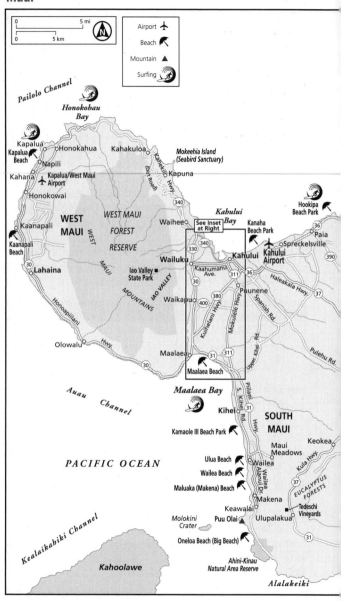

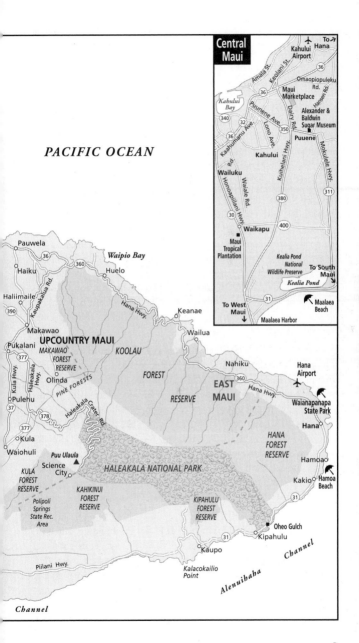

PACIFIC OCEAN

Central Maui

To Hana

Kahului Airport

Amala St.

Keolani St.

Omaopiopuleku Rd.

Maui Marketplace

Kahului Bay

Puunene Ave.

Lono Ave.

Dairy Rd.

Hansen Rd.

Alexander & Baldwin Sugar Museum

Puunene

Mokulele Hwy.

Kahului

Kaahumanu Ave.

Waiale Rd.

Kuihelani Hwy.

Wailuku

Honoapiilani Hwy.

Waikapu

Maui Tropical Plantation

Kealia Pond National Wildlife Preserve

To West Maui

To South Maui

Kealia Pond

Maalaea Beach

Maalaea Harbor

Pauwela

Waipio Bay

Haiku

Huelo

Haliimaile

Kaupakalua Rd.

Hana Hwy.

Keanae

Makawao

UPCOUNTRY MAUI

Wailua

Pukalani

MAKAWAO FOREST RESERVE

KOOLAU

Nahiku

Hana Airport

Kula Hwy.

Haleakala Hwy.

Olinda

PINE FORESTS

FOREST

EAST MAUI

Hana Hwy.

Waianapanapa State Park

Pulehu

Crater Rd.

Haleakala

RESERVE

Hana

Kula

Haleakala

HANA FOREST RESERVE

Waiohuli

Puu Ulaula

Science City

HALEAKALA NATIONAL PARK

Hamoao

Kakio

Hamoa Beach

KULA FOREST RESERVE

KAHIKINUI FOREST RESERVE

KIPAHULU FOREST RESERVE

Polipoli Springs State Rec. Area

Oheo Gulch

Kipahulu

Piilani Hwy.

Kaupo

Kalacokailio Point

Alenuihaha

Channel

Channel

3

architecture, a Frank Lloyd Wright building, and the always-endearing Bailey House Museum.

WEST MAUI

This is the fabled Maui you see on postcards. Jagged peaks, green valleys, a wilderness full of native species—the majestic West Maui Mountains are the epitome of earthly paradise. The beaches here are some of the islands' best. And it's no secret: This stretch of coastline along Maui's "forehead," from Kapalua to the historic port of Lahaina, is the island's most bustling resort area.

The coastal communities are listed from south to north below.

LAHAINA 🏵   This old whaling seaport teems with restaurants, T-shirt shops, and a gallery on nearly every block, but there's still lots of real history to be found amid the tourist development. This vintage village is a tame version of its former self, when whalers swaggered ashore in search of women and grog. The town is a great base for visitors: A few old hotels (like the restored 1901 Pioneer Inn on the harbor), quaint B&Bs, and a handful of oceanfront condos offer a variety of choices. This is the place to stay if you want to be in the center of things—restaurants, shops, and nightlife—but parking can be a problem.

KAANAPALI 🏵🏵   Farther north along the west Maui coast is Hawaii's first master-planned resort. Pricey mid-rise hotels, which line nearly 3 miles of lovely gold-sand beach, are linked by a landscaped parkway and separated by a jungle of plants. Golf greens wrap around the slope between beachfront and hillside properties. **Whalers Village** (a mall with pricey shops like Tiffany and Louis Vuitton, plus a great whale museum) and restaurants are easy to reach on foot along the waterfront walkway or via the resort shuttle, which also serves the small West Maui Airport to the north. Shuttles also go to Lahaina, 3 miles to the south, for shopping, dining, entertainment, and boat tours. Kaanapali is popular with convention groups and families.

FROM HONOKOWAI TO NAPILI   In the building binge of the 1970s, condominiums sprouted along this gorgeous coastline like mushrooms after a rain. Today these older ocean-side units offer excellent bargains for astute travelers. The great location—along sandy beaches, within minutes of both the Kapalua and the Kaanapali resort areas, and close to the goings-on in Lahaina—makes this area a great place to stay for value-conscious travelers. It feels more peaceful and residential than either Kaanapali or Lahaina.

In **Honokowai** and **Mahinahina** you'll find mostly older units that tend to be cheaper. There's not much shopping here aside from convenience stores, but you'll have easy access to the shops and restaurants of Kaanapali.

Kahana is a little more upscale than Honokowai and Mahinahina. Most of the condos here are big high-rise types, built more recently than those immediately to the south. You'll find a nice selection of shops and restaurants in the area, and Kapalua–West Maui Airport is nearby.

Napili is a much-sought-after area for condo seekers: It's quiet; has great beaches, restaurants, and shops; and is close to Kapalua. Units are generally more expensive here (although I've found a few affordable gems; see the Napili Bay entry on p. 52).

KAPALUA ℛ   North beyond Kaanapali and the shopping centers of Napili and Kahana, the road starts to climb, and the vista opens up to fields of silver-green pineapple and manicured golf fairways. Turn down the country lane of Pacific pines toward the sea, and you could only be in Kapalua. It's the very exclusive domain of the luxurious Ritz-Carlton Kapalua and expensive condos and villas, located next to two bays that are marine-life preserves (with fabulous surfing in winter).

Even if you don't stay here, you're welcome to come and enjoy Kapalua. There is public parking and beach access. The resort champions innovative environmental programs and also has an art school, a golf school, three golf courses, historic features, a collection of swanky condos and homes (many available for vacation rental at astronomical prices), and wide-open spaces that include a rainforest preserve—all open to the general public. Kapalua is a great place to stay put. However, if you plan to "tour" Maui, know that it's a long drive from here to get to many of the island's highlights. You might want to consider a more central place to stay because even Lahaina is a 15-minute drive away.

SOUTH MAUI

This is the hottest, sunniest, driest coastline on Maui—Arizona by the sea. Rain rarely falls, and temperatures stick around 85°F (29°C) year-round. On former scrubland from Maalaea to Makena, where cacti once grew wild and cows grazed, are now four distinct areas—Maalaea, Kihei, Wailea, and Makena—and a surprising amount of traffic.

MAALAEA If the western part of Maui were a head, Maalaea would be just under the chin. This windy oceanfront village centers around a small boat harbor (with a general store, a couple of restaurants, and a huge new mall) and the **Maui Ocean Center** ☆, an aquarium/ocean complex. This quaint region offers several condominium units to choose from, but visitors staying here should be aware that it is almost always very windy.

KIHEI   Kihei is less a proper town than a nearly continuous series of condos and minimalls lining South Kihei Road. This is Maui's best vacation bargain: Budget travelers flock to the eight sandy beaches along this scalloped, condo-packed, 7-mile stretch of coast. Kihei is neither charming nor quaint, but it does offer sunshine, affordability, and convenience. If you want a latte in the morning, fine beaches in the afternoon, and Hawaii Regional Cuisine in the evening, all at budget prices, head to Kihei.

WAILEA ☆   Only 3 decades ago, this was wall-to-wall scrub kiawe trees, but now Wailea is a manicured oasis of multimillion-dollar resort hotels strung along 2 miles of palm-fringed gold coast. It's like Beverly Hills by the sea, except California never had it so good: warm, clear water full of tropical fish; year-round sunshine and clear blue skies; and hedonistic pleasure palaces on 1,500 acres of black-lava shore. It's amazing what a billion dollars can do.

This is the playground of the private jet set. The planned resort development—practically a well-heeled town—has an upscale shopping village, three prized golf courses of its own and three more in close range, and a tennis complex. A growing number of large homes sprawls over the upper hillside (some offering excellent bed-and-breakfast units at reasonable prices).

Appealing natural features include the coastal trail, a 3-mile round-trip path along the oceanfront with pleasing views everywhere you look—out to sea and to the neighboring islands, or inland to the broad lawns and gardens of the hotels. The trail's south end borders an extensive garden of native coastal plants, as well as ancient lava-rock house ruins juxtaposed with elegant oceanfront condos. But the chief attractions, of course, are those five outstanding beaches (the best is Wailea).

MAKENA ☆   After passing through well-groomed Wailea, suddenly the road enters raw wilderness. After Wailea's overmanicured development, the thorny landscape is a welcome relief. Although beautiful, this is an end-of-the-road kind of place: It's a long drive from Makena to anywhere on Maui. If you want to tour a lot of the island, you might want to book somewhere else. But if you crave a quiet, relaxing respite, where the biggest trip of the day is from your bed to the gorgeous, pristine beach, Makena is your place.

Beyond Makena you'll discover Haleakala's last lava flow, which ran to the sea in 1790; the bay named for French explorer La Pérouse; and a chunky lava trail known as the King's Highway, which leads around Maui's empty south shore past ruins and fish camps. Puu Olai stands like Maui's Diamond Head on the shore, where a sunken crater shelters tropical fish, and empty golden-sand beaches stand at the end of dirt roads.

UPCOUNTRY MAUI

After a few days at the beach, you'll probably take notice of the 10,000-foot mountain in the middle of Maui. The slopes of Haleakala are home to cowboys, farmers, and other country people. They're all up here enjoying the crisp air, emerald pastures, eucalyptus, and flower farms of this tropical Olympus. You can see 1,000 tropical sunsets reflected in the windows of houses old and new, strung along a road that runs like a loose hound from Makawao, an old *paniolo*-(cowboy)-turned-New-Age village, to Kula, where the road leads up to the crater and **Haleakala National Park** 🐾🐾🐾. A stay upcountry is usually affordable, a chance to commune with nature, and a nice contrast to the sizzling beaches and busy resorts below.

MAKAWAO 🐾   Until recently, this small, two-street upcountry town consisted of little more than a post office, gas station, feed store, bakery, and restaurant/bar serving the cowboys and farmers living in the surrounding community. As the population of Maui started expanding in the 1970s, a health-food store popped up, followed by boutiques and a host of health-conscious restaurants. The result is an eclectic amalgam of old *paniolo* Hawaii and the baby-boomer trends of transplanted mainlanders. **Hui No'eau Visual Arts Center** (p. 164), Hawaii's premier arts collective, is definitely worth a peek. The only accommodations here are reasonably priced bed-and-breakfasts, perfect for those who enjoy great views and don't mind slightly chilly nights.

KULA 🐾   A feeling of pastoral remoteness prevails in this upcountry community of old flower farms, humble cottages, and new suburban ranch houses with million-dollar views that take in the ocean, isthmus, West Maui Mountains, Lanai, and Kahoolawe off in the distance. At night the lights run along the gold coast like a string of pearls, from Maalaea to Puu Olai. Kula sits at a cool 3,000 feet, just below the cloud line, and from here a winding road snakes its way up to Haleakala National Park. Everyone here grows something—Maui onions, carnations, orchids, and proteas, those strange-looking blossoms that look like *Star Trek* props. The local B&Bs cater to guests seeking cool tropical nights, panoramic views, and a rural upland escape. Here you'll find the true peace and quiet that only rural farming country can offer—yet you're still just 30 to 40 minutes away from the beach and an hour's drive from Lahaina.

EAST MAUI

THE ROAD TO HANA 🐾🐾   When old sugar towns die, they usually fade away in rust and red dirt. Not **Paia.** The tangle of electrical, phone, and cable wires hanging overhead symbolizes the town's ability to adapt to the times. Here, trendy restaurants, eclectic boutiques, and high-tech windsurf shops stand next door to the ma-and-pa grocery, fish market, and storefronts that have been serving customers since the plantation days. Hippies took over in the 1970s, and although their macrobiotic restaurants and old-style artists' co-op have made way for Hawaii Regional Cuisine and galleries featuring the works of renowned international artists, Paia still manages to maintain a pleasant vibe of hippiedom. The town's main attraction, though, is **Hookipa Beach Park,** where the wind that roars through the isthmus of Maui brings windsurfers from around the world.

Ten minutes down the road from Paia and up the hill from the Hana Highway—the connector road to the entire east side of Maui—sits **Haiku.** Once a pineapple-plantation village, complete with cannery (today a shopping complex), Haiku offers vacation rentals and B&Bs in a quiet, pastoral setting: the perfect base for those who want to get off the beaten path and experience a quieter side of Maui but don't want to feel too removed (the beach is only 10 min. away).

About 15 to 20 minutes past Haiku is the largely unknown community of **Huelo.** Every day thousands of cars whiz by on the road to Hana. But if you take the time to stop, you'll discover a hidden Hawaii, where Mother Nature is still sensual and wild, where ocean waves pummel soaring lava cliffs, and where serenity prevails. Huelo is not for everyone, but if you want the magic of a place still largely untouched by "progress," check in to a B&B or vacation rental here.

HANA 🐾🐾   Set between an emerald rainforest and the blue Pacific is a village probably best defined by what it lacks: golf courses, shopping malls, and McDonald's. Except for two gas stations and a bank with an ATM, you'll find little of what passes for progress here. Instead, you'll discover fragrant tropical flowers, the sweet taste of backyard bananas and papayas, and the easy calm and unabashed small-town aloha spirit of old Hawaii. What saved "Heavenly" Hana from the inevitable march of progress? The 52-mile **Hana Highway,** which winds around 600 curves and crosses more than 50 one-lane bridges on its way from Kahului. You can go to Hana for the day—it's a 3-hour drive (and a half-century away)—but 3 days are better. The tiny town has one hotel, a handful of great B&Bs, and some spectacular vacation rentals.

2 Visitor Information & Maps

For advance information on traveling in Maui, contact the **Maui Visitors Bureau,** 1727 Wili Pa Loop, Wailuku, Maui, HI 96793 (© **800/525-MAUI** or 808/244-3530; fax 808/244-1337; www. visitmaui.com).

The **Kaanapali Beach Resort Association** is at 2530 Kekaa Dr., Suite 1-B, Lahaina, HI 96761 (© **800/245-9229** or 808/661-3271; fax 808/661-9431; www.kaanapaliresort.com).

The state agency responsible for tourism is the **Hawaii Visitors and Convention Bureau (HVCB),** Suite 801, Waikiki Business Plaza, 2270 Kalakaua Ave., Honolulu, HI 96815 (© **800/GO-HAWAII** or 808/923-1811; www.gohawaii.com).

If you want information about working and living in Maui, contact the **Maui Chamber of Commerce,** 250 Alamaha St., Unit N-16A, Kahului, HI 96732 (© **808/871-7711;** www.mauichamber.com).

INFORMATION ON MAUI'S PARKS

NATIONAL PARKS   Maui has one national park: **Haleakala National Park,** P.O. Box 369, Makawao, HI 96768 (© **808/ 572-4400;** www.nps.gov/hale). For more information, see "Hiking" in chapter 4.

STATE PARKS   To find out more about state parks on Maui, contact the **Hawaii State Department of Land and Natural Resources,** 54 S. High St., Wailuku, HI 96793 (© **808/984-8109;** www.hawaii.gov), which provides information on hiking and camping. For free topographic trail maps, call the State Department of Forestry at © **808/984-8100.**

COUNTY PARKS   For information on Maui County Parks, contact **Maui County Parks and Recreation,** 1580-C Kaahumanu Ave., Wailuku, HI 96793 (© **808/270-7230;** www.co.maui.hi.us/departments/Parks/Recware).

3 Entry Requirements

PASSPORTS

For information on how to get a passport, go to **"Passports"** in the **"Fast Facts: Maui"** section, later in this chapter. For an up-to-date, country-by-country listing of passport requirements around the world, go to **http://travel.state.gov** and enter "foreign entry requirements" in the search box. International visitors can obtain a visa application at the same website. *Note:* Children are required to present a passport when entering the United States at airports. More information on obtaining a passport for a minor can be found at http://travel.state.gov.

VISAS

For specifics on how to get a visa, go to **"Visas"** in the **"Fast Facts: Maui"** section, later in this chapter.

The U.S. State Department has a **Visa Waiver Program (VWP)** allowing citizens of the following countries (at press time) to enter the United States without a visa for stays of up to 90 days: Andorra, Australia, Austria, Belgium, Brunei, Denmark, Finland, France, Germany, Iceland, Ireland, Italy, Japan, Liechtenstein, Luxembourg, Monaco, the Netherlands, New Zealand, Norway, Portugal, San Marino, Singapore, Slovenia, Spain, Sweden, Switzerland, and the United Kingdom. Canadian citizens may enter the United States without visas; they will need to show passports and proof of residence, however. *Note:* Any passport issued on or after October 26, 2006, by a VWP country must be an **e-Passport** for VWP travelers to be eligible to enter the U.S. without a visa. Citizens of these nations also need to present a round-trip air or cruise ticket upon arrival. E-Passports contain computer chips capable of storing

---

U.S. Entry: Passport Required

New regulations issued by the Homeland Security Department now require virtually every air traveler entering the U.S. to show a passport—and future regulations will cover land and sea entry as well. As of January 23, 2007, all persons, including U.S. citizens, traveling by air between the United States and Canada, Mexico, Central and South America, the Caribbean, and Bermuda are required to present a valid passport. Similar regulations for those traveling by land or sea (including ferries) are expected as early as January 1, 2008.

biometric information, such as the required digital photograph of the holder. (You can identify an e-Passport by the symbol on the bottom center cover of your passport.) If your passport doesn't have this feature, you can still travel without a visa if it is a valid passport issued before October 26, 2005, and includes a machine-readable zone, or between October 26, 2005, and October 25, 2006, and includes a digital photograph. For more information, go to **www. travel.state.gov/visa**.

Citizens of all other countries must have (1) a valid passport that expires at least 6 months later than the scheduled end of their visit to the United States, and (2) a tourist visa, which may be obtained without charge from any U.S. consulate.

As of January 2004, many international visitors traveling on visas to the United States will be photographed and fingerprinted on arrival at Customs in airports and on cruise ships in a program created by the Department of Homeland Security called **US-VISIT.** Exempt from the extra scrutiny are visitors entering by land or those (mostly in Europe; see p. 10) who don't require a visa for short-term visits. For more information, go to the Homeland Security website at **www.dhs.gov/dhspublic**.

CUSTOMS

For information on what you can bring into and take out of Maui, go to **"Customs"** in the **"Fast Facts: Maui"** section, later in this chapter.

4 When to Go

Most visitors don't come to Maui when the weather's best in the islands; rather, they come when it's at its worst everywhere else. Thus, the **high season**—when prices are up and resorts are booked to capacity—generally runs from mid-December through March or mid-April. The last 2 weeks of December in particular are the prime time for travel to Maui. Whale-watching season begins in January and continues through the rest of winter, sometimes lasting into May.

The **off seasons,** when the best bargain rates are available, are spring (mid-Apr to mid-June) and fall (Sept to mid-Dec)—a paradox, since these are the best seasons in terms of reliably great weather. If you're looking to save money, or if you just want to avoid the crowds, this is the time to visit.

Note: If you plan to come to Maui between the last week in April and the first week in May, be sure to book your accommodations, interisland air reservations, and car rental in advance. In Japan the last week of April is called **Golden Week,** because three Japanese holidays take place one after the other. The islands are especially busy with Japanese tourists during this time.

Due to the large number of families traveling in **summer** (June–Aug), you won't get the fantastic bargains of spring and fall. However, you'll still do much better on packages, airfare, and accommodations than you will in the winter months.

THE WEATHER

Because Maui lies at the edge of the tropical zone, it technically has only two seasons, both of them warm. The dry season corresponds to summer, and the rainy season generally runs during the winter, from November to March. Fortunately, it seldom rains for more than 3 days straight, and rainy days often just consist of a mix of clouds and sun, with very brief showers.

The **year-round temperature** usually varies no more than 15°, but it depends on where you are. Maui's **leeward** sides (the west and south) are usually hot and dry, whereas the **windward** sides (east and north) are generally cooler and moist. If you want arid, sun-baked, desertlike weather, go leeward. If you want lush, often wet, junglelike weather, go windward. Your best bets for total year-round sun are the Kihei-Wailea and Lahaina-Kapalua coasts.

Maui is also full of **microclimates,** thanks to its interior valleys, coastal plains, and mountain peaks. If you travel into the mountains, it can change from summer to winter in a matter of hours, because it's cooler the higher up you go. In other words, if the weather doesn't suit you, go to the other side of the island—or head into the hills.

HOLIDAYS

When Hawaii observes holidays, especially those over a long weekend, travel between the islands increases, interisland airline seats are fully booked, rental cars are at a premium, and hotels and restaurants are busier than usual.

Federal, state, and county government offices are closed on all federal holidays: January 1 (New Year's Day); third Monday in January (Martin Luther King Day); third Monday in February (Presidents' Day, Washington's Birthday); last Monday in May (Memorial Day); July 4th (Independence Day); first Monday in September (Labor Day); second Monday in October (Columbus Day); November 11 (Veterans Day); fourth Thursday in November (Thanksgiving Day); and December 25 (Christmas Day).

State and county offices also are closed on local holidays, including Prince Kuhio Day (Mar 26), honoring the birthday of Hawaii's first delegate to the U.S. Congress; King Kamehameha Day (June 11), a statewide holiday commemorating Kamehameha the Great, who united the islands and ruled from 1795 to 1819; and Admission Day (third Fri in Aug), which honors Hawaii's admission as the 50th state in the United States on August 21, 1959.

MAUI CALENDAR OF EVENTS

As with any schedule of upcoming events, the following information is subject to change; always confirm the details before you plan your schedule around an event. For an exhaustive list of events beyond those mentioned here, check **www.visitmaui.com**, **www.molokai-hawaii.com**, or **www.visitlanai.net** for events throughout Maui, or http://events.frommers.com, where you'll find a searchable, up-to-the-minute roster of what's happening in cities all over the world.

January

PGA Kapalua Mercedes Championship, Kapalua Resort. Top PGA golfers compete for $1 million. Call ☎ **808/669-2440** or visit www.kapaluamaui.com. Early January.

February

Whale Day Celebration, Kalama Park, Kihei. A daylong celebration in the park with a parade of whales, entertainment, a crafts fair, games, and food. Call ☎ **808/249-8811** or visit www.visitmaui.com. Early or mid-February.

March

Ocean Arts Festival, Lahaina. The entire town of Lahaina celebrates the annual migration of Pacific humpback whales with an Ocean Arts Festival in Banyan Tree Park. Artists display their best ocean-themed art for sale, and Hawaiian musicians and hula troupes entertain. Enjoy marine-related activities, games, and a Creature Feature touch-pool exhibit for children. Call ☎ **888/310-1117** or 808/667-9194, or visit www.visitlahaina.com. Mid-March.

Run to the Sun, Paia to Haleakala. The world's top ultramarathoners make the journey from sea level to the top of 10,000-foot Haleakala, some 37 miles. Call ☎ **808/280-4893** or visit www.virr.com. March 22, 2008.

April

Buddha Day, Lahaina Jodo Mission, Lahaina. Each year this historic mission holds a flower festival pageant honoring the birth of Buddha. Call ☎ **808/661-4303** or visit www.calendarmaui.com. Early April.

Banyan Tree Birthday Party, Lahaina. Come celebrate the birthday of Lahaina's famous Banyan Tree with a weekend of activities. Call ✆ **888/310-1117** or 808/667-9175, or visit www.visit lahaina.com. April 26 and 27, 2008.

East Maui Taro Festival, Hana. Here's your chance to taste taro in many different forms, from poi to chips. Also on hand are Hawaiian exhibits, demonstrations, and food booths. Call ✆ **808/ 264-3336** or visit www.calendarmaui.com. Generally late April.

May

Outrigger Canoe Season, all islands. From May to September nearly every weekend, canoe paddlers across the state participate in outrigger canoe races. Call ✆ **808/383-7790** or go to www. y2kanu.com for this year's schedule of events.

Annual Lei Day Celebration, Fairmont Kea Lani, Wailea. May Day is Lei Day in Hawaii, celebrated with lei-making contests, pageantry, arts and crafts, and concerts throughout the islands. Call ✆ **808/224-6042** or go to www.visitmaui.com. May 1.

International Festival of Canoes, west Maui. Celebration of the Pacific islands' seafaring heritage. Events include canoe paddling and sailing regattas, a luau feast, cultural arts demonstrations, canoe-building exhibits, and music. Call ✆ **888/310-1117** or visit www.mauicanoefest.com. Mid- to late May.

June

King Kamehameha Celebration, statewide. It's a state holiday with a massive floral parade, *hoolaulea* (parties), and much more. Call ✆ **888/310-1117** or 808/667-9194, or go to www.visit lahaina.com for Maui events; call ✆ **808/567-6361** for Molokai events. June 6 and 7, 2008.

Maui Film Festival, Wailea Resort. Five days and nights of screenings of premieres and special films, along with traditional Hawaiian storytelling, chants, hula, and contemporary music. Call ✆ **808/572-3456** or 808/579-9244, or go to www.maui filmfestival.com. Beginning the Wednesday before Father's Day, June 11 to June 15, 2008.

Hawaiian Slack Key Guitar Festival, Maui Arts and Cultural Center, Kahului. Great music performed by the best musicians in Hawaii. It's 5 hours long and absolutely free. Call ✆ **808/ 226-2697** or visit www.hawaiianslackkeyguitarfestivals.com. Late June.

July

Makawao Parade and Rodeo, Makawao, Maui. The annual parade and rodeo event have been taking place in this upcountry cowboy town for generations. Call ✆ **808/572-9565.** July 4.

Kapalua Wine and Food Festival, Kapalua. Famous wine and food experts and oenophiles gather at the Ritz-Carlton and Kapalua Bay hotels for formal tastings, panel discussions, and samplings of new releases. Call ✆ **800/KAPALUA** or go to www. kapaluaresort.com. Usually early July.

August

Maui Onion Festival, Whalers Village, Kaanapali, Maui. Everything you ever wanted to know about the sweetest onions in the world. Food, entertainment, tasting, and the Maui Onion Cook-Off. Call ✆ **808/661-4567** or go to www.whalersvillage.com. Early August.

Hawaii State Windsurf Championship, Kanaha Beach Park, Kahului. Top windsurfers compete. Call ✆ **808/877-2111.** Early August.

September

Aloha Festivals, various locations. Parades and other events celebrate Hawaiian culture. Call ✆ **800/852-7690** or 808/545-1771, or visit www.alohafestivals.com for a schedule of events.

A Taste of Lahaina, Lahaina Civic Center, Maui. Some 30,000 people show up to sample 40 signature entrees of Maui's premier chefs during this weekend festival, which includes cooking demonstrations, wine tastings, and live entertainment. The event begins Friday night with Maui Chefs Present, a themed dinner/cocktail party featuring about a dozen of Maui's best chefs. Call ✆ **888/310-1117** or 808/667-9194, or visit www.visit lahaina.com. Early September.

Maui Marathon, Kahului to Kaanapali, Maui. Runners line up at the Maui Mall before daybreak and head off for Kaanapali. Call ✆ **866/577-8379,** or visit www.virr.com or www.maui marathon.com. September 19, 20, and 21, 2008.

Maui County Fair, War Memorial Complex, Wailuku. The oldest county fair in Hawaii features a parade, amusement rides, live entertainment, and exhibits. Call ✆ **800/525-MAUI** or in July call 808/242-2721, or visit www.mauicountyfair.com. Last week in September or first week in October.

October

Aloha Festivals Ho'olaule'a, Lahaina. This all-day cultural festival, which culminates the end of Maui island's Aloha Festivals Week, is held at Banyan Tree Park and features Hawaiian food, music, and dance, along with arts and crafts on display and for sale. Call © **888/310-1117** or 808/667-9194 or visit www.visit lahaina.com. September or October.

Halloween in Lahaina, Maui. There's Carnival in Rio, Mardi Gras in New Orleans, and Halloween in Lahaina. Come to this giant costume party (some 20,000 people show up) on the streets of Lahaina; Front Street is closed off for the party. Call © **888/310-1117** or 808/667-9194, or go to www.visitlahaina.com. October 31.

November

Hula O Na Keiki, Kaanapali Beach Hotel, Kaanapali. Solo hula competition for children ages 5 to 17. In its 18th year, this weekend festival celebrates Hawaiian dance, arts, and music. Call © 808/661-0011 or visit www.kbhmaui.com. Early November.

Hawaii International Film Festival, various locations on Maui. A cinema festival with a cross-cultural spin, featuring filmmakers from Asia, the Pacific Islands, and the United States. Call © **808/ 550-8457** or visit www.hiff.org. Mid-November.

December

Hui Noeau Christmas House, Makawao. The festivities in the beautifully decorated Hui mansion include shopping, workshops and art demonstrations, children's activities and visits with Santa, holiday music, fresh-baked goods, and local foods. Call © **808/572-6560** or go to www.huinoeau.com. Late November and early December.

Festival of Lights, island-wide. Festivities include parades and tree-lighting ceremonies. Call © **808/667-9175** on Maui or 808/552-2800 on Molokai. Early December.

First Light 2008, Maui Arts and Cultural Center, Maui. The Academy of Motion Pictures holds major screenings of top films. Not to be missed. Call © **808/572-3456** or go to www. mauifilmfestival.com. Mid-December to early January.

5 Getting There

BY PLANE

If you think of the island of Maui as the shape of a head and shoulders of a person, you'll probably arrive on its neck, at **Kahului Airport.** If you're headed for Molokai or Lanai, you'll have to connect through Honolulu.

At press time seven airlines flew directly from the U.S. mainland to Kahului: **United Airlines** (✆ 800/241-6522; www.ual.com) offers daily nonstop flights from San Francisco and Los Angeles; **Aloha Airlines** (✆ 800/367-5250; www.alohaair.com) has nonstop service from Oakland, Sacramento, Orange County, and San Diego; **Hawaiian Airlines** (✆ 800/367-5320; www.hawaiianair.com) has direct flights from San Diego, Portland, and Seattle; **American Airlines** (✆ 800/433-7300; www.aa.com) flies direct from Los Angeles and San Jose; **Delta Airlines** (✆ 800/221-1212; www.delta.com) offers direct flights from San Francisco and Los Angeles; **America West** (✆ 800/327-7810; www.americawest.com) has nonstop service between Maui and Las Vegas; and **American Trans Air** (✆ 800/435-9282; www.ata.com) has direct flights from Los Angeles, San Francisco, and Phoenix.

The other carriers—including **Continental** (✆ 800/525-0280; www.continental.com) and **Northwest Airlines** (✆ 800/225-2525; www.nwa.com)—fly to Honolulu, where you'll have to pick up an interisland flight to Maui. (The airlines listed in the paragraph above also offer many more flights to Honolulu from additional cities on the mainland.) Both **Aloha Airlines** and **Hawaiian Airlines** offer jet service from Honolulu. See "Interisland Flights," below.

LANDING AT KAHULUI AIRPORT

If there's a long wait at baggage claim, step over to the state-operated **Visitor Information Center,** where you can pick up brochures and the latest issue of *This Week Maui,* which features great regional maps of the islands. After collecting your bags, step outside to the curbside rental-car pickup area. (All major rental companies have branches at Kahului; see "Getting Around Maui" later in this chapter.)

If you're not renting a car, the cheapest way to get to your hotel is **SpeediShuttle** (✆ 877/242-5777; www.speedishuttle.com), which can take you from Kahului Airport to any one of the major resorts between 5am and 11pm daily. Rates vary, but figure on $33 for one to Wailea (one-way), $46 one-way to Kaanapali, and $63 one-way to Kapalua. Be sure to call before your flight to arrange pickup.

You'll see taxis outside the airport terminal, but note that they are quite expensive—expect to spend around $60 to $75 for a ride from Kahului to Kaanapali and $50 from the airport to Wailea.

If possible, avoid landing on Maui between 3 and 6pm, when the working stiffs on Maui are "pau work" (finished with work) and a major traffic jam occurs at the first intersection.

IMMIGRATION & CUSTOMS CLEARANCE

Foreign visitors arriving by air, no matter what the port of entry, should cultivate patience and resignation before setting foot on U.S. soil. U.S. airports have considerably beefed up security clearances in the years since the terrorist attacks of September 11, 2001, and clearing Customs and Immigration can take as long as 2 hours.

People traveling by air from Canada, Bermuda, and certain Caribbean countries can sometimes clear Customs and Immigration at the point of departure, which is much faster.

INTERISLAND FLIGHTS

Aloha Airlines (✆ **800/367-5250** or 808/244-9071; www.aloha air.com) is the state's largest provider of interisland air transport service. It offers 15 regularly scheduled daily jet flights a day from Honolulu to Maui on their all-jet fleet of Boeing 737 aircraft.

Hawaiian Airlines (✆ **800/367-5320** or 808/871-6132; www. hawaiianair.com) is Hawaii's other interisland airline featuring jet planes.

In 2006 a new airline entered the Hawaiian market. Owned by Mesa Air Group (which has more than 1,000 flights to 166 cities across the U.S., Canada, and Mexico), **go!** (✆ **888/IFLYGO2;** www.iflygo.com) began service with 50-passenger Bombardier CRJ200 jets with service from Honolulu to Maui, Kauai, and both Hilo and Kona on the Big Island.

In 2007 visitors to Molokai and Lanai got not one but two new commuter airlines that began flying from Honolulu to Molokai and Lanai. go! started a new commuter service from Honolulu to Molokai and Lanai under the name **go!Express,** on their new fleet of Cessna Grand Caravan 208B planes. Another commuter airline, **Pacific Wings,** started operating a discount airline, **PW Express** (✆ **888/866-5022** or 808/873-0877; www.flypwx.com) with daily nonstop flights between Honolulu and Molokai and Lanai, plus flights from Kahului, Maui, and Molokai.

Island Air (✆ **800/323-3345** or 808/484-2222) serves Hawaii's small interisland airports on Maui, Molokai, and Lanai and operates deHavilland DASH-8 and DASH-6 turboprop aircraft. Although I have to tell you that I have not had stellar service from Island Air and would recommend you book on go!Express or PW Express if you are headed to Molokai or Lanai.

THE SUPERFERRY

As we went to press, the Hawaii legislature approved the long-awaited Superferry (www.hawaiisuperferry.com), scheduled to begin service between Honolulu and Kauai and Honolulu and Maui in summer 2007. If you buy tickets online at least 14 days in advance, fares are $44 off-peak (Tues–Thurs), $55 peak (Fri–Mon) one-way. The regular fare is $52 off-peak or $62 peak. Tickets for children (2–12) and seniors (62 and over) cost $41 off-peak, $51 peak. Tickets for infants under 2 cost $17.

Vehicles are charged separately, in addition to the passenger fares above. The fare for a car or SUV is $59 off-peak, $69 peak.

The 3-hour trip from Honolulu to Maui or Kauai will be offered once daily 6 days a week (no Sat service). The company hopes to add a second ferry in 2009 and a 4^1/$_2$-hour service from Honolulu to the Big Island.

6 Money & Costs

It's always advisable to bring money in a variety of forms on a vacation: a mix of cash, credit cards, and traveler's checks. You should also exchange enough petty cash to cover airport incidentals, tipping, and transportation to your hotel before you leave home, or withdraw money upon arrival at an airport ATM.

ATMs

Hawaii pioneered the use of **ATMs** more than 2 decades ago, and now they're everywhere. You'll find them at most banks, in supermarkets, at Longs Drugs, and in most resorts and shopping centers. **Cirrus** (© 800/424-7787; www.mastercard.com) and **PLUS** (© 800/843-7587; www.visa.com) are the two most popular networks; check the back of your ATM card to see which network your bank belongs to (most banks belong to both these days).

Be sure you know your personal identification number (PIN) and daily withdrawal limit before you depart. *Note:* Remember that many banks impose a fee every time you use a card at another bank's ATM, and that fee can be higher for international transactions (up to $5 or more) than for domestic ones (where they're rarely more than $2). In addition, the bank from which you withdraw cash may charge its own fee. To compare banks' ATM fees within the U.S., use **www.bankrate.com**.

CREDIT CARDS & DEBIT CARDS

Credit cards are the most widely used form of payment in the United States: **Visa** (Barclaycard in Britain), **MasterCard** (EuroCard in Europe, Access in Britain, Chargex in Canada), **American Express,**

Diners Club, and **Discover.** They also provide a convenient record of all your expenses and offer relatively good exchange rates. You can withdraw cash advances from your credit cards at banks or ATMs, but high fees make credit card cash advances a pricey way to get cash.

It's highly recommended that you travel with at least one major credit card. You must have a credit card to rent a car, and hotels and airlines usually require a credit card imprint as a deposit against expenses.

ATM cards with major credit card backing, known as **"debit cards,"** are now a commonly acceptable form of payment in most stores and restaurants. Debit cards draw money directly from your checking account. Some stores enable you to receive cash back on your debit card purchases as well. The same is true at most U.S. post offices.

Visitors from outside the U.S. should also find out whether their bank assesses a 1% to 3% fee on charges incurred abroad.

TRAVELER'S CHECKS

Though credit cards and debit cards are more often used, traveler's checks are still widely accepted in the U.S. Foreign visitors should make sure that traveler's checks are denominated in U.S. dollars; foreign-currency checks are often difficult to exchange.

You can buy traveler's checks at most banks. The most popular traveler's checks are offered by **American Express** (✆ **800/807-6233;** ✆ **800/221-7282** for card holders—this number accepts collect calls, offers service in several foreign languages, and exempts Amex gold and platinum cardholders from the 1% fee); **Visa** (✆ **800/732-1322**)—AAA members can obtain Visa checks for a $9.95 fee (for checks up to $1,500) at most AAA offices or by calling ✆ **866/339-3378;** and **MasterCard** (✆ **800/223-9920**).

Be sure to keep a copy of the traveler's check serial numbers separate from your checks in the event that they are stolen or lost. You'll get a refund faster if you know the numbers.

Another option is the new **prepaid traveler's check cards,** reloadable cards that work much like debit cards but aren't linked to your checking account. The **American Express Travelers Cheque Card,** for example, requires a minimum deposit ($300), sets a maximum balance ($2,750), and has a one-time issuance fee of $14.95. You can withdraw money from an ATM ($2.50 per transaction, not including bank fees), and the funds can be purchased in dollars, euros, or pounds. If you lose the card, your available funds will be refunded within 24 hours.

7 Travel Insurance

The cost of travel insurance varies widely, depending on the cost and length of your trip, your age and health, and the type of trip you're taking, but expect to pay between 5% and 8% of the vacation itself. You can get estimates from various providers through **Insure MyTrip.com.** Enter your trip cost and dates, your age, and other information, for prices from more than a dozen companies.

For **U.K. citizens,** insurance is always advisable when traveling in the States. Check **www.moneysupermarket.com**, which compares prices across a wide range of providers for single- and multi-trip policies. **The Association of British Insurers** (© 020/7600-3333; www.abi.org.uk) gives advice by phone and publishes *Holiday Insurance,* a free guide to policy provisions and prices. You might also shop around for better deals: Try **Columbus Direct** (© 0870/ 033-9988; www.columbusdirect.net).

TRIP-CANCELLATION INSURANCE

Trip-cancellation insurance will help retrieve your money if you have to back out of a trip or depart early, or if your travel supplier goes bankrupt. Trip cancellation traditionally covers such events as sickness, natural disasters, and State Department advisories. The latest news in trip-cancellation insurance is the availability of **expanded hurricane coverage** and the **"any-reason"** cancellation coverage—which costs more but covers cancellations made for any reason. You won't get back 100% of your prepaid trip cost, but you'll be refunded a substantial portion. **TravelSafe** (© 888/885-7233; www.travel safe.com) offers both types of coverage. Expedia also offers any-reason cancellation coverage for its air-hotel packages.

For details, contact one of the following recommended insurers: **Access America** (© 866/807-3982; www.accessamerica.com), **Travel Guard International** (© 800/826-4919; www.travel guard.com), **Travel Insured International** (© 800/243-3174; www.travelinsured.com), or **Travelex Insurance Services** (© 888/ 457-4602; www.travelex-insurance.com).

MEDICAL INSURANCE

Although it's not required of travelers, health insurance is highly recommended. Most health insurance policies cover you if you get sick away from home—but check your coverage before you leave.

International visitors should note that unlike many European countries, the United States does not usually offer free or low-cost medical care to its citizens or visitors. Doctors and hospitals are expensive, and in most cases will require advance payment or proof of coverage before they render their services. Good policies will cover the costs of an accident, repatriation, or death. Packages such as **Europ Assistance's "Worldwide Healthcare Plan"** are sold by European automobile clubs and travel agencies at attractive rates. **Worldwide Assistance Services, Inc.** (© **800/777-8710;** www. worldwideassistance.com) is the agent for Europ Assistance in the United States.

Though lack of health insurance may prevent you from being admitted to a hospital in nonemergencies, don't worry about being left on a street corner to die: The American way is to fix you now and bill the living daylights out of you later.

If you're ever hospitalized more than 150 miles from home, **MedjetAssist** (© **800/527-7478;** www.medjetassistance.com) will pick you up and fly you to the hospital of your choice in a medically equipped and staffed aircraft 24 hours day, 7 days a week. Annual memberships are $225 individual, $350 family; you can also purchase short-term memberships.

LOST-LUGGAGE INSURANCE

On flights within the U.S., checked baggage is covered up to $2,500 per ticketed passenger. On flights outside the U.S. (and on U.S. portions of international trips), baggage coverage is limited to approximately $9.07 per pound, up to approximately $635 per checked bag. If you plan to check items more valuable than what's covered by the standard liability, see if your homeowner's policy covers your valuables or get baggage insurance, such as Travel Guard's "BagTrak" product.

If your luggage is lost, immediately file a lost-luggage claim at the airport, detailing the luggage contents. Most airlines require that you report delayed, damaged, or lost baggage within 4 hours of arrival. The airlines are required to deliver luggage, once found, directly to your house or destination free of charge.

8 Specialized Travel Resources

TRAVELERS WITH DISABILITIES

Most disabilities shouldn't stop anyone from traveling in the U.S. There are more options and resources out there than ever before.

Travelers with disabilities are made to feel very welcome in Maui. Hotels are usually equipped with wheelchair-accessible rooms, and tour companies provide many special services. The **Hawaii Center**

for Independent Living, 414 Kauwili St., Suite 102, Honolulu, HI 96817 (© **808/522-5400;** fax 808/586-8129), can provide information.

The only travel agency in Hawaii specializing in needs for travelers with disabilities is **Access Aloha Travel** (© **800/480-1143;** www.accessalohatravel.com), which can book anything, including rental vans, accommodations, tours, cruises, airfare, and just about anything else you can think of.

The following travel agencies don't specialize in Hawaii travel, but they offer customized tours and itineraries for travelers with disabilities. **Flying Wheels Travel** (© **507/451-5005;** www.flying wheelstravel.com); **Access-Able Travel Source** (© **303/232-2979;** www.access-able.com); and **Accessible Journeys** (© **800/846-4537** or 610/521-0339; www.disabilitytravel.com).

For travelers with disabilities who wish to do their own driving, hand-controlled cars can be rented from **Avis** (© **800/331-1212;** www.avis.com) and **Hertz** (© **800/654-3131;** www.hertz.com). The number of hand-controlled cars in Hawaii is limited, so be sure to book well in advance. For wheelchair-accessible vans, contact **Accessible Vans of Hawaii,** 186 Mehani Circle, Kihei (© **800/303-3750** or 808/545-1143; fax 808/545-7657; www.accessaloha travel.com). Maui recognizes other states' windshield placards indicating that the driver of the car is disabled, so be sure to bring yours with you.

Vision-impaired travelers who use a Seeing Eye dog can now come to Hawaii without the hassle of quarantine. A recent court decision ruled that visitors with Seeing Eye dogs only need to present documentation that the dog is a trained Seeing Eye dog and has had rabies shots. For more information, contact the Animal Quarantine Facility (© **808/483-7171;** www.hawaii.gov/hdoa).

The **America the Beautiful—National Park and Federal Recreational Lands Pass—Access Pass** (formerly the **Golden Access Passport**) gives the visually impaired or those with permanent disabilities (regardless of age) free lifetime entrance to federal recreation sites administered by the National Park Service. This may include national parks, monuments, historic sites, recreation areas, and national wildlife refuges.

The American the Beautiful Access Pass can only be obtained in person at any NPS facility that charges an entrance fee. You need to show proof of medically determined disability. For more information, go to www.nps.gov/fees_passes.htm or call © **888/467-2757.**

Organizations that offer a vast range of resources and assistance to travelers with disabilities include **MossRehab** (© 800/CALL-MOSS; www.mossresourcenet.org); the **American Foundation for the Blind** (AFB; © 800/232-5463; www.afb.org); and **SATH** (Society for Accessible Travel & Hospitality; © 212/447-7284; www.sath.org). **AirAmbulanceCard.com** is now partnered with SATH and allows you to preselect top-notch hospitals in case of an emergency.

Access-Able Travel Source (© 303/232-2979; www.access-able.com) offers a comprehensive database on travel agents from around the world with experience in accessible travel; destination-specific access information; and links to such resources as service animals, equipment rentals, and access guides.

Many travel agencies offer customized tours and itineraries for travelers with disabilities. Among them are **Flying Wheels Travel** (© 507/451-5005; www.flyingwheelstravel.com); and **Accessible Journeys** (© 800/846-4537 or 610/521-0339; www.disability travel.com).

Flying with Disability (www.flying-with-disability.org) is a comprehensive information source on airplane travel. **Avis Rent a Car** (© 888/879-4273) has an "Avis Access" program that offers services for customers with special travel needs. These include specially outfitted vehicles with swivel seats, spinner knobs, and hand controls; mobility scooter rentals; and accessible bus service. Be sure to reserve well in advance.

Also check out the quarterly magazine *Emerging Horizons* (www.emerginghorizons.com), available by subscription ($16.95 per year in the U.S.; $21.95 outside the U.S.).

The "Accessible Travel" link at **Mobility-Advisor.com** (www.mobility-advisor.com) offers a variety of travel resources to persons with disabilities.

British travelers should contact **Holiday Care** (© 0845-124-9971 in the U.K. only; www.holidaycare.org.uk) to access a wide range of travel information and resources for people with disabilities as well as seniors.

GAY & LESBIAN TRAVELERS

Known for its acceptance of all groups, Hawaii welcomes gays and lesbians just as it does anybody else. For the latest information on the gay marriage issue, contact the **Hawaii Marriage Project** (© 808/532-9000).

Pacific Ocean Holidays, P.O. Box 88245, Honolulu, HI 96830 (© **800/735-6600** or 808/944-4700; www.gayhawaiivacations. com), offers vacation packages that feature gay-owned and gay-friendly lodgings. It also has a website (www.gayhawaii.com) with a list of gay-owned and gay-friendly businesses and links throughout the islands.

The **International Gay and Lesbian Travel Association (IGLTA;** © **800/448-8550** or 954/776-2626; www.iglta.org) is the trade association for the gay and lesbian travel industry. It offers an online directory of gay- and lesbian-friendly travel businesses and tour operators.

Many agencies offer tours and travel itineraries specifically for gay and lesbian travelers. **Above and Beyond Tours** (© **800/397-2681;** www.abovebeyondtours.com) are specialists in arranging tours in Australia for gay and lesbian visitors. San Francisco–based **Now, Voyager** (© **800/255-6951;** www.nowvoyager.com) offers worldwide trips and cruises, and **Olivia** (© **800/631-6277;** www. olivia.com) offers lesbian cruises and resort vacations.

Gay.com Travel (© **800/929-2268** or 415/644-8044; www.gay. com/travel or www.outandabout.com) is an excellent online successor to the popular *Out & About* print magazine. It provides regularly updated information about gay-owned, gay-oriented, and gay-friendly lodging, dining, sightseeing, nightlife, and shopping establishments in every important destination worldwide. British travelers should click on the "Travel" link at **www.uk.gay.com** for advice and gay-friendly trip ideas.

The Canadian website **GayTraveler (gaytraveler.ca)** offers ideas and advice for gay travel all over the world.

The following travel guides are available at many bookstores, or you can order them from any online bookseller: *Spartacus International Gay Guide, 35th Edition* (Bruno Gmünder Verlag; www.spartacusworld.com/gayguide) and *Odysseus: The International Gay Travel Planner, 17th Edition* (www.odyusa.com); and the *Damron* guides (www.damron.com), with separate, annual books for gay men and lesbians.

SENIOR TRAVEL

Discounts for seniors are available at almost all of Maui's major attractions, and occasionally at hotels and restaurants. Always inquire when making hotel reservations, and especially when you're buying your airline ticket—most major domestic airlines offer senior discounts.

Members of **AARP,** 601 E St. NW, Washington, DC 20049 (© **888/687-2277;** www.aarp.org), get discounts on hotels, airfares, and car rentals. AARP offers members a wide range of benefits, including *AARP: The Magazine* and a monthly newsletter. Anyone over 50 can join.

Some great, low-cost trips to Hawaii are offered to people 55 and older through **Elderhostel,** 75 Federal St., Boston, MA 02110 (© **800/454-5768;** www.elderhostel.org), a nonprofit group that arranges travel and study programs around the world. You can obtain a complete catalog of offerings by writing to Elderhostel, P.O. Box 1959, Wakefield, MA 01880-5959.

If you're planning to visit Haleakala National Park, you can save sightseeing dollars if you're 62 or older by picking up an **America the Beautiful—National Park and Federal Recreational Lands Pass—Senior Pass** (formerly the **Golden Age Passport**), which gives seniors 62 years or older lifetime entrance to all properties administered by the National Park Service—national parks, monuments, historic sites, recreation areas, and national wildlife refuges—for a one-time processing fee of $10. The pass must be purchased in person at any NPS facility that charges an entrance fee. Besides free entry, the American the Beautiful Senior Pass also offers a 50% discount on some federal-use fees charged for such facilities as camping, swimming, parking, boat launching, and tours. For more information, go to www.nps.gov/fees_passes.htm or call © **888/467-2757.**

Many reliable agencies and organizations target the 50-plus market. **Elderhostel** (© **800/454-5768;** www.elderhostel.org) arranges worldwide study programs for those age 55 or over. **ElderTreks** (© **800/741-7956** or 416/558-5000 outside North America; www.eldertreks.com) offers small-group tours to off-the-beaten-path or adventure-travel locations, restricted to travelers 50 and older.

Recommended publications offering travel resources and discounts for seniors include: the quarterly magazine *Travel 50 & Beyond* (www.travel50andbeyond.com) and the best-selling paperback *Unbelievably Good Deals and Great Adventures That You Absolutely Can't Get Unless You're Over 50 2005–2006, 16th Edition* (McGraw-Hill), by Joann Rattner Heilman.

FAMILY TRAVEL

Maui is paradise for children: beaches to frolic on, water to splash in, unusual sights to see, and a host of new foods to taste. Be sure to look for the "Kids" icon throughout the book.

The larger hotels and resorts have supervised programs for children and can refer you to qualified babysitters. You can also contact **People Attentive to Children** (**PATCH**; © **808/242-9232;** www.patchhawaii.org), which will refer you to individuals who have taken their training courses on child care. If you are traveling to Molokai or Lanai, call © **800/498-4145** or visit www.patch hawaii.org.

Baby's Away (© **800/942-9030** or 808/875-9030; www.babys away.com) rents cribs, strollers, highchairs, playpens, infant seats, and the like, to make your baby's vacation (and yours) much more enjoyable.

Recommended family travel websites include **Family Travel Forum** (www.familytravelforum.com), a comprehensive site that offers customized trip planning; **Family Travel Network** (www.familytravelnetwork.com), an online magazine that provides travel tips; **TravelWithYourKids.com** (www.travelwithyourkids.com), a comprehensive site written by parents for parents offering sound advice for long-distance and international travel with children; and **Family Travel Files** (www.thefamilytravelfiles.com), which offers an online magazine and a directory of off-the-beaten-path tours and tour operators for families.

Also look for *Frommer's Hawaii with Kids* (Wiley Publishing, Inc.).

9 Packages for the Independent Traveler

Booking an all-inclusive travel package that includes some combination of airfare, accommodations, rental car, meals, airport and baggage transfers, and sightseeing can be the most cost-effective way to travel to Maui. Package tours are not the same as escorted tours. They are simply a way to buy airfare and accommodations (and sometimes extras like sightseeing tours) at the same time.

When you're visiting Hawaii, a package can be a smart way to go. You can sometimes save so much money by buying all the pieces of your trip through a packager that your transpacific airfare ends up, in effect, being free. That's because packages are sold in bulk to tour operators, who then resell them to the public at a cost that drastically undercuts standard rates.

Good sources for packages include **More Hawaii for Less** (© **800/967-6687;** www.hawaii4less.com); **Outrigger**'s Ohana (Hawaiian for "family") hotels (© **800/462-6262;** www.ohanahotels.com) and the more upscale Outrigger resorts and condominiums

(© **800/OUTRIGGER;** www.outrigger.com); the **ResortQuest** chain (© **866/77-HAWAII;** www.resortquesthawaii.com); **American Airlines Vacations** (© 800/321-2121; www.aavacations.com), **Delta Vacations** (© 800/654-6559; www.deltavacations.com); **Continental Airlines Vacations** (© 800/301-3800; www.covacations.com); and **United Vacations** (© 888/854-3899; www.unitedvacations.com); and **online travel agencies** such as Expedia, Travelocity, Orbitz, Site59, and Lastminute.com.

Travel packages are also listed in the travel section of your local Sunday newspaper. Or check ads in the national travel magazines such as *Arthur Frommer's Budget Travel Magazine, Travel + Leisure, National Geographic Traveler,* and *Condé Nast Traveler.*

Packages, however, vary widely. Some offer a better class of hotels than others. Some offer the same hotels for lower prices. With some packagers, your choice of accommodations and travel days may be limited. Which package is right for you depends entirely on what you want. Be sure to **read the fine print.** Make sure you know *exactly* what's included in the price you're being quoted and what's not. Are hotel taxes and airport transfers included or will you have to pay extra? Before you commit to a package, make sure you know how much flexibility you have, say, if your kid gets sick or your boss suddenly asks you to adjust your vacation schedule. Some packagers require ironclad commitments, while others charge only minimal fees for changes or cancellations.

10 Getting Around Maui

The only way to really see Maui is by rental car. There's no real island-wide public transit. The best and most detailed road maps are published by *This Week* magazine, a free visitor publication available on Maui. Most rental-car maps are pretty good, too.

BY CAR

Maui has one of the least expensive car-rental rates in the country— about $47 a day (including all state tax and fees); the national average is about $56. Cars are usually plentiful on Maui, except on holiday weekends, which in Hawaii also means King Kamehameha Day, Prince Kuhio Day, and Admission Day (see "When to Go," earlier in this chapter). Rental cars are usually at a premium on Molokai and Lanai, so book well ahead.

All the major car-rental agencies have offices on Maui, usually at both Kahului and West Maui airports. They include: **Alamo**

(🖂 800/327-9633; www.goalamo.com), **Avis** (🖂 800/321-3712; www.avis.com), **Budget** (🖂 800/572-0700; www.budget.com), **Dollar** (🖂 800/800-4000; www.dollarcar.com), **Hertz** (🖂 800/654-3011; www.hertz.com), and **National** (🖂 800/227-7368; www.nationalcar.com). You might also want to check out **Breezenet.com,** which offers domestic car-rental discounts with some of the most competitive rates around.

There are also a few frugal car-rental agencies offering older cars at discount prices. **Word of Mouth Rent-a-Used-Car** 🖝, in Kahului (🖂 **800/533-5929** or 808/877-2436; www.mauirentacar.com), has older cars (Toyotas and Nissans from 1995 to 2004) that start at $27 a day (air-conditioned, four-door), including all taxes, with a 3-day minimum, or from $156 a week, free airport pickup and drop-off included. **Maui Cruisers,** in Wailuku (🖂 **877/749-7889** or 808/249-2319; www.mauicruisers.net), also offers free airport pickup and return on its 8- to 10-year-old Nissan Sentras and Toyota Corollas, with rentals starting at $31 a day (3-day minimum) or $175 a week (including tax and insurance).

To rent a car in Hawaii, you must be at least 25 years old and have a valid driver's license and a credit card.

If you're visiting from abroad and plan to rent a car in the United States, keep in mind that foreign driver's licenses are usually recognized in the U.S., but you should get an international one if your home license is not in English.

INSURANCE   Hawaii is a no-fault state, which means that if you don't have collision-damage insurance, you are required to pay for all damages before you leave the state, whether or not the accident was your fault. Your personal car insurance back home may provide rental-car coverage; find out before you leave home. Bring your insurance identification card if you decline the optional insurance, which usually costs from $12 to $20 a day. Obtain the name of your company's local claims representative before you go. Some credit card companies also provide collision-damage insurance for their customers; check with yours before you rent.

OTHER TRANSPORTATION OPTIONS

TAXIS   For island-wide 24-hour service, call **Alii Cab Co.** (🖂 808/661-3688 or 808/667-2605). You can also try **Kihei Taxi** (🖂 808/879-3000), **Wailea Taxi** (🖂 808/874-5000), or **Maui Central Cab** (🖂 808/244-7278) if you need a ride.

SHUTTLES   SpeediShuttle (℡ 877/242-5777; www.speedi shuttle.com) can take you between Kahului Airport and all the major resorts from 5am to 11pm daily (for details, see "Landing at Kahului Airport" under "Getting There," earlier in this chapter).

Holo Ka'a Public Transit is a public/private partnership that has convenient, economical, and air-conditioned shuttle buses. Maui Public Transit consists of seven public bus routes, all operated by Roberts Hawaii (℡ 808/871-4838; www.mauibus.com). These routes are funded by the County of Maui and provide service in and between various central, south, and west Maui communities. All of the routes are operated Monday through Saturday only. There is no service on Sunday. The routes go from as far south as Wailea up to as far north as Kapalua. Fares are $1 to $2.

FAST FACTS: Maui

American Express For 24-hour traveler's check refunds and purchase information, call ℡ 800/221-7282. Two local offices are located at the **Westin Maui** at Kaanapali Beach (℡ 808/ 661-7155).

Area Codes All of the islands are in the **808** area code. Note that if you're calling one island from another, you must dial 1-808 first, and you'll be billed at long-distance rates (often more expensive than calling the mainland).

Automobile Organizations Auto clubs will supply maps, suggested routes, guidebooks, accident and bail-bond insurance, and emergency road service. The **American Automobile Association (AAA)** is the major auto club in the United States. If you belong to an auto club in your home country, inquire about AAA reciprocity before you leave. You may be able to join AAA even if you're not a member of a reciprocal club; to inquire, call AAA (℡ 800/222-4357). AAA is actually an organization of regional auto clubs, so look under "AAA Automobile Club" in the White Pages of the telephone directory. AAA has a nationwide emergency road service telephone number (℡ 800/AAA-HELP).

Business Hours Most offices are open from 8am to 5pm. Bank hours are Monday through Thursday from 8:30am to 3pm, Friday from 8:30am to 6pm; some banks are open on Saturday. Shopping centers are open Monday through Friday from

10am to 9pm, Saturday from 10am to 5:30pm, and Sunday from 10am to 5 or 6pm.

Currency The most common bills are the $1 (a "buck"), $5, $10, and $20 denominations. There are also $2 bills (seldom encountered), $50 bills, and $100 bills (the last two are usually not welcome as payment for small purchases).

Coins come in seven denominations: 1¢ (1 cent, or a penny); 5¢ (5 cents, or a nickel); 10¢ (10 cents, or a dime); 25¢ (25 cents, or a quarter); 50¢ (50 cents, or a half dollar); the gold-colored Sacagawea coin, worth $1; and the rare silver dollar.

For additional information see "Money & Costs," p. 19.

Customs **What You Can Bring into Hawaii** Every visitor 21 years of age or older may bring in, free of duty, the following: (1) 1 liter of wine or hard liquor; (2) 200 cigarettes, 100 cigars (but not from Cuba), or 3 pounds of smoking tobacco; and (3) $100 worth of gifts. These exemptions are offered to travelers who spend at least 72 hours in the United States and who have not claimed them within the preceding 6 months. It is altogether forbidden to bring into the country foodstuffs (particularly fruit, cooked meats, and canned goods) and plants (vegetables, seeds, tropical plants, and the like). Foreign tourists may carry in or out up to $10,000 in U.S. or foreign currency with no formalities; larger sums must be declared to U.S. Customs on entering or leaving, which includes filing form CM 4790. For details regarding U.S. Customs and Border Protection, consult your nearest U.S. embassy or consulate, or **U.S. Customs** (*©* 202/927-1770; www.customs.ustreas.gov).

What You Can Take Home from Hawaii Canadian Citizens: For a clear summary of Canadian rules, write for the booklet *I Declare,* issued by the **Canada Border Services Agency** (*©* 800/461-9999 in Canada, or 204/983-3500; www.cbsa-asfc.gc.ca).

U.K. Citizens: For information, contact **HM Customs & Excise** at *©* 0845/010-9000 (from outside the U.K., 020/8929-0152), or consult their website at **www.hmce.gov.uk**.

Australian Citizens: A helpful brochure available from Australian consulates or Customs offices is *Know Before You Go.* For more information, call the **Australian Customs Service** at *©* 1300/363-263, or log on to **www.customs.gov.au**.

New Zealand Citizens: Most questions are answered in a free pamphlet available at New Zealand consulates and Customs offices: *New Zealand Customs Guide for Travellers, Notice no. 4.* For more information, contact **New Zealand Customs,** The Customhouse, 17–21 Whitmore St., Box 2218, Wellington (© **04/ 473-6099** or 0800/428-786; **www.customs.govt.nz**).

Dentists Emergency dental care is available at **Kihei Dental Center,** 1847 S. Kihei Rd., Kihei (© **808/874-8401**), or in Lahaina at **Aloha Lahaina Dentists,** 134 Luakini St. (in the Maui Medical Group Building; © **808/661-4005**).

Doctors No appointment is necessary at **West Maui Healthcare Center,** Whalers Village, 2435 Kaanapali Pkwy., Suite H-7 (near Leilani's restaurant), Kaanapali (© **808/667-9721**), which is open 365 days a year until 6pm. In Kihei call **Urgent Care,** 1325 S. Kihei Rd., Suite 103 (at Lipoa St., across from Star Market; © **808/879-7781**), open daily from 7am to 10pm; doctors here are on call 24 hours a day.

Drinking Laws The legal age for purchase and consumption of alcoholic beverages is 21 in Hawaii; proof of age is required and often requested at bars, nightclubs, and restaurants, so it's always a good idea to bring ID when you go out. Bars are allowed to stay open daily until 2am; places with cabaret licenses are able to keep the booze flowing until 4am. Grocery and convenience stores are allowed to sell beer, wine, and liquor 7 days a week.

Do not carry open containers of alcohol in your car or any public area that isn't zoned for alcohol consumption. The police can fine you on the spot. And nothing will ruin your trip faster than getting a citation for DUI ("driving under the influence"), so don't even think about driving while intoxicated.

Electricity Like Canada, the United States uses 110–120 volts AC (60 cycles), compared to 220–240 volts AC (50 cycles) in most of Europe, Australia, and New Zealand. Downward converters that change 220–240 volts to 110–120 volts are difficult to find in the United States, so bring one with you.

Embassies & Consulates All embassies are located in the nation's capital, Washington, D.C. Some consulates are located in major U.S. cities, and most nations have a mission to the United Nations in New York City. If your country isn't listed below, call for directory information in Washington, D.C. (© **202/555-1212**) or log on to **www.embassy.org/ embassies**.

The embassy of **Australia** is at 1601 Massachusetts Ave. NW, Washington, DC 20036 (② 202/797-3000; www.austemb.org). There are consulates in New York, Honolulu, Houston, Los Angeles, and San Francisco.

The embassy of **Canada** is at 501 Pennsylvania Ave. NW, Washington, DC 20001 (② 202/682-1740; www.canadian embassy.org). Other Canadian consulates are in Buffalo (New York), Detroit, Los Angeles, New York, and Seattle.

The embassy of **Ireland** is at 2234 Massachusetts Ave. NW, Washington, DC 20008 (② 202/462-3939; www.irelandemb.org). Irish consulates are in Boston, Chicago, New York, San Francisco, and other cities. See the website for a complete listing.

The embassy of **New Zealand** is at 37 Observatory Circle NW, Washington, DC 20008 (② 202/328-4800; www.nzemb. org). New Zealand consulates are in Los Angeles, Salt Lake City, San Francisco, and Seattle.

The embassy of the **United Kingdom** is at 3100 Massachusetts Ave. NW, Washington, DC 20008 (② 202/588-7800; www. britainusa.com). Other British consulates are in Atlanta, Boston, Chicago, Cleveland, Houston, Los Angeles, New York, San Francisco, and Seattle.

Emergencies Dial ② 911 for the police, an ambulance, or the fire department. For the **Poison Control Center**, call ② 800/362-3585.

Gasoline (Petrol) At press time, in the U.S. the cost of gasoline (also known as gas, but never petrol), is abnormally high (about $3.76 per gallon). Taxes are already included in the printed price. One U.S. gallon equals 3.8 liters or .85 imperial gallons. Fill-up locations are known as gas or service stations.

Hospitals For medical attention, go to **Maui Memorial Hospital**, in central Maui at 221 Mahalani, Wailuku (② 808/244-9056), or east Maui's **Hana Medical Center**, on Hana Highway (② 808/248-8924).

Lost & Found Be sure to tell all of your credit card companies the minute you discover your wallet has been lost or stolen, and file a report at the nearest police precinct. Your credit card company or insurer may require a police report number or record of the loss. Most credit card companies have an emergency toll-free number to call if your card is lost or stolen; they may be able to wire you a cash advance immediately or deliver an emergency credit card in a day or two.

Visa's U.S. emergency number is ✆ **800/847-2911** or 410/581-9994. American Express cardholders and traveler's check holders should call ✆ **800/221-7282**. MasterCard holders should call ✆ **800/307-7309** or 636/722-7111. For other credit cards, call the toll-free number directory at ✆ **800/555-1212.**

If you need emergency cash over the weekend when all banks and American Express offices are closed, you can have money wired to you via **Western Union** (✆ **800/325-6000;** www.westernunion.com).

Mail In Lahaina there is a U.S. post office at the Lahaina Civic Center, 1760 Honoapiilani Hwy.; in Kahului there's a branch at 138 S. Puunene Ave.; and in Kihei there's one at 1254 S. Kihei Rd. At press time domestic postage rates were 26¢ for a postcard and 41¢ for a letter. For international mail, a first-class letter of up to 1 ounce or postcard costs 90¢ (69¢ to Canada and Mexico). For more information go to **www.usps.com** and click on "Calculate Postage."

If you aren't sure what your address will be in the United States, mail can be sent to you, in your name, c/o General Delivery at the main post office of the city or region where you expect to be. (Call ✆ **800/275-8777** for information on the nearest post office.) The addressee must pick up mail in person and must produce proof of identity (driver's license, passport, and the like). Most post offices will hold your mail for up to 1 month and are open Monday to Friday from 8am to 6pm, Saturday from 9am to 3pm.

Always include zip codes when mailing items in the U.S. If you don't know your zip code, visit www.usps.com/zip4.

Passports **For Residents of Australia:** You can pick up an application from your local post office or any branch of Passports Australia, but you must schedule an interview at the passport office to present your application materials. Call the **Australian Passport Information Service** at ✆ **131-232,** or visit the government website at www.passports.gov.au.

For Residents of Canada: Passport applications are available at travel agencies throughout Canada or from the central **Passport Office,** Department of Foreign Affairs and International Trade, Ottawa, ON K1A 0G3 (✆ **800/567-6868;** www.ppt.gc.ca). *Note:* Canadian children who travel must have their own passport. However, if you hold a valid Canadian passport issued before December 11, 2001, that bears the name of your child, the passport remains valid for you and your child until it expires.

For Residents of Ireland: You can apply for a 10-year passport at the **Passport Office,** Setanta Centre, Molesworth Street, Dublin 2 (℡ **01/671-1633;** www.irlgov.ie/iveagh). Those under age 18 and over 65 must apply for a 3-year passport. You can also apply at 1A South Mall, Cork (℡ **021/272-525**) or at most main post offices.

For Residents of New Zealand: You can pick up a passport application at any New Zealand Passports Office or download it from their website. Contact the **Passports Office** at ℡ **0800/ 225-050** in New Zealand or 04/474-8100, or log on to www.passports.govt.nz.

For Residents of the United Kingdom: To pick up an application for a standard 10-year passport (5-year passport for children under 16), visit your nearest passport office, major post office, or travel agency or contact the **United Kingdom Passport Service** at ℡ **0870/521-0410** or search its website at www.ukpa.gov.uk.

Police In an emergency, dial ℡ **911** for police. For nonemergencies, call the district station in Lahaina (℡ **808/661-4441**) or Hana (℡ **808/248-8311**).

Smoking It's against the law to smoke in public buildings, including airports, shopping malls, grocery stores, retail shops, buses, movie theaters, banks, convention facilities, and all government buildings and facilities. Smoking is not allowed in restaurants, bars, and nightclubs. Most bed-and-breakfasts prohibit smoking indoors, and more and more hotels and resorts are becoming nonsmoking, even in public areas. Smoking is also prohibited within 20 feet of a doorway, window, or ventilation intake.

Taxes The United States has no value-added tax (VAT) or other indirect tax at the national level. Every state, county, and city may levy its own local tax on all purchases, including hotel and restaurant checks and airline tickets. These taxes will not appear on price tags. Hawaii's sales tax is 4%. The hotel-occupancy tax is 7.25%, and hoteliers are allowed by the state to tack on an additional .1666% excise tax. Thus, expect taxes of about 11.42% to be added to your hotel bill.

Time The continental United States is divided into **four time zones:** Eastern Standard Time (EST), Central Standard Time

(CST), Mountain Standard Time (MST), and Pacific Standard Time (PST). Alaska and Hawaii have their own zones. For example, when it's 9am in Los Angeles (PST), it's 7am in Honolulu (HST),10am in Denver (MST), 11am in Chicago (CST), noon in New York City (EST), 5pm in London (GMT), and 2am the next day in Sydney.

Daylight saving time is in effect from 2am on the second Sunday in March to 2am on the first Sunday in November, except in Arizona, Hawaii, the U.S. Virgin Islands, and Puerto Rico. Daylight saving time moves the clock 1 hour ahead of standard time.

Tipping Tips are a very important part of certain workers' income, and gratuities are the standard way of showing appreciation for services provided. (Tipping is certainly not compulsory if the service is poor!) In hotels tip **bellhops** at least $1 per bag ($2–$3 if you have a lot of luggage) and tip the **chamber staff** $1 to $2 per day (more if you've left a disaster area for him or her to clean up). Tip the **doorman** or **concierge** only if he or she has provided you with some specific service (for example, calling a cab for you or obtaining difficult-to-get theater tickets). Tip the **valet-parking attendant** $1 every time you get your car.

In restaurants, bars, and nightclubs, tip **service staff** 15% to 20% of the check, tip **bartenders** 10% to 15%, tip **checkroom attendants** $1 per garment, and tip **valet-parking attendants** $1 per vehicle.

As for other service personnel, tip **cabdrivers** 15% of the fare; tip **skycaps** at airports at least $1 per bag ($2–$3 if you have a lot of luggage); and tip **hairdressers** and **barbers** 15% to 20%.

Visas For information about U.S. visas, go to **http:// travel.state.gov** and click on "Visas." Or go to one of the following websites:

Australian citizens can obtain up-to-date visa information from the **U.S. Embassy Canberra,** Moonah Place, Yarralumla, ACT 2600 (© **02/6214-5600**) or by checking the U.S. Diplomatic Mission's website at **http://usembassy-australia.state. gov/consular**.

British subjects can obtain up-to-date visa information by calling the **U.S. Embassy Visa Information Line** (© **0891/200-290**) or by visiting the "Visas to the U.S." section of the American Embassy London's website at **www.usembassy.org.uk**.

Irish citizens can obtain up-to-date visa information through the **Embassy of the USA Dublin,** 42 Elgin Rd., Dublin 4, Ireland (*©* **353/1-668-8777**), or by checking the "Consular Services" section of the website at **http://dublin.usembassy.gov**.

Citizens of **New Zealand** can obtain up-to-date visa information by contacting the **U.S. Embassy New Zealand,** 29 Fitzherbert Terrace, Thorndon, Wellington (*©* **644/472-2068**), or get the information directly from the website at **http:// wellington.usembassy.gov**.

2

Where to Stay

Maui has accommodations to fit every taste and budget, from luxury oceanfront suites and historic bed-and-breakfasts to reasonably priced condos that will sleep a family of four.

The high season, during which rooms are always booked and rates are at the top end, runs from mid-December to March. A second high season, when rates are high but reservations are somewhat easier to get, is summer (late June to early Sept). The off seasons, with fewer tourists and cheaper rates, are April to early June and late September to mid-December.

Remember to add Hawaii's 11.42% accommodations tax to your final bill. Parking is free unless otherwise noted.

Important note: Before you book, be sure to read "The Island in Brief" in chapter 1, which will help you choose your ideal location.

1 Central Maui

KAHULUI
WAILUKU

Old Wailuku Inn at Ulupono 🌟🌟 *Finds*   This 1924 former plantation manager's home, lovingly restored by innkeepers Janice and Thomas Fairbanks, offers a genuine old Hawaii experience. The theme is Hawaii of the 1920s and 1930s, with decor, design, and landscaping to match. The spacious rooms are gorgeously outfitted with exotic ohia-wood floors, high ceilings, and traditional Hawaiian quilts. The mammoth bathrooms (some with claw-foot tubs, others with Jacuzzis) have plush towels and earth-friendly toiletries on hand. Recently, the owners added an additional building, the Vagabond House, a modern three-room complex in the inn's lavishly landscaped backyard. The rooms are decorated in island-designer Sig Zane's floral prints, with rare framed prints of indigenous Hawaiian flowers plus all the modern amenities you can imagine (including an ultraluxurious multihead shower). A full gourmet breakfast is served on the enclosed back lanai. You'll feel right at home lounging on the generous-size living-room sofa or watching the world go by from an old wicker chair on the lanai. The inn is located in the old historic area of Wailuku, just a few minutes' walk from the Maui County Seat Government Building, the courthouse, and a wonderful stretch of antiques shops.

2199 Kahookele St. (at High St., across from the Wailuku School), Wailuku, HI 96732. ℂ **800/305-4899** or 808/244-5897. Fax 808/242-9600. www.mauiinn. com. 10 units. $150–$190 double. Rates include full breakfast. Extra person $20. 2-night minimum. MC, V. **Amenities:** Jacuzzi; laundry service; dry cleaning. *In room:* A/C, TV/VCR, dataport, coffeemaker, high-speed Internet.

2 West Maui

LAHAINA
VERY EXPENSIVE

Outrigger Aina Nalu Resort ⓕ   Set on 9 acres in the middle of Lahaina, this property was totally renovated in 2005. Then the units were sold off to private owners and put into a rental pool. The result is a brand-new first-class property with all the latest appliances, new furniture, and 21st-century conveniences. The property isn't on the beach, but on a quiet side street (a rarity in Lahaina) and within walking distance of restaurants, shops, attractions, and the beach (just 3 blocks away). All of the good-size rooms, decorated in tropical-island style, are comfortable and quiet. The entire complex includes a sun deck and swimming pool, a barbecue, and a picnic area. The aloha-friendly staff will take the time to answer all of your questions.

660 Wainee St. (between Dickenson and Prison sts.), Lahaina, HI 96761. ℂ **800/ OUTRIGGER** or 808/667-9766. Fax 808/661-3733. www.outrigger.com. 197 units. $209–$229 studio with kitchenette; $269–$299 1-bedroom unit with kitchen (sleeps up to 4); $339–$359 2-bedroom with 1 bathroom and kitchen (sleeps 6); $349–$369 2-bedroom with 2 bathrooms and kitchen (sleeps 6). Extra rollaway bed $18. AE, DC, DISC, MC, V. Parking $5. **Amenities:** Outdoor pool; whirlpool; activities desk; laundry and dry cleaning. *In room:* A/C, TV, kitchenette in studio, full kitchen in 1- and 2-bedroom units, fridge, coffeemaker, hair dryer, iron, safe, washer and dryer in 1- and 2-bedroom units.

Puunoa Beach Estates ⓕⓕ ⓚⁱᵈˢ   If you're taking a family to Maui, consider these 10 gorgeous town houses in an exclusive 3-acre enclave on a white-sand beach. The individually owned and decorated units (1,700 sq. ft. and larger) all have private beachfront lanais, hardwood floors, marble bathrooms, and modern kitchens. Prices are high, but the amenity list has everything you should want for a first-class vacation rental in a dream location. It's within walking distance of the center of Lahaina, but the residential location makes you feel miles away.

45 Kai Pali Place, Lahaina, HI 96761. Managed by Classic Resorts. ☎ **800/ 642-6284** or 808/661-3339. Fax 808/667-1145. www.puunoabeachestates.com. 10 units. $750 2-bedroom unit (sleeps 4). 3-night minimum. AE, MC, V. **Amenities:** Outdoor pool; whirlpool; fitness center; sauna; complimentary snorkeling equipment; concierge; dry cleaning; barbecues; fax service; free Internet access; video library. *In room:* A/C, TV/VCR, dataport, full kitchen, fridge, coffeemaker, hair dryer, iron, safe, master bedroom w/whirlpool tub, washer/dryer, daily maid service.

EXPENSIVE

The Plantation Inn ★★ *Finds*   This charming Victorian-style inn, located a couple of blocks from the water, looks like it's been here 100 years or more, but it's actually of 1990s vintage—an artful deception. The rooms are romantic to the max, tastefully done with period furniture, hardwood floors, stained glass, and ceiling fans. There are four-poster canopy beds in some rooms, brass beds and wicker beds in others. All units are soundproof (a plus in Lahaina) and each comes with a private lanai; the suites have kitchenettes. Also on the property are a pavilion lounge and an outstanding French restaurant (guests get a discount). Breakfast is served around the pool and in the elegant pavilion lounge.

174 Lahainaluna Rd. (between Wainee and Luakini sts., 1 block from Hwy. 30), Lahaina, HI 96761. ☎ **800/433-6815** or 808/667-9225. Fax 808/667-9293. www.theplantationinn.com. 19 units, some bathrooms with shower only. $160–$225 double; suites from $245. Check the website for great package deals. Rates include full breakfast. Extra person $25. AE, DC, DISC, MC, V. **Amenities:** Acclaimed restaurant and bar (Gerard's, p. 80); large outdoor pool; Jacuzzi; concierge; activities desk; coin-op washer/dryers. *In room:* A/C, TV/VCR, kitchenette (in suites), fridge, hair dryer, iron, safe.

MODERATE

Guest House ★★ *Finds*   This is one of Lahaina's great bed-and-breakfast deals: a charming house with more amenities than the expensive Kaanapali hotels just down the road. The roomy home features parquet floors and floor-to-ceiling windows; its swimming pool—surrounded by a deck and comfortable lounge chairs—is larger than some at high-priced condos. Every guest room has a quiet lanai and a romantic hot tub. Guests share the large, well-equipped kitchen and computers with high-speed Internet access. The Guest House also operates Trinity Tours and offers discounts on car rentals and many island activities. Tennis courts are nearby, and the nearest beach is about a block away. Scuba divers are welcome here and are provided with places to store their gear.

1620 Ainakea Rd. (off Fleming Rd., north of Lahaina town), Lahaina, HI 96761. ☎ **800/ 621-8942** or 808/661-8085. Fax 808/661-1896. www.mauiguesthouse.com. 4 units. $129 single; $149 double. Rates include full breakfast. MC, V. Take Fleming Rd. off Hwy.

Lahaina & Kaanapali Accommodations & Attractions

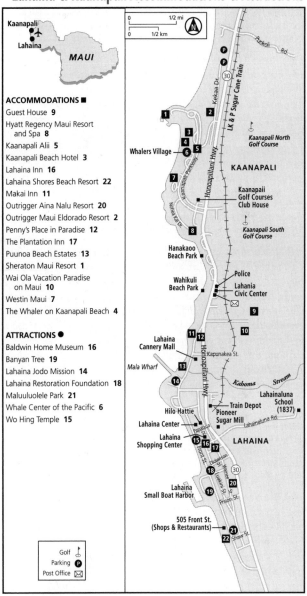

ACCOMMODATIONS ■

Guest House **9**
Hyatt Regency Maui Resort
  and Spa **8**
Kaanapali Alii **5**
Kaanapali Beach Hotel **3**
Lahaina Inn **16**
Lahaina Shores Beach Resort **22**
Makai Inn **11**
Outrigger Aina Nalu Resort **20**
Outrigger Maui Eldorado Resort **2**
Penny's Place in Paradise **12**
The Plantation Inn **17**
Puunoa Beach Estates **13**
Sheraton Maui Resort **1**
Wai Ola Vacation Paradise
  on Maui **10**
Westin Maui **7**
The Whaler on Kaanapali Beach **4**

ATTRACTIONS ●

Baldwin Home Museum **16**
Banyan Tree **19**
Lahaina Jodo Mission **14**
Lahaina Restoration Foundation **18**
Maluuluolele Park **21**
Whale Center of the Pacific **6**
Wo Hing Temple **15**

Golf
Parking
Post Office

30; turn left on Ainakea; it's 2 blocks down. **Amenities:** Huge outdoor pool; free water-sports equipment; concierge; activities desk; car-rental desk; self-service washer/dryers. *In room:* A/C, TV/VCR/DVD, fridge, free high-speed wireless Internet, Jacuzzi.

Lahaina Inn 🅐   If you like old hotels that have genuine historical touches, you'll love this place. As in many old hotels, some of these Victorian antiques–stuffed rooms are small; if that's a problem for you, ask for a larger unit. All come with private bathrooms and lanais. The best room in the house is no. 7, which overlooks the beach, the town, and the island of Lanai; you can watch the action below or close the door and ignore it. There's an excellent, though unaffiliated, restaurant in the same building (David Paul's Lahaina Grill, p. 79), with a bar downstairs.

127 Lahainaluna Rd. (near Front St.), Lahaina, HI 96761. 🕐 **800/669-3444** or 808/661-0577. Fax 808/667-9480. www.lahainainn.com. 12 units (most with shower only). $130–$170 double; from $180 suite. AE, MC, V. Next-door parking $7/day. **Amenities:** Bar; concierge; activities desk. *In room:* A/C, hair dryer, iron.

Lahaina Shores Beach Resort 🅐   First there's the location, right on the beach; second there's the location, away from the hustle and bustle of downtown Lahaina; and third there's the location, next door to the 505 Front St. restaurants (with charging privileges) and shops. This recently upgraded condominium project (of studios and one-bedroom units) resembles an old plantation home with arched colonnades at the entry and an open-air, beachfront lobby. From the moment you step into the airy units (ranging in size from 550 sq. ft. to 1,430 sq. ft.), you'll feel like you are home. The units all have full kitchens, large lanais, and ocean or mountain views. Ask for an oceanfront unit for that terrific view of the ocean with the island of Lanai in the distance.

475 Front St., Lahaina, HI 96761. 🕐 **800/628-6699** or 808/661-4835. www.lahaina shores.com. 145 units. $200–$260 studio double; $275–$325 1-bedroom double; $325–$360 1-bedroom penthouse double. AE, MC, V. Parking $5. **Amenities:** Outdoor pool; tennis courts (across the street); whirlpool spa; concierge; coin-op washer/dryers; dry cleaning; barbecue grill; beach activities. *In room:* A/C, TV, full kitchen, fridge, coffeemaker, iron, hair dryer.

Wai Ola Vacation Paradise on Maui 🅐   Just 2 blocks from the beach, in a quiet, residential development behind a tall concrete wall, lies this lovely retreat, with shade trees, sitting areas, gardens, a pool, an ocean mural, and a range of accommodations (a small studio, a couple of suites inside the home, a separate honeymoon cottage, a one-bedroom apartment, or the entire 5,000-sq.-ft. house). Kim and Jim Wicker are the hosts of this vacation paradise and are more than willing to provide any information you need to make your vacation fabulous. Every unit has a welcome fruit basket when you arrive, plus beans for the coffeemaker. Kim loves to bake, and sometimes surprises her guests with "a little something" from her kitchen. You'll also find a deck, barbecue facilities, and an outdoor wet bar on the property. There's a great beach just a 3-minute drive away and tennis courts are nearby.

1565 Kuuipo St. (P.O. Box 12580), Lahaina, HI 96761. © 800/492-4652 or 808/661-7901. Fax 808/661-1119. www.waiola.com. 5 units. Studio $129–$149; suite $139; 1-bedroom apt $139; honeymoon cottage $179; entire house $725–$900. Extra person $15. AE, DISC, MC, V. **Amenities:** Outdoor pool; Jacuzzi; complimentary use of watersports equipment; free self-service washer/dryers. *In room:* A/C, TV/DVD/VCR, dataport, kitchenette, fridge, coffeemaker, hair dryer, iron.

INEXPENSIVE

Makai Inn *Value   Budget travelers take note:* Here's a small apartment complex located right on the water (no white-sand beach out front, but what do you want at these eye-popping prices?). You can take a 10-minute stroll to the closest white-sand beach or a 20-minute walk to the center of Lahaina town. The units are small (400 sq. ft.) but clean and filled with everything you should need for your vacation: full kitchens, views of the ocean (in most units), and separate bedrooms, all in a quiet neighborhood. There's a public phone by the office (none in the rooms, and no TVs either). I recommend the Ginger Hideaway unit, with windows on two sides overlooking the ocean, for just $156. Families will like the Pineapple "Sweet," the only two-bedroom unit (800 sq. ft.), for just $156.

1415 Front St., Lahaina, HI 96761. © 808/662-3200. Fax 808/661-9027. www.makaiinn.net. 18 units. $99–$156 double. Extra person $17. MC, V. **Amenities:** Coin-op washer/dryer. *In room:* Kitchen, no phone.

Penny's Place in Paradise *Finds   No attention to detail has been spared in this Victorian-style bed-and-breakfast, just 50 feet from the water with a fabulous view from the front porch of Molokai and Lanai. Each of the four rooms is uniquely decorated, with themes ranging from contemporary Hawaii to formal Victorian. Guests are welcome to use the balcony kitchenette (fridge, microwave, toaster, coffeemaker, and ice machine). The only problem is the location—a small island bounded by Honoapiilani Highway on one side and busy Front Street on the other. The house is soundproof, and air-conditioning in each room drowns out the noise outside. Recently Penny enclosed the outside lanai area so you can enjoy your breakfast without the highway noise.

1440 Front St., Lahaina, HI 96761. © 877/431-1235 or 808/661-1068. Fax 808/667-7102. www.pennysplace.net. 4 units. $98–$147 double. Rates include continental breakfast Mon–Sat. 3-night minimum. AE, DISC, MC, V. *In room:* A/C, TV, iron, wireless Internet.

KAANAPALI

VERY EXPENSIVE

Hyatt Regency Maui Resort & Spa ⭑⭑ (Kids)   Spa goers will love this resort. Hawaii's first oceanfront spa, the Spa Moana, opened here in 2000 with some 9,000 square feet of facilities. Book your treatment before you leave home—this place is popular.

The management has poured some $19 million in renovations into rooms in this fantasy resort, the southernmost of the Kaanapali beachfront properties. It certainly has lots of imaginative touches: a collection of exotic species (pink flamingos, unhappy-looking penguins, and an assortment of loud parrots and macaws in the lobby), nine waterfalls, and an eclectic Asian and Pacific art collection. The ½-acre outdoor pool features a 150-foot lava tube slide, a cocktail bar under the falls, a "honeymooner's cave," and a swinging rope bridge. There's even a children-only pool with its own beach, tidal pools, and fountains, and a "Camp Hyatt" children's program offering young guests a range of activities, from "Olympic Games" to a scavenger hunt. There's also a game room for kids with video games, pool, Ping-Pong, and air hockey.

The rooms, spread out among three towers, are pleasantly outfitted with an array of amenities and have very comfortable separate sitting areas and private lanais with eye-popping views. The latest, most comfortable bedding is now standard in every room (including fluffy feather beds). Two Regency Club floors have a private concierge, complimentary breakfast, sunset cocktails, and snacks.

200 Nohea Kai Dr., Lahaina, HI 96761. ℭ **800/233-1234** or 808/661-1234. Fax 808/667-4498. www.maui.hyatt.com. 806 units. $385–$700 double; $580–$785 Regency Club; from $850 suite. Mandatory $15 resort fee for access to new Moana Athletic Club, daily local newspaper, local and toll-free phone calls, in-room coffee and tea, in-room safe, and 1-hr. tennis court time per day. Extra person $50 ($75 in Regency Club rooms). Children 18 and under stay free in parent's room using existing bedding. Packages available. AE, DC, DISC, MC, V. Valet parking $10, free self-parking. **Amenities:** 5 restaurants; 2 bars; a 1/2-acre outdoor pool; 36-hole golf course; 6 tennis courts; health club w/weight room; state-of-the-art spa; Jacuzzi; watersports equipment rentals; bike rentals; year-round children's program; game room; concierge; activities desk; car-rental desk; business center; shopping arcade; salon; room service; in-room or spa massage; babysitting; coin-op washer/dryers; laundry service; dry cleaning; concierge-level rooms. *In room:* A/C, TV, dataport, minibar, fridge, coffeemaker, hair dryer, iron, safe, high-speed Internet ($10/day), 2-line phone.

Kaanapali Alii ⭑⭑ (Kids)   The height of luxury, these oceanfront condominium units sit on 8 landscaped acres right on Kaanapali Beach. Kaanapali Alii combines all the amenities of a luxury hotel (including a 24-hr. front desk) with the convenience of a condominium to make a stay here memorable. Each of the one-bedroom (1,500-sq.-ft.) and two-bedroom (1,900-sq.-ft.) units is impeccably decorated and comes with all the comforts of home (fully equipped kitchen, washer/dryer, lanai, two full bathrooms) and then some (room service, daily maid service, complimentary local newspaper). The beachside recreation area includes a swimming pool, plus a separate children's pool, whirlpool, gas barbecue grills and picnic areas, exercise rooms, saunas, and tennis courts. You can even take yoga classes on the lawn.

50 Nohea Kai Dr., Lahaina, HI 96761. ℂ **800/642-6284** or 808/661-3330. Fax 808/667-1145. www.kaanapali-alii.com. 264 units. $405–$675 1-bedroom unit for 4; $575–$830 2-bedroom for 6. AE, DC, DISC, MC, V. Free parking. **Amenities:** Poolside cafe; 2 outdoor pools; 36-hole golf course; 3 lighted tennis courts; fitness center; Jacuzzi; watersports equipment rentals; children's program; game room; concierge; activities desk; room service; in-room massage; babysitting; same-day dry cleaning. *In room:* A/C, TV, dataport, kitchen, fridge, coffeemaker, hair dryer, iron, safe, washer/dryer.

Sheraton Maui Resort 𝒞𝒞 (Kids) Terrific facilities for families and fitness buffs and a premier beach location make this beautiful resort an all-around great place to stay. The grande dame of Kaanapali Beach is built into the side of a cliff on the curving, white-sand cove next to Black Rock (a lava formation that rises 80 ft. above the beach), where there's excellent snorkeling. After its recent renovation, the resort is virtually new, with six buildings of six stories or less set in well-established tropical gardens. The lobby has been elevated to take advantage of panoramic views, while a new lagoonlike pool features lava-rock waterways, wooden bridges, and an open-air whirlpool.

The new emphasis is on family appeal, with a class of rooms dedicated to those traveling with kids. These "family suites" have three beds, a sitting room with full-size couch, and two TVs, both equipped with Nintendo. In addition, there's the Keiki Aloha program, with fun activities ranging from Hawaiian games to visits to nearby attractions. Children 12 and younger eat free when dining with one adult.

2605 Kaanapali Pkwy., Lahaina, HI 96761. ℂ **866/716-8109** or 808/661-0031. Fax 808/661-0458. www.sheraton-maui.com. 510 units. $470–$735 double; from $860 suite. Extra person $70. Children 17 and under stay free in parent's room using existing bedding. Resort fee of $17, plus tax for high-speed Internet access in guest rooms, self-parking, free local calls and credit card calls up to 60 min., free valet parking on the day of arrival. AE, DC, DISC, MC, V. Valet parking $5. **Amenities:** 2 restaurants; 2 poolside bars; indoor lounge; weekly luau show; nightly sunset cliff-dive ceremony; lagoon-style pool; beachfront snorkeling at Black Rock; 36-hole golf course; 3 tennis courts; fitness center; day spa; Jacuzzi; watersports equipment rentals; children's program; lobby and poolside concierge; car-rental desk; business center; room service; babysitting; coin-op washer/dryers; same-day laundry service and dry cleaning. *In room:* A/C, TV w/PlayStation, dataport, fridge, coffeemaker, hair dryer, iron, safe, high-speed Internet.

Westin Maui 🐸 *Kids*   The 758-room Westin Maui recently built a $5-million spa and gym. To further add to the healthy environment, smoking is no longer allowed in guest rooms. I love the fabulous custom-designed, pillow-top "heavenly beds," which come with a choice of five different pillows. If that doesn't give you sweet dreams, nothing will. Once you get up, head to the aquatic playground—an 87,000-square-foot pool area with five free-form heated pools joined by swim-through grottoes, waterfalls, and a 128-foot-long water slide. The fantasy theme extends from the estatelike grounds into the interior's public spaces, which are filled with the shrieks of tropical birds and the splash of waterfalls. The $2-million art collection makes a pleasing backdrop for all the action. Most of the rooms in the two 11-story towers overlook the aquatic playground, the ocean, and the island of Lanai in the distance.

2365 Kaanapali Pkwy., Lahaina, HI 96761. **©** **888/625-4949** or 808/667-2525. Fax 808/661-5764. www.westinmaui.com. 758 units. $485–$710 double; from $1,100 suite. Extra person $70. Resort fee of $18 for free local calls, use of fitness center and spa, coffee and tea, a souvenir shopping bag, shuttle services to golf and tennis facilities, in-room high-speed Internet access, self-parking, and local paper. AE, DC, DISC, MC, V. Valet parking $15. **Amenities:** 5 restaurants; 3 bars; 5 free-form outdoor pools; 36-hole golf course; tennis courts; health club and spa w/aerobics, steam baths, sauna, massages, and body treatments; Jacuzzi; watersports equipment rentals; bike rental; children's program; game room; concierge; activities desk; car-rental desk; business center; shopping arcade; salon; room service; in-room and spa massage; babysitting; same-day laundry service and dry cleaning. *In room:* A/C, TV, dataport, minibar, fridge, coffeemaker, hair dryer, iron, safe, high-speed Internet access.

EXPENSIVE

Outrigger Maui Eldorado Resort 🐸 *Kids*   These spacious condominium units—each with full kitchen, washer/dryer, and daily maid service—were built at a time when land in Kaanapali was cheap, contractors took pride in their work, and visitors expected large, spacious units with views from every window. You'll find it hard to believe that this was one of Kaanapali's first properties in the late 1960s; this first-class choice still looks like new. The Outrigger chain has managed to keep prices down to reasonable levels, especially in spring and fall. This is a great choice for families, with big units, grassy areas that are perfect for running off excess energy, and a beachfront (with beach cabanas and a barbecue area) that's usually safe for swimming. Tennis courts are nearby.

2661 Kekaa Dr., Lahaina, HI 96761. © **800/688-7444** or 808/661-0021. Fax 808/667-7039. www.outrigger.com. 204 units. $249–$299 studio double; $299–$349 1-bedroom unit (up to 4); $425–$539 2-bedroom (up to 6). Numerous packages available, including 5th night free, rental-car packages, senior rates, and more. Parking $5. AE, DC, DISC, MC, V. **Amenities:** 3 outdoor pools; 36-hole golf course; concierge/activities desk; car-rental desk; some business services; washer/dryers. *In room:* A/C, TV, dataport, kitchen, fridge, coffeemaker, hair dryer, iron, safe, washer/dryer.

The Whaler on Kaanapali Beach 🌟🌟

In the heart of Kaanapali, right on the world-famous beach, lies this oasis of elegance, privacy, and luxury. The relaxing atmosphere strikes you as soon as you enter the open-air lobby, where light reflects off the dazzling koi in the meditative lily pond. No expense has been spared on these gorgeous accommodations; each unit has a full kitchen, washer/dryer, marble bathroom, 10-foot beamed ceilings, and blue-tiled lanai. Every unit boasts spectacular views of Kaanapali's gentle waves or the humpback peaks of the West Maui Mountains. Next door is Whalers Village, with numerous restaurants, bars, and shops. Kaanapali Golf Club's 36 holes are across the street.

2481 Kaanapali Pkwy. (next to Whalers Village), Lahaina, HI 96761. © **866/77-HAWAII** or 808/661-4861. Fax 808/661-8315. www.resortquesthawaii.com. 360 units. $255–$330 studio double; $360–$415 1-bedroom unit (up to 4 people); $305–$760 2-bedroom (up to 6 people). Check website for specials. AE, DC, DISC, MC, V. Parking $10 per day. **Amenities:** Outdoor pool; tennis courts; refurbished fitness room; Hinamana Salon & Spa (which offers massages, pedicures, and manicures); Jacuzzi; concierge desk; activities desk; coin-op washer/dryers. *In room:* A/C, TV/VCR/DVD, kitchen, fridge, coffeemaker, hair dryer, iron, safe, washer/dryer, free dial-up Internet access (fee charged for wireless access).

MODERATE

Kaanapali Beach Hotel 🌟 *Value*

It's older and less high-tech than its upscale neighbors, but the Kaanapali has an irresistible local style and a real Hawaiian warmth that's missing from many other Maui hotels. Three low-rise wings, which border a fabulous stretch of beach, are set around a wide, grassy lawn with coco palms and a whale-shaped pool. The spacious, spotless motel-like rooms are done in wicker and rattan, with Hawaiian-style bedspreads and a lanai that looks toward the courtyard and the beach. The beachfront rooms are separated from the water only by Kaanapali's landscaped walking trail.

As part of the hotel's extensive Hawaiiana program, you can learn to cut pineapple, weave lauhala, even dance the *real* hula. The children's program is complimentary. Service is some of the friendliest around.

2525 Kaanapali Pkwy., Lahaina, HI 96761. © **800/262-8450** or 808/661-0011. Fax 808/667-5978. www.kbhmaui.com. 430 units. $195–$335 double; from $275 suite. Extra person $30. Car, golf, bed-and-breakfast, and romance packages available, as well as senior discounts. AE, DC, DISC, MC, V. Valet parking $11, self-parking $9. **Amenities:** 2 restaurants; bar (poolside; it fixes a mean piña colada); outdoor pool; 36-hole golf course nearby; access to tennis courts; watersports equipment rentals; children's program; concierge/guest services; activities desk; convenience shops; salon; babysitting; coin-op washer/dryers. *In room:* A/C, TV, fridge, coffeemaker, iron, safe.

HONOKOWAI, KAHANA & NAPILI
EXPENSIVE
Napili Kai Beach Resort ★★ *(Finds)*   Just south of the Kapalua Resort lies this comfortable oceanfront complex. The one- and two-story units with double-hipped Hawaii-style roofs face their very own gold-sand beach, which is safe for swimming. Many units have a view of the Pacific, with Molokai and Lanai in the distance. Those who prefer air-conditioning should book into the Honolua Building, where you'll get a fully air-conditioned room set back from the shore around a grassy, parklike lawn and pool. Most (but not all) units have a fully stocked kitchenette. On-site pluses include daily maid service, even in the condo units; two shuffleboard courts; barbecue areas; complimentary morning coffee and afternoon tea; weekly lei making, hula lessons, and horticultural tours; and a free weekly mai tai party. There are three nearby championship golf courses, excellent tennis courts, shopping, and yummy restaurants at the adjacent Kapalua Resort.

5900 Honoapiilani Rd. (at the extreme north end of Napili, next to Kapalua), Lahaina, HI 96761. © **800/367-5030** or 808/669-6271. Fax 808/669-0086. www.napilikai.com. 162 units. $220–$260 hotel room double; $275–$360 studio double (sleeps 3–4); $415–$500 1-bedroom suite (sleeps up to 5); $585–$755 2-bedroom (sleeps up to 7). Packages available. AE, DISC, MC, V. **Amenities:** Restaurant; bar; 4 outdoor pools; 2 18-hole putting greens (w/free golf putters for guest use); tennis courts nearby (and complimentary use of tennis rackets); good-size fitness room; Jacuzzi; complimentary watersports equipment; free children's activities at Easter, June 15–Aug 31, and Christmas; concierge; activities desk; babysitting; coin-op washer/dryers; laundry; dry cleaning. *In room:* A/C (most units), TV, kitchenette (most units), fridge, coffeemaker, hair dryer, iron, safe.

MODERATE
Kahana Sunset ★★ *(Kids)*   Lying in the crook of a sharp horseshoe curve on Lower Honoapiilani Road is this series of wooden condo units, stair-stepping down a hill to a postcard-perfect white-sand beach. The unique location, nestled between the coastline and the road above, makes this a very private place to stay. In the midst of

Where to Stay & Dine from Honokowai to Kapalua

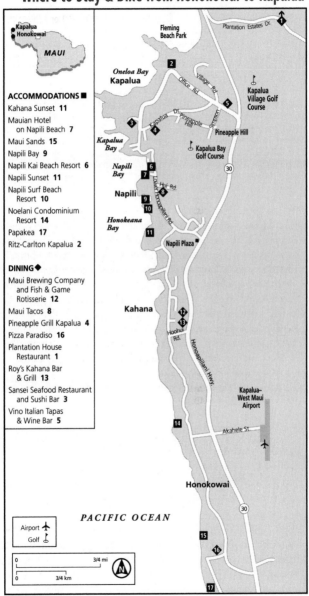

MAUI

Kapalua
Honokowai

ACCOMMODATIONS ■

Kahana Sunset **11**

Mauian Hotel
on Napili Beach **7**

Maui Sands **15**

Napili Bay **9**

Napili Kai Beach Resort **6**

Napili Sunset **11**

Napili Surf Beach
Resort **10**

Noelani Condominium
Resort **14**

Papakea **17**

Ritz-Carlton Kapalua **2**

DINING ◆

Maui Brewing Company
and Fish & Game
Rotisserie **12**

Maui Tacos **8**

Pineapple Grill Kapalua **4**

Pizza Paradiso **16**

Plantation House
Restaurant **1**

Roy's Kahana Bar
& Grill **13**

Sansei Seafood Restaurant
and Sushi Bar **3**

Vino Italian Tapas
& Wine Bar **5**

Fleming
Beach Park

Plantation Estates Dr.

Oneloa Bay
Kapalua

Office Rd.

Village Rd.

Kapalua
Village Golf
Course

Kapalua Dr.

Pineapple Hill

Simpson Rd.

Pineapple Hill

Kapalua Bay

Kapalua Bay
Golf Course

30

Napili Bay

Napili

Lower Honoapiilani Rd.

Hui Rd.

Honokeana Bay

Napili Plaza

Kahana

Hoohui Rd.

Honoapiilani Hwy.

Kapalua–
West Maui
Airport

Akahele St.

30

Honokowai

PACIFIC OCEAN

Airport ✈
Golf ⛳

0   3/4 mi
0   3/4 km

N

the buildings sits a grassy lawn with a small pool and Jacuzzi; down by the sandy beach are gazebos and picnic areas. The units feature full kitchens, washer/dryers, large lanais with terrific views, and sleeper sofas. This is a great complex for families: The beach is safe for swimming, the grassy area is away from traffic, and the units are roomy.

4909 Lower Honoapiilani Hwy. (at the northern end of Kahana, almost in Napili). Book with Premier Properties, c/o P.O. Box 10219, Lahaina, HI 96761. ℂ **800/ 669-1488** or 808/669-8011. Fax 808/669-9170. www.kahanasunset.com. 79 units. $155–$275 1-bedroom unit (sleeps up to 4); $210–$440 2-bedroom (sleeps up to 6). AE, MC, V. From Hwy. 30, turn makai (toward the ocean) at the Napili Plaza (Napilihau St.), then left on Lower Honoapiilani Rd. **Amenities:** 2 outdoor pools (1 just for children); concierge. *In room:* TV/VCR/DVD, kitchen, coffeemaker, iron, safe (in some units), washer/dryer.

Mauian Hotel on Napili Beach ✿
The Mauian is perched above a beautiful ½-mile-long white-sand beach with great swimming and snorkeling; there's a pool with chaise longues, umbrellas, and tables on the sun deck, and the verdant grounds are bursting with tropical color. The rooms feature hardwood floors, Indonesian-style furniture, and big lanais with great views. Thoughtful little touches include fresh flowers, plus chilled champagne for guests celebrating a special occasion. There are no phones or TVs in the rooms, but the large *ohana* (family) room does have a TV with a VCR, complimentary Internet access, and an extensive library. There's complimentary coffee, and phones and fax service are available in the business center. Great restaurants are just a 5-minute walk away, and Kapalua Resort is up the street. The nightly sunsets off the beach are spectacular.

5441 Lower Honoapiilani Rd. (in Napili), Lahaina, HI 96761. ℂ **800/367-5034** or 808/669-6205. Fax 808/669-0129. www.mauian.com. 44 units. $155–$230 double (sleeps up to 4). Extra person $10. Children under 5 stay free in parent's room. AE, DISC, MC, V. **Amenities:** Outdoor pool; golf course nearby; tennis courts nearby; activities desk; coin-op washer/dryers; shuffleboard court. *In room:* Kitchen, fridge, coffeemaker, no phone.

Napili Surf Beach Resort ✿ *Finds*
This well-maintained, superbly landscaped condo complex has a great location on Napili Beach. Facilities include two pools, three shuffleboard courts, and three gas barbecue grills. The well-furnished units (all with full kitchens) were renovated in 2004 with new carpet and new beds, and some units even have all-new kitchens. Free daily maid service, a rarity in condo properties, keeps the units clean. Management encourages socializing: In addition to weekly mai tai parties and coffee socials, the resort hosts annual shuffleboard and golf tournaments, as

well as get-togethers on July 4th, Thanksgiving, Christmas, and New Year's.

50 Napili Place (off Lower Honoapiilani Rd., in Napili), Lahaina, HI 96761. © **800/ 541-0638** or 808/669-8002. Fax 808/669-8004. www.napilisurf.com. 53 units (some with shower only). $111–$237 studio double (sleeps 3); $190–$336 1-bed-room double (sleeps 4). Extra person $15. No credit cards. **Amenities:** 2 outdoor pools; shuffleboard; barbecue grills; coin-op washer/dryers. *In room:* TV/VCR, full kitchen, fridge, coffeemaker, iron, safe.

Noelani Condominium Resort *Kids* This oceanfront condo is a great value, whether you stay in a studio or a three-bed-room unit (ideal for large families). Everything is first-class, from the furnishings to the oceanfront location. Though it's on the water, there's no sandy beach here (despite the photos posted on their web-site)—but next door is a sandy cove at the county park, which opened in 2001. There's good snorkeling off the cove, which is fre-quented by spinner dolphins and turtles in summer and humpback whales in winter. All units feature complete kitchens, entertainment centers, and spectacular views (all except the studio units also have their own washer/dryers and dishwashers). My favorites are in the Anthurium Building, where the condos have oceanfront lanais just 20 feet from the water. Frugal travelers will love the deluxe studios in the Orchid Building, with great ocean views for just $125. Guests are invited to a continental breakfast orientation on their first day and mai tai parties at night. There are also oceanfront barbecue grills for guest use.

4095 Lower Honoapiilani Rd. (in Kahana), Lahaina, HI 96761. © **800/367-6030** or 808/669-8374. Fax 808/669-7904. www.noelani-condo-resort.com. 50 units. $125–$175 studio double; $167–$197 1-bedroom unit (sleeps up to 4); $257–$290 2-bedroom (sleeps up to 6); $317–$357 3-bedroom (sleeps up to 8). Rates include continental breakfast on 1st morning. Extra person $20. Children under 18 stay free in parent's room. Packages for honeymooners, seniors, and AAA members available. 3-night minimum. AE, MC, V. **Amenities:** 2 freshwater swimming pools (1 heated for night swimming); access to nearby health club; oceanfront Jacuzzi; concierge; activities desk; car-rental desk; coin-op washer/dryers. *In room:* TV/VCR, kitchen, fridge, coffeemaker, hair dryer, iron, safe, washer/dryer (in larger units).

INEXPENSIVE

Maui Sands The Maui Sands was built back when property wasn't as expensive and developers took the extra time and money to sur-round their condos with lush landscaping. It's hard to get a unit with a bad view: All face either the ocean (with views of Lanai and Molokai) or tropical gardens blooming with brilliant heliconia, hibiscus, and sweet-smelling ginger. Each roomy unit has a big lanai and a full kitchen. With two big bedrooms, plus space in the living room for a fifth person (or even a sixth), the larger units are good deals for families. There's a narrow beach out front.

Maui Resort Management, 3600 Lower Honoapiilani Rd. (in Honokowai), Lahaina, HI 96761. ☎ 800/367-5037 or 808/669-1900. Fax 808/878-8790. www.mauiresort management.com. 76 units. $100–$165 1-bedroom unit (sleeps up to 3); $190–$220 2-bedroom (sleeps 5). 7-night minimum. MC, V. **Amenities:** Outdoor pool; coin-op washer/dryers. *In room:* A/C, TV, kitchen, fridge, coffeemaker.

Napili Bay *ℱ* *Finds*   One of Maui's best bargains is this small, two-story complex right on Napili's beautiful ½-mile white-sand beach. It's perfect for a romantic getaway: The atmosphere is comfortable and relaxing, the ocean lulls you to sleep at night, and birdsong wakes you in the morning. The beach here is one of the best on the coast, with great swimming and snorkeling—in fact, it's so beautiful that people staying at much more expensive resorts down the road frequently haul all their beach paraphernalia here for the day. The studio apartments are definitely small, but they pack in everything you need to feel at home, from a full kitchen to a comfortable queen-size bed, and a roomy lanai that's great for watching the sun set over the Pacific. There's no air-conditioning, but louvered windows and ceiling fans keep the units fairly cool during the day. There are lots of restaurants and a convenience store within walking distance, and you're about 10 to 15 minutes away from Lahaina and some great golf courses.

33 Hui Dr. (off Lower Honoapiilani Hwy., in Napili). c/o Aloha Condos Hawaii, P.O. Box 396681, Keauhou, HI 96740. ☎ 877/782-5642. www.alohacondos.com. 33 units. $120–$235 double. Cleaning fee $85. 5-night minimum. MC, V. **Amenities:** Coin-op washer/dryers. *In room:* TV, kitchen, fridge, coffeemaker.

Papakea *Value*   Just a mile down the beach from Kaanapali lie these low-rise buildings, surrounded by manicured, landscaped grounds and ocean views galore. Palm trees and tropical plants dot the property, a putting green wraps around two kidney-shaped pools, and a footbridge arches over a lily pond brimming with carp. Each pool has its own private cabana with sauna, Jacuzzi, and barbecue grills; a poolside shop rents snorkel gear for exploring the offshore reefs. All units have big lanais and washer/dryers. The studios have pull-down beds to save space during the day. Definitely a good value.

Maui Resort Management, 3600 Lower Honoapiilani Rd. (in Honokowai), Lahaina, HI 96761. ☎ 800/367-5037 or 808/669-1900. Fax 808/669-8790. www.mauigetaway. com. 364 units. $115–$135 studio double; $165–$220 1-bedroom unit (sleeps up to 4); $190–$270 2-bedroom (sleeps up to 6). 7-night minimum. MC, V. **Amenities:** 2 outdoor pools; 3 tennis courts; 2 Jacuzzis; watersports equipment rental; washer/dryer. *In room:* A/C, TV/VCR, kitchen, fridge, coffeemaker, washer/dryer.

KAPALUA
VERY EXPENSIVE

Ritz-Carlton Kapalua ★★ *Kids*   This Ritz is a complete universe, one of those resorts where you can happily sit by the ocean with a book for 2 whole weeks and never leave the grounds. It rises proudly on a knoll, in a singularly spectacular setting between the rainforest and the sea.

The style is fancy plantation, elegant but not imposing. The public spaces are open, airy, and graceful, with plenty of tropical foliage and landscapes by artist Sarah Supplee that recall the not-so-long-ago agrarian past. Rooms are up to the usual Ritz standard, outfitted with marble bathrooms, private lanais, and in-room fax capability. The Ritz Kids program offers a variety of educational activities and sports.

The excellent Banyan Tree Restaurant has a new chef, and the relaxing spa has just undergone extensive renovation and has a new menu of Hawaiian-influenced treatments. The resort's Hawaiian cultural program is one of Maui's best, with twice weekly movies and "talk story," along with other events.

As we went to press, the investment partnership that recently purchased this property plans to sell 107 suites in the hotel to individual buyers; some will be available to guests and some will remained privately owned and occupied. The hotel announced that it would close the property for some $95 million in renovations and hoped to reopen for Christmas 2007. Contact the hotel for details.

1 Ritz-Carlton Dr., Kapalua, HI 96761. © **800/262-8440** or 808/669-6200. Fax 808/669-1566. www.ritzcarlton.com. 548 units. $505–$675 double; $700–$875 Club Floor double; from $675 suite; from $815 Club Floor suite. Extra person $50 ($100 in Club Floor rooms). Resort fee of $18 for use of fitness center, steam room and sauna, selected wellness classes, preferred tee times, Aloha Friday festivities, cultural history tours, self-parking, resort shuttle service, signing privileges at selected restaurants and shops in the resort, tennis, morning coffee at the Lobby Lounge, use of the 9-hole putting green, tennis and basketball courts, and games of bocce ball on the lawn. Wedding/honeymoon, golf, and other packages available. AE, DC, DISC, MC, V. Valet parking $15, free self-parking. **Amenities:** 4 restaurants; 4 bars (including 1 serving drinks and light fare next to the beach); outdoor pool; access to the Kapalua Resort's 3 championship golf courses (each w/its own pro shop), golf teaching academy, and deluxe tennis complex; fitness room; spa; 2 outdoor hot tubs; watersports equipment rentals; bike rentals; children's program; game room; concierge; activities desk; car-rental desk; business center; shopping arcade; salon; room service; in-room and spa massage; babysitting; same-day laundry and dry cleaning; concierge-level rooms (some of Hawaii's best, w/top-drawer service and amenities). *In room:* A/C, TV, dataport, coffeemaker, hair dryer, iron, high-speed Internet $14/day.

3 South Maui

MAALAEA

I recommend two booking agencies that rent a host of condominiums and unique vacation homes in the Kihei/Wailea/Maalaea area: **Kihei Maui Vacation** (② 800/541-6284 or 808/879-7581; www.kmvmaui.com) and **Condominium Rentals Hawaii** (② 800/367-5242 or 808/879-2778; www.crhmaui.com).

KIHEI
EXPENSIVE

Hale Pau Hana Resort *Kids* Located on the sandy shores of Kamaole Beach Park but separated from the white-sand beach by a velvet green manicured lawn, this is a great condo resort for families. Each of the large units has a private lanai, a terrific ocean view, and a complete kitchen. The management goes above and beyond, personally greeting each guest and acting as your own concierge service. Guests can mingle at the free coffee hour every morning, or at the pupu parties with local Hawaiian entertainment held twice a week at sunset. The location is in the heart of Kihei, close to shopping, restaurants, and activities.

2480 S. Kihei Rd., Kihei, HI 96753. ② **800/367-6036** or 808/879-2715. Fax 808/875-0238. www.hphresort.com. 79 units. $237–$323 1-bedroom unit; $373–$486 2-bedroom. MC, V. **Amenities:** Pool; concierge; coin-op laundry; barbecue. *In room:* A/C in bedrooms, TV, full kitchens, fridge, coffeemaker, hair dryer, iron, safe.

Maui Coast Hotel *R* This place stands out as one of the few hotels in Kihei (which is largely full of affordable condo complexes rather than traditional hotels or resorts). Ask about the room/car packages: The Maui Coast's Extra Value package gives you a rental car for just a few dollars more than the regular room rate. It's a great location, about a block from Kamaole Beach Park I, with plenty of bars, restaurants, and shopping within walking distance and a golf course nearby. The rooms offer extras such as sitting areas, whirlpool tubs, ceiling fans, and private lanais.

2259 S. Kihei Rd. (1 block from Kamaole Beach Park I), Kihei, HI 96753. ② **800/895-6284** or 808/874-6284. Fax 808/875-4731. www.mauicoasthotel.com. 265 units. $265 double; $295 suite; $325 1-bedroom unit (sleeps up to 4). Children 17 and under stay free in parent's room using existing bedding. Rollaway bed $20. Packages available. AE, DC, DISC, MC, V. **Amenities:** Restaurant; pool bar w/nightly entertainment; outdoor pool (plus children's wading pool); 2 night-lit tennis courts; fitness room; concierge; activities desk; room service; washer/dryers; laundry service; dry cleaning. *In room:* A/C, TV, fridge, coffeemaker, hair dryer, iron, safe.

Where to Stay & Dine in South Maui

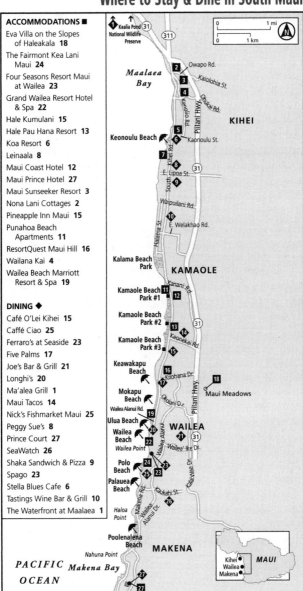

ACCOMMODATIONS ■

Eva Villa on the Slopes
of Haleakala **18**

The Fairmont Kea Lani
Maui **24**

Four Seasons Resort Maui
at Wailea **23**

Grand Wailea Resort Hotel
& Spa **22**

Hale Kumulani **15**

Hale Pau Hana Resort **13**

Koa Resort **6**

Leinaala **8**

Maui Coast Hotel **12**

Maui Prince Hotel **27**

Maui Sunseeker Resort **3**

Nona Lani Cottages **2**

Pineapple Inn Maui **15**

Punahoa Beach
Apartments **11**

ResortQuest Maui Hill **16**

Wailana Kai **4**

Wailea Beach Marriott
Resort & Spa **19**

DINING ◆

Café O'Lei Kihei **15**

Caffé Ciao **25**

Ferraro's at Seaside **23**

Five Palms **17**

Joe's Bar & Grill **21**

Longhi's **20**

Ma'alea Grill **1**

Maui Tacos **14**

Nick's Fishmarket Maui **25**

Peggy Sue's **8**

Prince Court **27**

SeaWatch **26**

Shaka Sandwich & Pizza **9**

Spago **23**

Stella Blues Cafe **6**

Tastings Wine Bar & Grill **10**

The Waterfront at Maalaea **1**

ResortQuest Maui Hill ⓡ If you can't decide between the privacy of a condo and the conveniences of a hotel, try this place. Maui Hill gives you the best of both worlds. Located on a hill above the heat of Kihei town, this large, Spanish-style resort (with stucco buildings, red-tile roofs, and arched entries) combines all the amenities and activities of a hotel—pool, hot tub, tennis courts, Hawaiiana classes, maid service, and more—with large luxury condos that have full kitchens and plenty of privacy. Nearly all units have ocean views, dishwashers, washer/dryers, queen-size sofa beds, and big lanais. Beaches, restaurants, and shops are within easy walking distance, a golf course is nearby, and barbecue grills are provided for guests' use. The management here goes out of its way to make sure your stay is perfect.

2881 S. Kihei Rd. (across from Kamaole Park III, between Keonekai St. and Kilohana Dr.), Kihei, HI 96753. ⓒ **866/77-HAWAII** or 808/879-6321. Fax 808/879-8945. www.resortquesthawaii.com. 140 units. $220–$325 1-bedroom apt, $275–$410 2-bedroom, $405–$525 3-bedroom. Extra person $30. AE, DC, DISC, MC, V. **Amenities:** Outdoor pool; putting green; tennis courts; Jacuzzi; concierge; activities desk; car-rental desk; coin-op washer/dryers; laundry service; dry cleaning. *In room:* A/C, TV/VCR, kitchen, fridge, coffeemaker, hair dryer, iron, safe, washer/dryer.

MODERATE

Eva Villa on the Slopes of Haleakala ⓡⓡ *Finds* True to its name, this three-unit bed-and-breakfast is located on ½-acre of lushly landscaped property at the top of the Maui Meadows subdivision. From the rooftop lanai, guests have a spectacular view of the sunset behind Kahoolawe and Lanai and of the West Maui Mountains. Hosts Rick and Dale Pounds have done their best to make this one of Maui's classiest vacation rentals. From the continental breakfast stocked in the unit's kitchen (fresh island fruit, juice, bread, muffins, jam, and coffee/tea) to the decor of the suites to the heated pool, Jacuzzi, and individual barbecue facilities, this is a great place to stay. The location couldn't be better: just a few minutes' drive to Kihei's sunny beaches, golf courses, tennis, and shopping, and restaurants in Kihei and Wailea. Each unit is a roomy 600 square feet. The separate cottage has a living room, full kitchen, and separate bedroom; the poolside studio is a one-room unit with a huge kitchen; and the poolside suite has two bedrooms and a kitchenette. You can't go wrong here.

815 Kumulani Dr., Kihei, HI 96753. ⓒ **800/824-6409** or 808/874-6407. Fax 808/874-6407. www.mauibnb.com. 3 units. $145–$175 double. Extra person $15. No credit cards. **Amenities:** Heated outdoor pool; Jacuzzi. *In room:* TV/DVD, kitchen or kitchenette, fridge, coffeemaker, washer/dryer in cottage, wireless Internet.

Leinaala ⓡ *Value* From Kihei Road, you can't see Leinaala amid the jumble of buildings, but this oceanfront boutique condo offers excellent accommodations at 1980s prices. The building is set back from the water, with a county park—an oasis of green grass and tennis courts—in between. A golf course lies nearby. The units are compact but filled with everything you need: a full kitchen, sofa bed, and oceanview lanai. (Hideaway beds are available if you need one.)

998 S. Kihei Rd., Kihei, HI 96753. ⓒ **800/822-4409** or 808/879-2235. Fax 808/874-6144. www.mauicondo.com. 24 units. $130–$160 1-bedroom double; $175–$205 2-bedroom unit (sleeps up to 4). 4-night minimum. No credit cards. **Amenities:** Outdoor pool; coin-op washer/dryers. *In room:* A/C, TV, kitchen, fridge, coffeemaker.

Maui Sunseeker *(Finds)*   This former budget property, located just across the street from a terrific white-sand beach, has a new management team who have spiffed up the studio and one-bedroom units with custom furniture, and added air-conditioning and several amenities not usually seen at small properties (like high-speed Internet access and concierge services). The units have been tastefully redecorated. The one-bedrooms, which have a pullout sofa in the living room and new appliances in the kitchen, are a deal during low season. All units have private lanais with ocean views with the beach just a few steps away, and there's a gas barbecue for guests' use. The new owners also bought the apartment complex next door, revamping everything and putting slate in the bathroom and new tile on the floor, buying new furniture, and repainting. The units are small, but the lanais are large, the price is right, and the beach is just across the street. There's also a gas barbecue available. Plus there's a rooftop lanai where you can sit in the hot tub and enjoy great ocean views.

551 S. Kihei Rd., P.O. Box 276, Kihei, HI 96753. ⓒ **800/532-MAUI** or 808/879-1261. Fax 808/874-3877. www.mauisunseeker.com. 16 units. $120–$160 hotel room double; $120–$170 studio double; $150–$200 Junior Suite double; $155–$205 Premium Junior Suite double; $135–$225 1-bedroom double. Extra person $15. AE, DISC, MC, V. **Amenities:** Hot tub; concierge; coin-op washer/dryers; same-day laundry service. *In room:* A/C, TV/VCR, full kitchen (1-bedroom) or kitchenette (studio), coffeemaker, hair dryer, answering machine, high-speed Internet.

Punahoa Beach Apartments ⓡ *(Value)*   Book this place! I can't put it any more simply than that. The location—off noisy, traffic-ridden Kihei Road, on a quiet side street with ocean frontage—is fabulous. A grassy lawn rolls about 50 feet down to the beach, where there's great snorkeling just offshore and a popular surfing spot next door; shopping and restaurants are all within walking distance. All of the beautifully decorated units in this small, four-story building have fully equipped kitchens and lanais with great ocean views. Rooms go quickly in winter, so reserve early.

2142 Iliili Rd. (off S. Kihei Rd., 300 ft. from Kamaole Beach I), Kihei, HI 96753. ℂ **800/564-4380** or 808/879-2720. Fax 808/875-9147. www.punahoabeach.com. 13 units. $116–$150 studio double; $160–$231 1-bedroom double; $198–$263 2-bedroom double; $188–$258 1-bedroom penthouse. Extra person $15. 5-night minimum. AE, MC, V. **Amenities:** Coin-op washer/dryer. *In room:* TV, kitchen, fridge, coffeemaker, iron.

INEXPENSIVE

Hale Kumulani ✿ *Finds*   At the top of Maui Meadows subdivision, right on the Wailea border and about a 5-minute drive to the beach, lies this ½-acre property, surrounded by a 40,000-acre wilderness area with two quaint units. The first is a darling one-room cottage with full kitchen, wood flooring, high-beam ceilings, living-room area (with king-size bed and full-size guest sofa/futon), large deck, and outdoor shower. Underneath the main house, but with its own entrance and complete privacy, is the waterfall suite. It has a full kitchen, two bedrooms and two bathrooms, and a living/dining area that opens to a landscaped area with a waterfall plus banana and papaya trees. (It's also wheelchair-accessible.) Both units have access to the organic vegetable garden, numerous fruit trees, and beach equipment. Hosts Ron and Merry couldn't be more gracious in helping you navigate around the island. They also have a full-size crib, stroller, and junior beds available for kids.

874 Kumulani Dr., Maui Meadows, Kihei, HI 96753. ℂ **808/891-0425.** Fax 808/ 891-0269. www.cottagemaui.com. 2 units. $155 cottage double; $175 suite double. 4-night minimum. MC, V. **Amenities:** 6 championship golf courses within 5 miles; aquatic center w/3 pools nearby (a 7-min. drive). *In room:* TV/DVD, kitchen, fridge, coffeemaker, hair dryer, iron, washer/dryer, Wi-Fi.

Koa Resort ✿ *Kids*   Located just across the street from the ocean, Koa Resort consists of five two-story wooden buildings on more than 5½ acres of landscaped grounds. The spacious, privately owned one-, two-, and three-bedroom units are decorated with care and come fully equipped, right down to the dishwasher and disposal in the kitchens. There's plenty of room for families, who can enjoy the tennis courts, pool, and putting green. The larger condos have both showers and tubs; the smaller units have showers only. All feature large lanais, ceiling fans, and washer/dryers. For maximum peace and quiet, ask for a unit far from Kihei Road. Bars, restaurants, and a golf course are nearby.

811 S. Kihei Rd. (between Kulanihakoi St. and Namauu Place). c/o Bello Realty, P.O. Box 1776, Kihei, HI 96753. ℂ **800/541-3060** or 808/879-3328. Fax 808/875-1483. www.bellomaui.com. 54 units, some with shower only. High season $115 1-bedroom unit, $120–$130 2-bedroom, $180–$200 3-bedroom; low season $99 1-bedroom,

SOUTH MAUI

59

$100–$110 2-bedroom, $160–$180 3-bedroom. MC, V. **Amenities:** Outdoor pool; 18-hole putting green; 2 tennis courts; Jacuzzi. *In room:* TV, kitchen, fridge, coffee-maker, iron, safe, washer/dryer.

Nona Lani Cottages ⊛ *(Finds)*   Picture this: a grassy expanse dotted with eight cottages tucked among palm, fruit, and sweet-smelling flower trees, right across the street from a white-sand beach. This is one of the great hidden deals in Kihei. The cottages are tiny but contain everything you'll need: a small but complete kitchen, twin beds that double as couches in the living room, a separate bedroom with a queen-size bed, and a lanai with table and chairs. The real attraction, however, is the garden setting next to the beach. There are no phones in the cabins, but there's a public one by the check-in area.

If the cabins are booked, or if you want a bit more luxury, you might opt for one of the private guest rooms. These beautiful units feature plush carpet, koa bed frames, air-conditioning, lanais, and private entrances. The industrious Kong family, hosts here, also run Happy Valley Hale Maui, hostel accommodations on the other side of the island in Happy Valley, next to Wailuku.

455 S. Kihei Rd. (just south of Hwy. 31; P.O. Box 655), Kihei, HI 96753. ℂ **800/733-2688** or 808/879-2497. www.nonalanicottages.com. 11 units. $90–$100 double; $100–$120 cottage. Extra person $12–$15. 3-night minimum for rooms, 4-night minimum for cottages. No credit cards. **Amenities:** Coin-op washer/dryers. *In room:* A/C, TV, kitchen (in cottages), fridge, coffeemaker, no phone.

Pineapple Inn Maui ⊛⊛ *(Finds)*   Opened at the end of 2004, this charming inn (only four rooms, plus a darling two-bedroom cottage) is an exquisite find, with terrific prices. Located in the residential Maui Meadows area, with panoramic ocean views, this two-story inn (one side of the building is the owner's home) boasts gorgeous landscaping, with tropical flowers and plants and a lily pond in the front and a giant saltwater pool and Jacuzzi overlooking the ocean. Each of the rooms is soundproof and expertly decorated, with a small kitchenette stocked with juice, pastries, and drinks on your arrival. There's also an incredible view off your own private lanai. If you need more room, they also offer a darling two-bedroom, one-bathroom cottage (wood floors, beautiful artwork) with a full kitchen (even a dishwasher), separate bedrooms, and a private lanai. The cottage is landscaped for maximum privacy.

3170 Akala Dr., Kihei, HI 96753. ℂ **877/212-MAUI (6284)** or 808/298-4403. www.pineappleinnmaui.com. 5 units. $109–$139 double; $185 cottage for 4. 3-night minimum for rooms, 6-night minimum for cottage. No credit cards. **Amenities:** Large saltwater pool; Jacuzzi; complimentary laundry facilities. *In room:* A/C, TV/VCR, kitchenette (in rooms), full kitchen (in cottage), fridge, coffeemaker, hair dryer, no phone (in rooms), wireless Internet access.

Wailana Kai ★ *Value*   Bello Realty has added this renovated, two-story, 10-unit, one- and two-bedroom apartment complex to its collection. As of this writing, one-bedroom units start at $90, but this is a deal that will not last long. Once they get a reputation, the prices most likely will go up. Located at the end of a cul-de-sac and just a 1-minute walk to the beach, the property was totally renovated in 2004 with two types of units: standard (perfectly acceptable, clean, with new paint, furniture, and more) and deluxe (the ones I recommend, for only a few dollars more). All units have full kitchens and soundproof concrete walls, and the second floor has ocean views.

34 Wailana Place. c/o Bello Realty, P.O. Box 1776, Kihei, HI 96753. © 800/ 541-3060 or 808/879-3328. Fax 808/875-1483. www.bellomaui.com. 10 units. $90–$110 1-bedroom unit; $110–$125 2-bedroom. MC, V. **Amenities:** Outdoor pool; coin-op washer/dryers. *In room:* TV/VCR, kitchen, fridge, coffeemaker, iron.

WAILEA

For a complete selection of condo units throughout Wailea and Makena, contact **Destination Resorts Hawaii** (© **800/367-5246** or 808/879-1595; fax 808/874-3554; www.drhmaui.com).

VERY EXPENSIVE

The Fairmont Kea Lani Maui ★★★   At first glance this blinding-white complex of arches and turrets may look a bit out of place in tropical Hawaii (it's actually a close architectural cousin of Las Hadas, the Arabian Nights fantasy resort in Manzanillo, Mexico). But once you enter the flower-filled lobby and see the big blue Pacific outside, there's no doubt you're in Hawaii.

This is the place to get your money's worth. For the price of a hotel room, you get an entire suite—plus a few extras. Each unit in this all-suite luxury hotel has a kitchenette, a living room with entertainment center and sofa bed, a marble wet bar, an oversize marble bathroom with separate shower big enough for a party, a spacious bedroom, and a large lanai that overlooks the pools, lawns, and white-sand beach.

The villas are definitely out of a fantasy. The rich and famous stay in these 2,000-square-foot two- and three-bedroom beach bungalows, each with its own plunge pool and gourmet kitchen.

4100 Wailea Alanui Dr., Wailea, HI 96753. © **800/659-4100** or 808/875-4100. Fax 808/875-1200. www.fairmont.com/kealani. 450 units. $475–$1,000 suite (sleeps up to 4); from $1,900 villa. Valet parking $15, complimentary self-parking. AE, DC, DISC, MC, V. **Amenities:** 4 restaurants (including Nick's Fishmarket Maui, p. 94) plus gourmet bakery and deli; 3 bars (w/sunset cocktails and entertainment at the Caffè Ciao Restaurant); 2 large swimming lagoons connected by a 140-ft. water slide and swim-up bar, plus an adult pool; closer by is Wailea Golf Club's 3

18-hole championship golf courses, as well as the nearby Makena and Elleair golf courses; use of Wailea Tennis Center's 11 courts (3 lit for night play) and a pro shop; fine 24-hr. fitness center; excellent full-service spa; 2 whirlpools; watersports equipment rentals; year-round children's program; seasonal (summer and holidays) game room; concierge; activities desk; business center; shopping arcade; full-service salon; 24-hr. room service; in-room and spa massage; babysitting; complimentary self-service laundry; same-day laundry service and dry cleaning. *In room:* A/C, TV/DVD/VHS, dataport, kitchenette, fridge, coffeemaker, hair dryer, iron, safe, CD player, high-speed Internet $14/day, microwave.

Four Seasons Resort Maui at Wailea ☺☺☺ *Kids*   If money's no object, this is the place to spend it. It's hard to beat this modern version of a Hawaiian palace by the sea, with a relaxing, casual atmosphere. Although it sits on a glorious beach between two other hotels, you won't feel like you're on chockablock resort row: The Four Seasons inhabits its own separate world, thanks to an open courtyard of pools and gardens. Amenities are first-rate here, including outstanding restaurants, an excellent spa, and a wonderful activities program for kids (complimentary, of course). In fact, this may be the most kid-friendly hotel on Maui, with cookies and milk on arrival, children's menus in all restaurants, and complimentary baby gear (cribs, strollers, and even toilet-seat locks).

The spacious (about 600 sq. ft.) rooms feature furnished lanais (nearly all with ocean views) that are great for watching whales in winter and sunsets year-round. The grand bathrooms contain deep marble tubs, showers for two, and lighted French makeup mirrors.

Service is attentive but not cloying. At the pool, guests lounge in Casbah-like tents, pampered with special touches like iced Evian and chilled towels.

The fabulous spa has an incredible menu of treatments ranging from traditional Hawaiian to craniosacral to ayurvedic massage offered in 13 treatment rooms and three ocean-side *hales*.

The ritzy neighborhood surrounding the hotel is home to great restaurants and shopping, the Wailea Tennis Center (known as Wimbledon West), and six golf courses—not to mention that great beach, with gentle waves and islands framing the view on either side.

3900 Wailea Alanui Dr., Wailea, HI 96753. © 800/334-MAUI (6284) or 808/874-8000. Fax 808/874-2222. www.fourseasons.com/maui. 380 units. $425–$880 double; $960–$1,060 club floor; from $790 suite. Packages available. Extra person $100 ($250 in Club Floor rooms). Children under 18 stay free in parent's room. Valet parking $12. AE, DC, MC, V. **Amenities:** 3 restaurants (including Spago, p. 94); 3 bars (w/nightly entertainment); 3 fabulous outdoor pools; putting green; use of Wailea Golf Club's 3 18-hole championship golf courses, as well as the nearby Makena and Elleair golf courses; 2 on-site tennis courts (lit for night play); use of Wailea Tennis Center's 11 courts (3 lit for night play); health club featuring outdoor cardiovascular equipment (w/individual television/video players); excellent spa; 2 whirlpools (1 for adults only); beach pavilion w/watersports gear rentals and 1-hr. free use of snorkel equipment; complimentary use of bicycles; fabulous year-round kids' program; one of Maui's best concierge desks; activities desk; car-rental desk; business center; shopping arcade; salon; room service; in-room, spa, or ocean-side massage; babysitting; same-day laundry service and dry cleaning; concierge-level rooms. *In room:* A/C, TV, dataport, minibar, fridge, coffeemaker, hair dryer, iron, safe, high-speed Internet ($10/day).

Grand Wailea Resort Hotel & Spa 𝕲𝕲𝕲   *Spa aficionados take note:* Hawaii's largest (50,000 sq. ft.) and most elaborate spa is located here, with every kind of body treatment you can imagine. Treatments include use of the numerous baths, hot tubs, mineral pools, saunas, steam rooms, and other relaxation amenities in the his-and-her spa area.

Built at the pinnacle of Hawaii's brief fling with fantasy megaresorts, the Grand Wailea is extremely popular with families, incentive groups, and conventions. It has a Japanese restaurant decorated with real rocks hewn from the slopes of Mount Fuji; 10,000 tropical plants in the lobby; an intricate pool system with slides, waterfalls, and rapids; a restaurant in a man-made tide pool; and nothing but oceanview, amenity-filled rooms. It's all crowned with a $30-million collection of original art, much of it created expressly for the hotel by Hawaii artists and sculptors. Though minimalists may be put off, there's no denying that the Grand Wailea is plush, professional, and pampering, with all the diversions you could imagine. Oh, and did I mention the fantastic beach out front?

All the rooms and suites are now nonsmoking. Smoking is limited to the private lanais outside the rooms.

3850 Wailea Alanui Dr., Wailea, HI 96753. ℂ **800/888-6100** or 808/875-1234. Fax 808/874-2442. www.grandwailea.com. 780 units. $575–$950 double; from $1,800 suite; concierge (Na Pua) tower from $1,200. Resort fee $20 for lei greeting on arrival, welcome drink, local calls, coffee in room, use of spa, pools, admission to scuba-diving clinics and water aerobics, art and garden tours, nightly turndown service, high-speed Internet access, self-parking, and shuttle service to Wailea area. Extra person $50 ($100 in Na Pua Tower). AE, DC, DISC, MC, V. **Amenities:** 6 restaurants; 7 bars (including a nightclub w/laser-light shows); 2,000-ft.-long Activity Pool, featuring a swim/ride through mountains and grottoes; use of Wailea Golf Club's 3 18-hole championship golf courses, as well as the nearby Makena and Elleair golf courses; use of Wailea Tennis Center's 11 courts (3 lit for night play) and a pro shop; complete fitness center; Hawaii's largest spa; Jacuzzi; watersports equipment rentals; children's program; game room; concierge; activities desk; car-rental desk; business center; shopping arcade; salon; room service; in-room and spa massage; babysitting; same-day laundry service and dry cleaning; concierge-level rooms; dive and windsurf lessons. *In room:* A/C, TV, dataport, kitchenette, minibar, fridge ($25 per stay fee), coffeemaker, hair dryer, iron, safe, high-speed Internet.

EXPENSIVE

Wailea Beach Marriott Resort & Spa ⭐⭐   This classic, open-air, 1970s-style hotel in a tropical garden by the sea gives you a sense of what Maui was like before the big resort boom. It was the first resort built in Wailea (in 1976), and it remains the most Hawaiian of them all. Airy and comfortable, with touches of Hawaiian art throughout and a terrific aquarium that stretches forever behind the front desk, it just feels right.

What's truly special about this hotel is how it fits into its environment without overwhelming it. Eight buildings, all low-rise except for an eight-story tower, are spread along 22 gracious acres of lawns and gardens spiked by coco palms, with lots of open space and ½ mile of oceanfront property on a point between Wailea and Ulua beaches. The vast, parklike expanses are a luxury on this now-crowded coast.

The entire hotel has undergone a $60-million renovation, so it looks like it was just built. The small Mandara Spa offers a large list of treatments, from relaxing massages to aroma wraps to rejuvenating facials in a very Zen atmosphere.

3700 Wailea Alanui Dr., Wailea, HI 96753. ℂ **800/367-2960** or 808/879-1922. Fax 808/874-8331. www.waileamarriott.com. 545 units. $435–$800 single/double; from $850 suite. Extra person $40. Packages available. Resort fee $15 plus tax per night for self parking, high-speed Internet access, local phone calls, daily sunset appetizer, luau and snorkel gear rental discounts, and free kids' meals with purchase of adult entree. AE, DC, DISC, MC, V. **Amenities:** 2 restaurants; 2 bars; outdoor swimming pools; use of Wailea Golf Club's 3 18-hole championship golf courses; use of Wailea Tennis Center's 11 courts (3 lit for night play) and a pro shop; fitness center; full-service Mandara Spa & Salon w/steam rooms and whirlpools; watersports equipment rentals; children's program (plus kids-only pool and recreation center); concierge; activities desk; business center; shopping arcade; salon; room service; in-room or outdoor massages; babysitting; same-day laundry service and dry cleaning. *In room:* A/C, flatscreen TV, 4-outlet technology console, coffeemaker, hair dryer, iron, safe, ergonomic desk and chair, wet bar.

MAKENA

Maui Prince Hotel ⭐⭐   If you're looking for a vacation in a beautiful, tranquil spot with a golden-sand beach, here's your place. But if you plan to tour Maui, you might try another hotel. The Maui Prince is at the end of the road, far, far away from anything else on the island, so sightseeing in other areas would require a lot of driving.

When you first see the stark-white hotel, it looks like a high-rise motel stuck in the woods—but only from the outside. Inside, you'll discover an atrium garden with a koi-filled waterfall stream, an ocean view from every room, and a simple, clutter-free decor. Rooms are small but come with private lanais with great views.

5400 Makena Alanui, Makena, HI 96753. ℭ **800/321-6284** or 808/874-1111. Fax 808/879-8763. www.mauiprincehotel.com. 310 units. $355–$525 double; from $700 suite. Extra person $60. Packages available. AE, DC, MC, V. **Amenities:** 4 restaurants (including Prince Court, p. 96); 2 bars w/local Hawaiian music nightly; 2 outdoor pools (adults' and children's); 36-hole golf course (designed by Robert Trent Jones, Jr.); 6 Plexipave tennis courts (2 lit for night play); fitness room; Jacuzzi; watersports equipment rentals; children's program; concierge; activities desk; shopping arcade; salon; room service; in-room massage; babysitting; same-day laundry service and dry cleaning. *In room:* A/C, TV, dataport, fridge, hair dryer, iron, safe.

4 Upcountry Maui

MAKAWAO, OLINDA & HALIIMAILE
EXPENSIVE

Aloha Cottage 𝒦𝒦 *Finds*   Hidden in the secluded rolling hills of Olinda on a 5-acre parcel of manicured, landscaped tropical foliage are two separate cottages, both designed and decorated by the hosts, Ron and Ranjana Serle. The Thai Tree House ($245 a night) resembles an upscale Thai home with high vaulted ceilings, teak floors, and a king-size cherrywood bed in the center of the room. The private deck and private soaking tub make this a very romantic lodging. As fabulous as the Thai Tree House is, the Bali Bungalow ($318) is even better. Up a private driveway through a bamboo archway, the Balinese cottage features an octagonal design with multifaceted skylights, a large marble shower built for two, hand-carved teak cabinets in the kitchen area, and Oriental carpets on the hardwood floors. Out on the private deck is a soaking tub for two. Ranjana can arrange weddings, prepare a private dinner, set up personal massages, and even organize a private yoga session for two.

1879 Olinda Rd., Makawao, HI 96765. ℭ **888/328-3330** or 808/573-8555. Fax 808/573-2551. www.alohacottage.com. 2 cottages. $245–$318 double. 3-night minimum. MC, V. *In room:* TV/VCR, kitchen, fridge, coffeemaker, hair dryer, iron, safe, CD player, private soaking tub.

MODERATE

Olinda Country Cottages & Inn 𝒦𝒦 *Finds*   This charming property is set on the slopes of Haleakala in the crisp, clean air of Olinda, on an 8½-acre farm dotted with the surreal protea plants and surrounded by 35,000 acres of ranchland (with miles of great hiking trails). The 5,000-square-foot country home, outfitted with a professional eye to detail, has large windows with incredible panoramic views of all of Maui. Upstairs are two guest rooms with country furnishings and separate entryways. Connected to the main house, but with its own private entrance, the Pineapple Suite has a full kitchen, an antiques-filled living room, and a marble-tiled full bathroom. A separate 1,000-square-foot cottage is the epitome of cozy country luxury, with a fireplace, a queen-size bedroom, cushioned window seats (with great sunset views), and cathedral ceilings. My favorite, the 950-square-foot Hidden Cottage (located in a truly secluded spot surrounded by protea flowers) features three decks, 8-foot French glass doors, a full kitchen, a washer/dryer, and a private tub for two on the deck.

Restaurants are a 15-minute drive away in Makawao, and beaches are another 15 minutes beyond that. Once ensconced, however, you may never want to leave this enchanting inn.

2660 Olinda Rd. (near the top of Olinda Rd., a 15-min. drive from Makawao), Makawao, HI 96768. © 800/932-3435 or 808/572-1453. Fax 808/573-5326. www.mauibnbcottages.com. 5 units. $140 double; $140 suite double; $195–$245 cottage for 2 (sleeps up to 5). Extra person $25. 2-night minimum for rooms and suite, 3-night minimum for cottages. No credit cards. *In room:* TV, kitchen (in cottages), fridge, coffeemaker, washer/dryer (in cottages).

INEXPENSIVE

Banyan Tree House ⚑ *Finds*   Huge monkeypod trees (complete with swing and hammock) extend their branches over this 2½-acre property like a giant green canopy. The restored 1920s plantation manager's house is decorated with Hawaiian furniture from the 1930s. The house can accommodate a big family or a group of friends; it has three spacious bedrooms with big, comfortable beds and three marble-tiled bathrooms. A fireplace stands at one end of the huge living room, a large lanai runs the entire length of the house, and the hardwood floors shine throughout. The four smaller guest cottages have been totally renovated and also feature hardwood floors and marble bathrooms.

New additions to this grand property include a full-size swimming pool and Jacuzzi. The quiet neighborhood and old Hawaii ambience give this place a comfortable, easygoing atmosphere. Restaurants and shops are just minutes away in Makawao, and the beach is a 15-minute drive away—but this place is so relaxing that you may find yourself wanting to do nothing more than lie in the hammock and watch the clouds float by.

3265 Baldwin Ave. (next to Veteran's Cemetery, less than a mile below Makawao), Makawao, HI 96768. © 808/572-9021. Fax 808/573-5072. www.hawaii-mauirentals.com. 5 units. $155 double in house double; $150–$184 cottage for 2. Extra person $20. Children age 12 and under stay in parent's room for $10. 3-night minimum for house. No credit cards. **Amenities:** Outdoor pool; Jacuzzi; babysitting; small charge for washer/dryer. *In room:* TV (in some cottages), kitchen or kitchenette, fridge, coffeemaker.

Hale Ho'okipa Inn Makawao *⚡ Finds*   Step back in time at this 1924 plantation-style home, rescued by owner Cherie Attix in 1996 and restored to its original charm (on the State and National Historic Registers). Cherie lovingly refurbished the old wooden floors, filled the rooms with furniture from the 1920s, and hung works by local artists on the walls. The result is a charming, serene place to stay, just a 5-minute walk from the shops and restaurants of Makawao, 15 minutes from beaches, and an hour's drive from the top of Haleakala. The guest rooms have separate outside entrances and private bathrooms. The house's front and back porches are both wonderful for sipping tea and watching the sun set. The Kona Wing is a two-bedroom suite with private bathroom and use of the kitchen.

32 Pakani Place, Makawao, HI 96768. ⓒ **877/572-6698** or ⓒ/fax 808/572-6698. www.maui-bed-and-breakfast.com. 4 units (2 with shower only). $115–$145 double; $160–$175 suite with full kitchen. Rates include continental breakfast. Extra person $10. MC, V. From Haleakala Hwy., turn left on Makawao Ave., then turn right on the 5th street on the right off Makawao Ave. (Pakani Place); 2nd to the last house on the right (green house with white picket fence and water tower). *In room:* A/C, TV, hair dryer, Internet.

KULA

Lodgings in Kula are the closest options to the entrance of Haleakala National Park (about 60 min. away).

MODERATE

Malu Manu *⚡⚡ Finds*   This is one of the most romantic places to stay on Maui, with a panoramic view of the entire island from the front door. Tucked into the side of Haleakala Volcano at 4,000 feet is this old Hawaiian estate with a single-room log cabin (built as a writer's retreat in the early 1900s) and a 35-year-old family home. The writer's cabin has a full kitchen, a fireplace, and antiques galore. The two-bedroom, 2½-bathroom home also has antiques, koa walls, and beautiful eucalyptus floors. It's an ideal retreat for a romantic couple, a family, or two couples traveling together. The 7-acre property is filled with native forest, organic gardens (help yourself to lemons, avocados, and whatever else is ripe), a paddle-tennis court, and a Japanese-style outdoor soaking tub. If you're a dog person, you can also enjoy getting to know the resident golden retriever, Alohi. This is one of the closest accommodations to Haleakala; restaurants are about a 15-minute drive away.

446 Cooke Rd., Kula, HI 96790 (mailing address: P.O. Box 175, Kula, HI 96790). ⓒ **888/878-6161** or 808/878-6111. www.mauisunrise.com. 2 units. $150 double in log cabin; $185 double in 2-bedroom house. Extra person $10. 3-night minimum.

MC, V. **Amenities:** Hot tub; paddle-tennis court; in-room massage; laundry facilities. *In room:* Kitchen, fridge, coffeemaker, iron.

INEXPENSIVE

Kula Cottage *(Finds)*   I can't imagine having a less-than-fantastic vacation here. Tucked away on a quiet street amid a large grove of blooming papaya and banana trees, Cecilia and Larry Gilbert's romantic honeymoon cottage is very private—it even has its own driveway and carport. The 700-square-foot cottage has a full kitchen (complete with dishwasher), and three huge closets that offer enough storage space for you to move in permanently. An outside lanai has a big gas barbecue and an umbrella-covered table and chairs. Cecilia delivers a continental breakfast daily. Groceries and a small takeout lunch counter are within walking distance. It's a 30-minute drive to the beach.

40 Puakea Place (off Lower Kula Rd.), Kula, HI 96790. © **808/878-2043** or 808/871-6230. Fax 808/871-9187. www.kulacottage.com. 1 unit. $95 double. 2-night minimum. Rate includes continental breakfast. No credit cards. *In room:* TV, kitchen, fridge, coffeemaker, washer/dryer.

Kula Lynn Farm Bed & Bath *(Kids)*   The Coons, the same great family that runs Maui's best sailing adventure on the *Trilogy,* offer this spectacular 1,600-square-foot unit on the ground floor of a custom-built pole house. From its location on the slopes of Haleakala, the panoramic view alone—across Maui's central valley, with the islands of Lanai and Kahoolawe in the distance—is worth the price. Wall-to-wall windows and high ceilings add to the spacious feeling throughout. It's the perfect place for a family, with two bedrooms, two bathrooms, and two queen-size sofa beds in the living room. The spare-no-expense, European-style kitchen boasts top appliances and Italian marble floors. This place should appeal to those who enjoy a quiet location and such activities as barbecuing on the lanai and watching the sun set.

2114 Naalae Rd. (P.O. Box 847), Kula, HI 96790. © **808/878-6176.** Fax 808/878-6320. captcoon@hawaiiantel.net. 1 unit. $119 double. 5-night minimum. Rate includes breakfast fixings. Extra person $20. No credit cards. *In room:* TV/DVD, kitchen, fridge, coffeemaker, iron.

5 East Maui: On the Road to Hana

KUAU

The Inn at Mama's Fish House *(★★)*   The fabulous location (nestled in a coconut grove on secluded Kuau Beach), beautifully decorated interior (with rattan furniture and works by Hawaiian artists), and extras such as gas barbecues, 27-inch TVs, and lots of beach toys, make this place a gem for those seeking a centrally located vacation rental. All this and the fabulous Mama's Fish House restaurant is just next door. The one-bedrooms are nestled in a tropical jungle, with red ginger surrounding the garden patio, and the two-bedrooms face the beach. Both have terra-cotta floors, complete kitchens (even dishwashers), sofa beds, and laundry facilities.

799 Poho Place (off the Hana Hwy. in Kuau), Paia, HI 96779. (C) **800/860-HULA** or 808/579-9764. Fax 808/579-8594. www.mamasfishhouse.com. 6 units. $225 1-bedroom unit (sleeps up to 4); $475 2-bedroom (up to 6). 3-night minimum. AE, DISC, MC, V. **Amenities:** Restaurant. *In room:* A/C, TV/VCR, kitchen, fridge, coffeemaker, hair dryer, iron, washer/dryer.

HAIKU

Maui Dream Cottages *Value*   Essentially a vacation rental, this country estate is located atop a hill overlooking the ocean. The grounds are dotted with fruit trees (bananas, papayas, and avocados, all free for the picking), and the front lawn is comfortably equipped with a double hammock, chaise longues, and table and chairs. One cottage has two bedrooms, a full kitchen, a washer/dryer, and an entertainment center. The other is basically the same but with only one bedroom (plus a sofa bed in the living room). They're both very well maintained and comfortably outfitted with furniture that's attractive but casual. The Haiku location is quiet and restful and offers the opportunity to see how real islanders live. However, you'll have to drive a good 20 to 25 minutes to restaurants in Makawao or Paia. Hookipa Beach is about a 20-minute drive, and Baldwin Beach (good swimming) is 25 minutes away.

265 W. Kuiaha Rd. (1 block from Pauwela Cafe), Haiku, HI 96708. (C) **808/ 575-9079.** Fax 808/575-9477. www.mauidreamcottage.com. 2 units (shower only). $560/week double. Extra person $10. 7-night minimum. MC, V. *In room:* TV, kitchen, fridge, coffeemaker, washer/dryer.

Pilialoha B&B Cottage *(Finds)*   The minute you arrive at this split-level country cottage, located on a large lot with half-century-old eucalyptus trees, you'll see owner Machiko Heyde's artistry at work. Just in front of the quaint cottage (which is great for couples but can sleep up to five) is a garden blooming with some 200 varieties of roses. You'll find more of Machiko's handiwork inside. There's a queen-size bed in the master bedroom, a twin bed in a small adjoining room, and a queen-size sofa bed in the living room. A large lanai extends from the master bedroom. There's a great movie collection for rainy days or cool country nights, and a garage. Machiko delivers breakfast daily; if you plan on an early morning ride to the top of Haleakala, she'll make sure you go with a thermos of coffee and her homemade bread.

2512 Kaupakalua Rd. (½ mile from Kokomo intersection), Haiku, HI 96708. © **808/ 572-1440.** Fax 808/572-4612. www.pilialoha.com. 1 unit. $130 double. Extra person $20. 3-night minimum. Rates include continental breakfast. MC, V. **Amenities:** Complimentary use of beach toys (including snorkel equipment); washer/dryer. *In room:* TV, kitchenette, fridge, coffeemaker.

Wild Ginger Falls 🌺🌺 *Finds*   This cozy, romantic, intimate cottage, hidden in Miliko Gulch, overlooks a stream with a waterfall, bamboo, sweet-smelling ginger, and banana trees. It's perfect for honeymooners, lovers, and fans of Hawaiiana art. The moment you step into this 400-square-foot, artistically decorated Hawaiian cottage (with additional 156-sq.-ft. screened deck), you will be delighted at the memorabilia (ukulele tile, canoe paddle, and the like) found throughout. The cottage has a full kitchen with everything you need for cooking. The comfy queen-size bed opens to the living area. The screened porch has a table, chairs, and a couch, perfect for curling up with a good book. Outside there's a barbecue, plus plenty of beach toys to borrow. Your hosts are Bob, a ceramics artist (with his creations on display throughout the cottage), and his wife, Sunny, who manages Dolphin Galleries (where she buys artwork for the cottage).

355 Kaluanui Rd., Makawao, HI 96768. ©/fax **808/573-1173.** www.wildginger falls.com. 1 unit. $135–$145 double. 3-night minimum. No credit cards. *In room:* TV/VCR, kitchen, fridge, coffeemaker, hair dryer, iron, washer/dryer.

HUELO/WAILUA

Huelo Point Flower Farm *Finds*   Here's a little Eden by the sea on a spectacular, remote, 300-foot sea cliff near a waterfall stream. This estate overlooking Waipio Bay has two guest cottages, a guesthouse, and a main house available for rent. The studio-size Gazebo Cottage has three glass walls that make the most of the cottage's oceanfront location, a koa-wood captain's bed, a TV, a stereo, a kitchenette, a private oceanside patio, a private hot tub, and a half bathroom with outdoor shower. The new 900-square-foot Carriage House apartment sleeps four and has glass walls facing the mountain and sea, plus a kitchen, a den, decks, and a loft bedroom. The two-bedroom main house contains an exercise room, a fireplace, a sunken Roman bath, cathedral ceilings, and other extras. On-site is a natural pool with a waterfall and an oceanfront hot tub. You're welcome to pick fruit, vegetables, and flowers from the extensive garden. Homemade scones, tree-ripened papayas, and fresh-roasted coffee start your day. The secluded location, off the crooked road to Hana, is just a half-hour from Kahului, or about 20 minutes from Paia's shops and restaurants.

Off Hana Hwy., between mile markers 3 and 4. P.O. Box 791808, Paia, HI 96779. © 808/572-1850. www.mauiflowerfarm.com. 4 units. $225 cottage double; $240 carriage house double; $395 guesthouse double; $495 main house for 4. Extra person $20–$35. 2-night minimum for smaller houses, 5-night minimum for main house. No credit cards. **Amenities:** Outdoor pool; 3 Jacuzzis; washer/dryer. *In room:* TV, kitchenette (in cottage), kitchen (in houses), fridge, coffeemaker, hair dryer.

Kailua Maui Gardens *Finds*   In the middle of nowhere lies this nearly 2-acre tropical botanical garden with a main house and several bungalows dotting the property. Just a couple of miles down the serpentine Hana Highway from Huelo, in the remote area of Kailua, is an unlikely place for accommodations (it's a 30-min. drive to the nearest beach and 1 hr. to Hana), but for those who want to get away from it all, this could be your place. The small cabanas range from a two-bedroom cottage with a full kitchen to compact accommodations with basic kitchenette amenities. The Main House has three bedrooms and a full kitchen. They all face out into gorgeous gardens. In the midst of the botanical garden is a pool, with a cabana and covered barbecue area, and a hot tub. The garden sits right on the Hana Highway, so ask for a unit away from the road. Unfortunately, they have a 2-night minimum. Even if you don't stay here, stop by and visit the garden—hosts Keone and Cheryl love to show people their piece of paradise.

Located between mile markers 5 and 6 on the Hana Hwy. (S.R. 1, Box 9, Haiku, HI 96708). © **808/572-9726.** Fax 808/572-8845. www.kailuamauigardens.com. 7 units. $125–$175 double; $425 house for 6. 2-night minimum. AE, DC, MC, V. **Amenities:** Outdoor pool; 2 hot tubs; laundry facilities. *In room:* TV, kitchen or kitchenette, fridge, coffeemaker, wireless Internet access.

6 At the End of the Road in East Maui: Hana

To locate the following accommodations, see the "Hana" map on p. 151.

EXPENSIVE

Hotel Hana-Maui *★★★* *Kids*   This hotel sits on 66 rolling seaside acres and offers a wellness center, two pools, and access to one of the best beaches in Hana. This is the atmosphere, the landscape, and the culture of old Hawaii set in 21st-century accommodations. Every unit is excellent, but my favorites are the Sea Ranch Cottages (especially units 215–218 for the best views), where individual duplex bungalows look out over the craggy shoreline to the rolling surf. You step out of the oversize, open, airy units (with floor-to-ceiling sliding doors) onto a huge lanai with views that will stay with you long after your tan has faded. These comfy units have been totally redecorated with every amenity you can think of, and you won't be nickel-and-dimed for things like coffee and water—everything they give you, from the homemade banana bread to the bottled water, is complimentary. Cathedral ceilings, a plush feather bed, a giant-size soaking tub, Hawaiian artwork, bamboo hardwood floors—this is luxury. The white-sand beach (just a 5-min. shuttle away), top-notch wellness center with some of the best massage therapists in Hawaii, and numerous activities (horseback riding, mountain biking, tennis, pitch-and-putt golf) all add up to make this one of the top resorts in the state. There's no TV in the rooms, but the Club Room has a giant-screen TV, plus VCR and Internet access. I highly recommend this little slice of paradise.

5031 Hana Hwy. (P.O. Box 9), Hana, Maui, HI 96713. ℂ **800/321-HANA** or 808/248-8211. Fax 808/248-7202. www.hotelhanamaui.com. 66 units. $475–$525 Bay Cottages double; $625–$1,075 Sea Ranch Cottages double; $1,575 2-bedroom suite for 4; 2-bedroom Plantation Guest House from $4,000. Extra person $140. AE, DC, DISC, MC, V. **Amenities:** Restaurant (w/Hawaiian entertainment twice a week); bar (entertainment 4 times a week); 2 outdoor pools; complimentary use of the 3-hole practice golf courses (clubs are complimentary); complimentary tennis courts; fitness center; full-service spa; game room; concierge; activities desk; car-rental desk; business center; small shopping arcade; salon; room service; babysitting; laundry service. *In room:* Dataport, kitchenette, fridge, coffeemaker, hair dryer, iron, safe.

MODERATE

Ekena ⊛   Just one glance at the 360-degree view and you can see why hosts Robin and Gaylord gave up their careers on the mainland and moved here. This 8½-acre piece of paradise in rural Hana boasts ocean and rainforest views; the floor-to-ceiling glass doors in the spacious Hawaiian-style pole house bring the outside in. The elegant two-story home is exquisitely furnished, from the comfortable U-shaped couch that invites you to relax and take in the view to the top-of-the-line mattress on the king-size bed. The fully equipped kitchen has everything you should need to cook a gourmet meal. Only one floor (and one two-bedroom unit) is rented at any one time to ensure privacy. The grounds are impeccably groomed and dotted with tropical plants and fruit trees. Hiking trails into the rainforest start right on the property, and beaches and waterfalls are just minutes away. Robin places fresh flowers in every room and makes sure you're comfortable; after that, she's available to answer questions, but she also respects your privacy.

Off Hana Hwy., above Hana Airport (P.O. Box 728), Hana, HI 96713. ℂ **808/ 248-7047.** Fax 808/248-7853. www.ekenamaui.com. 2 units. $225 for 2;

$295–$400 for 4. Extra person $35. 3-night minimum. MC, V. **Amenities:**
Washer/dryers. *In room:* TV/DVD, kitchen, fridge, coffeemaker, iron, CD player.

Hamoa Bay Bungalow *⟨R⟩ ⟨Finds⟩*   Down a country lane guarded by
two Balinese statues stands a little bit of Indonesia in Hawaii: a carefully crafted bungalow and an Asian-inspired two-bedroom house
overlooking Hamoa Bay. This enchanting retreat is just 2 miles
beyond Hasegawa General Store on the way to Kipahulu. It sits on
4 verdant acres within walking distance of Hamoa Beach (which
author James Michener considered one of the most beautiful in the
Pacific). The 600-square-foot Balinese-style cottage is distinctly
tropical, with giant elephant-bamboo furniture from Indonesia,
batik prints, a king-size bed, a full kitchen, and a screened porch
with hot tub and shower. Hidden from the cottage is a 1,300-
square-foot home with a soaking tub and private outdoor stone
shower. It offers an elephant-bamboo king-size bed in one room, a
queen-size bed in another, a screened-in sleeping porch, a full
kitchen, and wonderful ocean views.

P.O. Box 773, Hana, HI 96713. © 808/248-7884. Fax 808/248-7853.
www.hamoabay.com. 2 units. $225 cottage (sleeps only 2); $285 house for 2; $395
house for 4. 3-night minimum. MC, V. **Amenities:** Hot tub; washer/dryers. *In room:*
TV/DVD, kitchen, fridge, coffeemaker, iron, CD player.

Hana Hale Inn *⟨Finds⟩*   Hana Inn sits on a historic site with ancient
fishponds and a cave mentioned in ancient chants. Host John takes
excellent care of the ponds (you're welcome to watch him feed the
fish at 5pm daily) and is fiercely protective of the hidden cave ("It's
not a tourist attraction, but a sacred spot"). There's access to a
nearby rocky beach, which isn't good for swimming but makes a
wonderful place to watch the sunset. All accommodations include
fully equipped kitchens, bathrooms, bedrooms, living/dining areas,
and private lanais. Next to the fishpond, the Royal Lodge, a 2,600-
square-foot architectural masterpiece built entirely of Philippine
mahogany, has large skylights the entire length of the house and can
be rented as a house or two separate units. The cottages range from
the separate two-level Tree House cottage (with Jacuzzi tub for two,
a Balinese bamboo bed, small kitchen/living area, and deck upstairs)
to the Pond Side Bungalow (with private outdoor Jacuzzi tub and
shower).

P.O. Box 374, Hana, HI 96713. © 808/248-7641. www.hanahaleinn.com. 5 units.
$145–$260 double. Extra person $15. 2-night minimum. MC, V. **Amenities:** Jacuzzi.
In room: TV/DVD, kitchen, fridge, coffeemaker, Jacuzzi (in all but 1 unit).

Hana Oceanfront 🍴🍴   Just across the street from Hamoa Bay, Hana's premier white-sand beach, lie these two plantation-style units, impeccably decorated in old Hawaii decor. My favorite unit is the romantic cottage, complete with a front porch where you can sit and watch the ocean; a separate bedroom (with a bamboo sleigh bed), plus a pullout sofa for extra guests; top-notch kitchen appliances; and comfy living room. The 1,000-square-foot vacation suite, located downstairs from hosts Dan and Sandi's home (but totally soundproof—you'll never hear them) has an elegant master bedroom with polished bamboo flooring, a spacious bathroom with custom hand-painted tile, and a fully appointed gourmet kitchen. Outside is a 320-square-foot lanai. The units sit on the road facing Hana's most popular beach, so there is traffic during the day. At night the traffic disappears, the stars come out, and the sound of the ocean soothes you to sleep.

P.O. Box 843, Hana, HI 96713. © **808/248-7558.** Fax 808/248-8034. www.hana oceanfrontcottages.com. 2 units. $250–$275 double. 3-night minimum. MC, V. **Amenities:** Barbecue area. *In room:* TV/VCR/DVD, full gourmet kitchen, fridge, coffee maker, hair dryer, iron, stereo/CD player.

Heavenly Hana Inn 🍴🍴 *Finds*   This place on the Hana Highway, just a stone's throw from the center of Hana town, is a little bit of heaven, where no attention to detail has been spared. Each suite has a sitting room with futon and couch, polished hardwood floors, and separate bedroom with a raised platform bed (with an excellent, firm mattress). The black-marble bathrooms have huge tubs. Flowers are everywhere, ceiling fans keep the rooms cool, and the delicious gourmet breakfast—worth splurging for—is served in a setting filled with art. The grounds are done in Japanese style with a bamboo fence, tiny bridges over a meandering stream, and Japanese gardens.

P.O. Box 790, Hana, HI 96713. © /fax **808/248-8442.** www.heavenlyhanainn.com. 3 units. $190–$260 suite. Full gourmet breakfast available for $17 per person. 2-night minimum. AE, DISC, MC, V. No children under age 15 accepted. *In room:* TV, no phone.

INEXPENSIVE

Hana's Tradewinds Cottages 🍴 *Value*   Nestled among the ginger and heliconias on a 5-acre flower farm are two separate cottages, each with full kitchen, carport, barbecue, private hot tub, TV, ceiling fans, and sofa bed. The studio cottage sleeps up to four; a bamboo shoji blind separates the sleeping area (with queen-size bed) from the sofa bed in the living room. The Tradewinds cottage has two bedrooms (with a queen-size bed in one room and two twins in the other), one bathroom (shower only), and a huge front porch. The atmosphere is quiet and relaxing, and hostess Rebecca Buckley, who has been in business for a decade, welcomes families (she has two children, a cat, and a very sweet golden retriever). You can use the laundry facilities at no extra charge.

135 Alalele Place (the airport road), P.O. Box 385, Hana, HI 96713. Ⓒ **800/ 327-8097** or 808/248-8980. Fax 808/248-7735. www.hanamaui.net. 2 units. $175 studio double; $175 2-bedroom double. Extra person $15. 2-night minimum. AE, DISC, MC, V. **Amenities:** Washer/dryer. *In room:* TV, kitchen, fridge, coffeemaker, no phone.

Waianapanapa State Park Cabins *Value*   These 12 rustic cabins are the best lodging deal on Maui. Everyone knows it, too—so make your reservations early (up to 6 months in advance). The cabins are warm and dry and come complete with kitchen, living room, bedroom, and bathroom with hot shower; furnishings include bedding, linen, towels, dishes, and very basic cooking and eating utensils. Don't expect luxury—this is a step above camping, albeit in a beautiful tropical jungle setting. The key attraction at this 120-acre beach park is the unusual horseshoe-shaped black-sand beach on Pailoa Bay, popular for shore fishing, snorkeling, and swimming. There's a caretaker on-site, along with restrooms, showers, picnic tables, shoreline hiking trails, and historic sites. But bring mosquito protection—this *is* the jungle, after all.

Off Hana Hwy. Reservations: State Parks Division, 54 S. High St., Room 101, Wailuku, HI 96793. Ⓒ **808/984-8109.** 12 cabins. $45 for 4 (sleeps up to 6). Extra person $5. 5-night maximum. No credit cards. *In room:* Kitchen, fridge, coffeemaker, no phone.

3

Where to Dine

With soaring visitor statistics and a glamorous image, the Valley Isle is fertile ground for Hawaii's famous enterprising chefs, as well as an international name or two. But some things haven't changed: You can still dine well at Lahaina's open-air waterfront watering holes, where the view counts for 50% of the experience. There are still budget eateries, but not many; Maui's old-fashioned, multigenerational mom-and-pop diners are disappearing, eclipsed by the flashy newcomers, or clinging to the edge of existence in the older neighborhoods of central Maui, such as lovable Wailuku. Although you'll have to work harder to find them in the resort areas, you won't have to go far to find creative cuisine, pleasing style, and stellar dining experiences.

In the listings below, reservations are not necessary unless otherwise noted.

1 Central Maui

KAHULUI
MODERATE

Mañana Garage ★★ *Finds* LATIN AMERICAN   Chef Ed Santos is serving up some incomparable fare at this central Maui hot spot. The industrial motif features table bases like hubcaps, a vertical garage door as a divider for private parties, blown-glass chandeliers, and gleaming chrome and cobalt walls with orange accents. The menu is brilliantly conceived and executed. Fried green tomatoes are done just right and served with slivered red onions. Three different kinds of seviche perfectly balance flavors and textures: lime, cilantro, chile, coconut, and fresh fish. They even have barbecued ribs. Mañana Garage has introduced exciting new flavors to Maui's dining scene—if you are on this side of the island, don't miss this incredible experience.

33 Lono Ave., Kahului. © 808/873-0220. Reservations recommended. Lunch main courses $7–$13; dinner main courses $16–$31. AE, DISC, MC, V. Mon, Wed, and Sat 11am–1:30am; Tues and Thurs 11am–9pm; Fri 11am–10:30pm; Sun 5–9pm.

Marco's Grill & Deli ITALIAN   Located in the thick of central Maui, where the roads to upcountry, west, and south Maui converge, Marco's is popular among area residents for its homemade Italian fare and friendly informality. Everything—from the meatballs, sausages, and burgers to the sauces, salad dressings, and ravioli—is made in-house. The 35 different choices of hot and cold sandwiches and entrees are served all day. Some favorites include vodka rigatoni with imported prosciutto, and simple pasta with marinara sauce. This is one of those comfortable neighborhood fixtures favored by all generations. The antipasto salad and roasted peppers are taste treats, but the meatballs and Italian sausage are famous in central Maui. It also has a full bar.

Dairy Center, 395 Dairy Rd., Kahului. ✆ 808/877-4446. Main courses $11–$27. AE, DISC, MC, V. Daily 7:30am–10pm.

INEXPENSIVE

Down to Earth *Value* ORGANIC HEALTH FOOD   If you are looking for a healthy alternative to fast foods, here's your place. Healthful organic ingredients, 90% vegan, appear in scrumptious salads, lasagna, chili, curries, and dozens of tasty dishes, presented at hot and cold serve-yourself stations. Stools line the counters in the simple dining area, where a few tables are available for those who don't want takeout. The food is great: millet cakes, mock tofu chicken, curried tofu, and Greek salad, everything organic and tasty, with herb-tamari marinades and pleasing condiments such as currants or raisins, apples, and cashews. (The fabulous tofu curry has apples, raw cashews, and raisins.) The food is sold by the pound, but you can buy a hearty, wholesome plate for $7. Vitamin supplements, health-food products, fresh produce, and cosmetics fill the rest of the store.

305 Dairy Rd., Kahului. ✆ 808/877-2661. www.downtoearth.org. Self-serve hot buffet and salad bar; food sold by the pound. Average $6–$8 for a plate. AE, MC, V. Mon–Sat 7am–9pm; Sun 8am–8pm.

Ichiban *Finds* JAPANESE/SUSHI   What a find: an informal neighborhood restaurant that serves inexpensive, home-cooked Japanese food *and* good sushi at realistic prices. Local residents consider Ichiban a staple for breakfast, lunch, or dinner and a haven of comforts: egg-white omelets; great saimin; combination plates of teriyaki chicken, teriyaki meat, *tonkatsu* (pork cutlet), rice, and pickled cabbage; chicken yakitori; and sushi—everything from unagi and scallop to California roll. The sushi items may not be cheap, but like the specials, such as steamed opakapaka, they're a good value. I love the tempura, miso soup, and spicy ahi hand roll.

Kahului Shopping Center, 47 Kaahumanu Ave., Kahului. © **808/871-6977**. Main courses $5–$6 breakfast, $7.95–$12 lunch (combination plates $9.95), $6.95–$30 dinner (combination dinner $13, dinner specials from $8.95). AE, DC, MC, V. Mon–Fri 7am–2pm; Sat 10:30am–2pm; Mon–Sat 5–9pm. Closed 2 weeks around Christmas and New Year's.

WAILUKU
MODERATE

Class Act ★ GLOBAL   Part of a program run by the distinguished Food Service Department of Maui Community College, now housed in a new state-of-the-art, $15-million culinary facility (with floor-to-ceiling windows at one end, exhibition kitchen at the other end) is this "classroom" restaurant, with a huge following. Student chefs show their stuff with a flourish and pull out all the stops to give you a dining experience you will long remember. Linen, china, servers in ties and white shirts, and a four-course lunch make this a unique value. The appetizer, soup, salad, and dessert are set, but you can choose between the regular entrees and a heart-healthy main course prepared in the culinary tradition of the week. The menu roams the globe with highlights of Italy, Mexico, Maui, Napa Valley, France, New Orleans, and other locales. The filet mignon of French week is popular, as are the New Orleans gumbo and Cajun shrimp, the sesame-crusted mahimahi on taro-leaf pasta, the polenta flan with eggplant, and the bean and green chile *chilaquile*.

Maui Community College, 310 Kaahumanu Ave., Wailuku. © **808/984-3280**. http://mauiculinary.com/academy/class_act.cfm. Reservations recommended. 4-course lunch $25. MC, V. Wed and Fri 11am–12:15pm (last seating). Closed June–Aug for summer vacation. Menu and cuisine type change weekly.

A Saigon Cafe ★★ *Finds* VIETNAMESE   Jennifer Nguyen has stuck to her guns and steadfastly refused to erect a sign, but diners find their way here anyway. That's how good the food is. Fans drive from all over the island for her crisped, spiced Dungeness crab, her steamed opakapaka with ginger and garlic, and her wok-cooked Vietnamese specials tangy with spices, herbs, and lemon grass. There are a dozen different soups, cold and hot noodles (including the popular beef noodle soup called pho), and chicken and shrimp cooked in a clay pot. You can create your own Vietnamese "burritos" from a platter of tofu, noodles, and vegetables that you wrap in rice paper and dip in garlic sauce. Among my favorites are the savory and refreshing shrimp lemon grass and the tofu curry, swimming in herbs and vegetables straight from the garden. The Nhung Dam— a hearty spread of basil, cucumbers, mint, romaine, bean sprouts, pickled carrots, turnips, and vermicelli, wrapped in rice paper and dipped in a legendary sauce—is cooked at your table.

1792 Main St., Wailuku. ☎ **808/243-9560.** Main courses $6.50–$17. DC, MC, V. Mon–Sat 10am–9:30pm; Sun 10am–8:30pm. Heading into Wailuku from Kahului, go over the bridge and take the 1st right onto Central Ave., then the 1st right on Nani St. At the next stop sign, look for the building with the neon sign that says OPEN.

INEXPENSIVE

AK's Café 🌟🌟 *Value*   HEALTHY/PLATE LUNCHES   Chef Elaine Rothermel has a winner with this tiny cafe in the industrial district of Wailuku. It may be slightly off the tourist path, but the creative cuisine coming out of the kitchen makes it well worth the effort to find this delicious eatery. Prices are so eye-popping cheap, you might find yourself wandering back here during your vacation. Lunches feature everything from grilled chicken with Thai sauce to fish tacos to hamburger steak to seared ahi sandwich with tempura eggplant. Dinner specials include chicken Marsala over noodles, crab cakes with papaya beurre blanc, tofu napoleon with ginger basil sauce, and Hunan lamb chops. There are plenty of heart-healthy options from which to choose (low in sugar, salt, and fat).

1237 Lower Main St., Wailuku. ☎ **808/244-8774.** www.akscafe.com. Plate lunches $6.75–$9.50; dinners $11–$18. MC, V. Tues–Fri 10:30am–2pm; Tues–Sat 5–9pm. Live Hawaiian music Fri–Sat nights.

Maui Bake Shop   BAKERY/DELI   Sleepy Vineyard Street has seen many a mom-and-pop business come and go, but Maui Bake Shop is here to stay. Maui native Claire Fujii-Krall and her husband, baker José Krall (who was trained in the south of France), are turning out buttery brioches, healthful nine-grain and two-tone rye breads, focaccia, strudels, sumptuous fresh-fruit gâteaux, puff pastries, and dozens of other baked goods and confections. The breads are baked in one of Maui's oldest brick ovens, installed in 1935; a high-tech European diesel oven handles the rest. The front window displays more than 100 bakery and deli items, among them salads, a popular eggplant marinara focaccia, homemade quiches, and an inexpensive calzone filled with chicken, pesto, mushroom, and cheese. Homemade soups (clam chowder, minestrone, cream of asparagus) team up nicely with sandwiches on freshly baked bread. Save room for the Ultimate Dessert: white-chocolate macadamia-nut cheesecake.

2092 Vineyard St. (at N. Church St.), Wailuku. ☎ **808/242-0064.** Most items under $7. AE, DISC, MC, V. Tues–Fri 6:30am–2:30pm; Sat 7am–1pm.

2 West Maui

LAHAINA
VERY EXPENSIVE

David Paul's Lahaina Grill ✸✸ NEW AMERICAN   Even after David Paul Johnson's departure, this Lahaina hot spot has maintained its popularity. It's still filled with chic, tanned diners in stylish aloha shirts, and there's still attitude aplenty at the entrance. The signature items remain: tequila shrimp and firecracker rice, Kona-coffee-roasted rack of lamb, Maui-onion-crusted seared ahi, and kalua duck quesadilla. As always, a special custom-designed chef's table can be arranged with 72 hours notice for larger parties. The ambience—black-and-white tile floors, pressed-tin ceilings, eclectic 1890s decor—is striking, and the bar, despite not having an ocean view, is the busiest spot in Lahaina.

127 Lahainaluna Rd. ⓒ **808/667-5117.** Reservations required. Main courses $29–$43; tasting menu $76. AE, DC, DISC, MC, V. Daily 6–10pm. Bar daily 5:30pm–midnight (sometimes earlier if it's slow).

The Feast at Lele ✸✸ POLYNESIAN   The owners of Old Lahaina Luau have teamed up with chef James McDonald's culinary prowess (I'O and Pacific'O), placed it in a perfect outdoor oceanfront setting, and added the exquisite dancers of the Old Lahaina Luau. The result: a culinary and cultural experience that sizzles. As if the sunset weren't heady enough, dances from Hawaii, New Zealand, Tahiti, and Samoa are presented, up close and personal, in full costumed splendor. Chanting, singing, drumming, dancing, the swish of ti-leaf skirts, the scent of plumeria—it's a full adventure, even for the most jaded luau aficionado. Guests sit at white-clothed, candlelit tables set on the sand (unlike the luau, where seating is en masse) and dine on entrees from each island: imu-roasted kalua pig from Hawaii, Maori fishcake from New Zealand, poisson cru from Tahiti, and beef with breadfruit from Samoa. Particularly mesmerizing is the evening's opening: A softly lit canoe carries three people ashore to the sound of conch shells.

505 Front St. ⓒ **886/244-5353** or 808/667-5353. www.feastatlele.com. Reservations a must. Set 5-course menu $105 adults, $75 children 2–12. AE, DISC, MC, V. Apr 1–Sept 30 daily 6–9pm; Oct 1–Mar 31 daily 5:30–8:30pm.

EXPENSIVE

Chez Paul ✸✸ *Finds* FRENCH   Chez Paul is located in the middle of nowhere, in Olowalu Village (a blip on the highway—if you blink you'll miss it). But it's worth the drive to this classic French restaurant, under the helm of chef Patrick Callarec (formerly of the Ritz-Carlton's Anuenue Room). Look forward to such delights as wild-mushroom-and-brie pastry in an aged port-wine sauce, just to get started. Or choose their signature dish of crispy duck with local fruits or fresh island fish in a champagne-and-cream sauce. Don't miss the pineapple-and-vanilla crème brûlée, served in a pineapple shell. The dress here is Maui casual, which means anything short of tank tops and shorts. Chez Paul has recently added lunch on Sunday starting at 11am.

Olowalu Village, Honoapiilani Hwy., Olowalu. © **808/661-3843**. www.chezpaul. net. Reservations recommended. Main courses $29–$44. DISC, MC, V. Daily 5:30–9pm; Sun also 11am–2:30pm.

Gerard's ★★★ *Finds* FRENCH   The charm of Gerard's—soft lighting, Edith Piaf on the sound system, excellent service—is matched by a menu of uncompromising standards. After more than 2½ decades in Lahaina, Gerard Reversade never runs out of creative offerings, yet stays true to his French roots. Roasted opakapaka with star anise, fennel fondue, and hints of orange and ginger is a stellar entree on a menu of winners. The Kona lobster and avocado salad promises ecstasy, and the spinach salad with scallops is among the finest I've tasted. Gerard's has an excellent appetizer menu, with shiitake and oyster mushrooms in puff pastry, fresh ahi and smoked salmon carpaccio, and a very rich, highly touted escargot ragout with burgundy butter and garlic cream. The restaurant is a frequent winner of the *Wine Spectator* Award of Excellence and the *Wine Enthusiast* 2006 Award of Distinction.

In The Plantation Inn, 174 Lahainaluna Rd. © **808/661-8939**. www.gerards maui.com. Reservations recommended. Main courses $30–$50. AE, DC, DISC, MC, V. Daily 6–9pm.

I'o ★ PACIFIC RIM   I'O is a fantasy of sleek curves and etched glass, co-owned by chef James McDonald. He offers an impressive selection of appetizers (his strong suit) and some lavish Asian-Polynesian interpretations of seafood, such as his "rainbow catch," fresh fish of the day topped with lemon-grass pesto, tomatoes, truffle oil, and goat cheese fondue sauce, or his "scallops ala bondage," scallops wrapped in sage and jalapeño bacon and roasted Japanese eggplant served with a *ponzu* cream sauce. Unless you're sold on a particular entree, my advice is to go heavy on the superb appetizers, especially the blackened ahi tower (a tower of ahi, avocado, fruit, and tomatoes), shredded pork in a quesadilla with pepper-jack cheese, or the Siamese shashi rolls—spicy tempura portobello mushroom with an

Where to Dine in Lahaina & Kaanapali

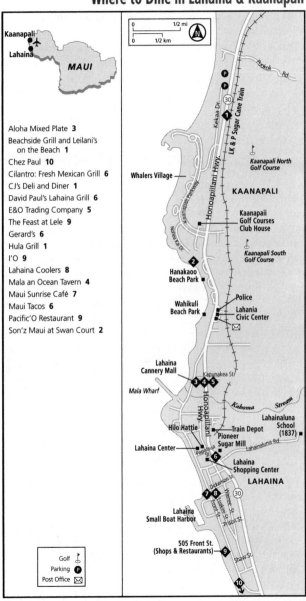

Aloha Mixed Plate **3**
Beachside Grill and Leilani's on the Beach **1**
Chez Paul **10**
Cilantro: Fresh Mexican Grill **6**
CJ's Deli and Diner **1**
David Paul's Lahaina Grill **6**
E&O Trading Company **5**
The Feast at Lele **9**
Gerard's **6**
Hula Grill **1**
I'O **9**
Lahaina Coolers **8**
Mala an Ocean Tavern **4**
Maui Sunrise Café **7**
Maui Tacos **6**
Pacific'O Restaurant **9**
Son'z Maui at Swan Court **2**

MAUI

Kaanapali
Lahaina

0   1/2 mi
0   1/2 km

Akokoli Rd

LK & P Sugar Cane Train
Kekaa Dr.
Honoapiilani Hwy.
(30)

Kaanapali North Golf Course

Whalers Village

KAANAPALI

Kaanapali Golf Courses Club House

Kaanapali South Golf Course

Kaanapali Parkway
Nohea Kai Dr.

Hanakaoo Beach Park

Police

Wahikuli Beach Park

Lahaina Civic Center

Lahaina Cannery Mall

Kapunakea St.

Mala Wharf

Kahoma Stream

Honoapiilani Hwy.

Hilo Hattie

Train Depot
Pioneer Sugar Mill

Lahainaluna School (1837)

Lahaina Center

Papalaua St.

Lahaina Shopping Center

Lahainaluna Rd.

LAHAINA

Dickenson St.
Waine'e St.
Luakini St.
Front St.
Prison St.

Lahaina Small Boat Harbor

(30)

505 Front St. (Shops & Restaurants)

Shaw St.

Golf
Parking **P**
Post Office ✉

orange-mint dipping sauce. Chef McDonald also owns Pacific'O (see review below) and is the chef for The Feast at Lele (reviewed above).

505 Front St. ℂ 808/661-8422. www.iomaui.com. Reservations recommended. Main courses $28–$36. AE, DC, DISC, MC, V. Daily 5:30–10pm.

Pacific'O Restaurant ☆ PACIFIC RIM/CONTEMPORARY PACIFIC

You can't get any closer to the ocean than the tables here, which are literally on the beach. With good food complementing this sensational setting, foodies and aesthetes have much to enjoy. The split-level dining starts near the entrance, with a long bar (where you can also order lunch or dinner) and a few tables along the railing. Steps lead down to the outdoor tables, where the award-winning seafood dishes come to you with the backdrop of Lanai across the channel. Favorites include the coconut macadamia-nut-crusted catch of the day or the pasta moana—fresh fish with bay scallops, rock shrimp, shiitake mushrooms, roasted peppers, and snap peas in a lobster-Alfredo sauce served over orecchiette (the little ears) pasta. If you like seafood, sunsets, and touches of India and Indonesia in your fresh-from-the-sea dining choices, you should be happy here.

505 Front St. ℂ 808/667-4341. www.pacificomaui.com. Reservations recommended. Main courses $9–$15 lunch, $26–$36 dinner. AE, DC, MC, V. Daily 11:30am–4pm and 5:30–10pm.

MODERATE

E&O Trading Company ECLECTIC SOUTHEAST ASIAN ☆☆

Value   From the wok fountain sculpture out front to the billowing tentlike fabrics lining the walls, you feel like you have entered another, more exotic world. Each branch of this tiny regional chain has its own unique signature and decor. The feel at the Lahaina Cannery location is straight out of the Arabian Nights. The menu, with both small plates (so you can try a range of dishes) and larger portions, will have something for everyone, and the prices are easy on your wallet. Must-try items include the sweet corn fritters with chile soy dipping sauce, any of the many assortments of satays, green papaya-ginger salad, mango-mustard glazed spareribs, five-spice marinated duck breast (with sweet potato croquettes and plum wine sauce), and any of the five different kinds of naan (Indian flat bread). There's entertainment every evening from 4 to 6pm and live music on Thursday from 4:30 to 6:30pm. On Saturday the restaurant becomes the Feng Shui Lounge from 10pm to 2am, with music by a DJ (and sometimes a cover; call to check).

Lahaina Cannery Mall, 1221 Honoapiilani Hwy. ℂ 808/667-1818. www.eotrading. com. Reservations recommended. Small plates $4–$15; big plates $17–$30. MC, V. Daily 4–10pm.

Mala An Ocean Tavern ⭐⭐ (Value) LOCAL/SEAFOOD   Perched right on the ocean, this tiny "tavern" is the brainchild of Mark and Judy Ellman, owners of Maui Tacos and Penne Pasta Café. They use healthy, organically grown food and fresh fish to make intriguing culinary dishes. The atmosphere could not be more enticing, with just a handful of tables out on the oceanfront lanai and several more tables in the warmly decorated interior. The staff is helpful and efficient, and the food is outstanding. If you are in the mood, ask for their exotic martini menu. You can pick from "tavern food" such as an ahi burger or cheeseburger, one of the tempting salads (the beet and Kula goat cheese salad is divine), or something off the "big plate" menu (such as wok-fried moi fish or glazed baby back ribs). Don't miss Saturday and Sunday brunch (I recommend their "killer" French toast). *Warning:* This is a popular place, so avoid prime lunch and dinner hours if you can.

1307 Front St. (across from the Lahaina Cannery's Safeway Store). © 808/ 667-9394. www.malaoceantavern.com. Small plates $5–$17; big plates $15–$26. Brunch $6–$12. MC, V. Mon–Fri 11am–10pm; Sat 9am–10pm; Sun 9am–9pm.

INEXPENSIVE
Aloha Mixed Plate ⭐ (Value) PLATE LUNCHES/BEACHSIDE GRILL   Look for the festive turquoise-and-yellow, plantation-style front with the red corrugated-iron roof and adorable bar, tiny and busy, directly across from the Lahaina Cannery Mall. Grab a picnic table at ocean's edge, in the shade of large kiawe and milo trees, where you can watch the bobbing sailboats and two islands on the near horizon. (On the upper level, there are umbrellas and plumeria trees—just as charming.) Then tuck into inexpensive mahimahi, kalua pig and cabbage, shoyu chicken, teriyaki beef, and other local plate-lunch specials, all at budget-friendly prices, served with macaroni salad and rice. The shoyu chicken is the best I've had—fork tender and tasty—and the spicy chicken drumettes come from a fabled family recipe. (The bestsellers are the coconut prawns and Aloha Mixed Plate of shoyu chicken, teriyaki beef, and mahimahi.) I don't know of anywhere else where you can order a mai tai with a plate lunch and enjoy table service with an ocean view.

1285 Front St. © 808/661-3322. www.alohamixedplate.com. Main courses $4.95–$14. MC, V. Daily 10:30am–10pm.

Cilantro: Fresh Mexican Grill ⭐ (Finds) MEXICAN   This is Maui's best bet for fabulous Mexican food at frugal prices (and the winner of the Taste of Lahaina Award for the last 3 years). And, believe it or not, this fast-food restaurant serves fresh, healthy food.

The chef and owner is Paris Nabavi, creator of Maui's Pizza Paradiso Italian Kitchen. He wanted the "challenge of something different," so he took off to Mexico to find out how the Mexicans used to cook in "the old days." He's back on Maui with this unbelievably delicious eatery where everything is made from scratch. Even the corn tortillas are handmade daily. Signature dishes include the citrus-and-herb-marinated chipotle rotisserie chicken, the veggie Mariposa salad, and the popular mother-clucker flautas. Plus there's lip-smacking "al pastor" style adobo pork. All this at budget-pleasing prices. It's a great place to take the kids: Los Niños menu items are under $4.75.

170 Papalaua Ave. ⓒ 808/667-5444. www.cilantrogrill.com. Entrees $3.95–$13. DISC, MC, V. Mon–Sat 11am–9pm; Sun 11am–8pm.

Lahaina Coolers 🍴 AMERICAN/INTERNATIONAL   A huge marlin hangs above the bar, epic wave shots and wall sconces made of surfboard fins fill the walls, and open windows line three sides of this ultracasual indoor/outdoor restaurant. This is a great breakfast joint, with feta-cheese Mediterranean omelets, huevos rancheros, and fried rice made with jasmine rice, Kula vegetables, and Portuguese sausage. There are three types of eggs Benedict: the classic, a vegetarian version (with Kula vegetables—excellent), and the Local, with Portuguese sausage and sweetbread. At lunch burgers rule and the sandwiches, from grilled portobellos to the classic tuna melt, are ideal for casual Lahaina. Made fresh daily, the pasta is prepared Asian-style (with chicken and spicy Thai peanut sauce), with pesto, or vegetarian (in a spicy Creole sauce). Pizzas, pastas, fresh catch, steak, and enchiladas round out the entrees. Everything can be prepared vegetarian upon request.

180 Dickenson St. ⓒ 808/661-7082. www.lahainacoolers.com. Breakfast $8.25–$10; lunch main courses $7.50–$11; dinner main courses $10–$22. AE, DC, DISC, MC, V. Daily 8am–2am (full menu until midnight).

Maui Sunrise Café *Value* GOURMET DELI/CAFE   If you want to know where to find the best breakfasts or the most filling lunches on a budget, follow the surfers to this teeny-tiny cafe located on Front Street, next door to the library. Eat in the patio garden out back or take your lunch to the beach. You'll find huge breakfasts, delicious gourmet sandwiches, and filling lunch plates all at bargain prices. It's tough to find a parking spot nearby (and you can't park at the library), but you'll probably want a brisk walk after eating here anyway.

693A Front St. ⓒ 808/661-8558. Breakfast under $10; lunch $6–$10. No credit cards. Daily 6am–6pm.

KAANAPALI
EXPENSIVE

Son'z Maui at Swan Court ✸✸✸ CONTEMPORARY EURO-PEAN/HAWAIIAN REGIONAL   For 30 years the Swan Court was *the* dining experience at the Hyatt Regency Maui. When Tri-Star Restaurant Group CEO Aaron Placourakis (who also owns Nick's Fishmarket, p. 94) took over this restaurant, he and executive chef Geno Sarmiento knew they wanted to hit a home run every night with the cuisine. The restaurant already had perhaps the most romantic location in Maui, overlooking a man-made lagoon with white and black swans swimming by and the rolling surf of the Pacific in the distance. The culinary team's creative dishes, coupled with fresh local ingredients (Kula corn and strawberries, Ono Farms avocados, Hana hearts of palm, Maui Cattle Company beef, fresh Hawaiian fish, and sweet Maui onions), top-notch service, and the relaxing atmosphere make this gem one of Maui's best restaurants. My personal picks from the very tempting menu are the Maui Surf-ing Goat Cheese ravioli appetizer with Kula corn, edamame, Hamakua mushrooms, prosciutto, and a sherry vinegar pan sauce, and, for a main course, either the Hawaiian opakapaka picatta (with artichokes, caper berries, Lison lemon, sweet-potato hash browns, and tomato purée) or the seared scallops BLT (with bacon and poached cherry tomatoes in a Caesar salad emulsion, served with truffled potato chips). They also serve a beautiful breakfast buffet.

Hyatt Regency Maui Resort & Spa, 200 Nohea Kai Dr. ✆ 808/667-4506. www. sonzmaui.com. Reservations necessary for dinner. Breakfast buffet $25; entrees $14–$22; dinner entrees $30–$42. AE, DC, DISC, MC, V. Daily 6:30am–11am and 5:30–10pm.

MODERATE

Beachside Grill and Leilani's on the Beach STEAK/SEAFOOD   The Beachside Grill is the informal, less-expensive room downstairs on the beach, where folks wander in off the sand for a frothy beer and a burger. Leilani's is the dinner-only room, with more-expensive but still not outrageously priced steak and seafood offerings. At Leilani's you can order everything from fresh fish prepared four different ways to filet mignon, barbecued ribs to fried coconut prawns. All of this, of course, comes with an ocean view. There's live Hawaiian music every afternoon except Friday, when the Rock 'n' Roll Aloha Friday set gets those decibels climb-ing. Free concerts are usually offered on a stage outside the restau-rant on the last Sunday of the month.

In Whalers Village, 2435 Kaanapali Pkwy. ⒸⓃ 808/661-4495. www.leilanis.com. Reservations suggested for dinner. Lunch and dinner (Beachside Grill) $8–$15; dinner (Leilani's) $18–$31. AE, DC, DISC, MC, V. Beachside Grill daily 11am–11pm (bar daily until 12:30am). Leilani's daily 5–10pm.

Hula Grill *R* HAWAII REGIONAL/SEAFOOD   Who wouldn't want to tuck into a wood-grilled ahi steak or a lemon-ginger roasted chicken at this bistro on the beach at Kaanapali? If you aren't that hungry, you have a choice of sandwiches, entrees, pizza, appetizers, and salads. There's happy-hour entertainment and Hawaiian music daily. For those wanting a more casual atmosphere, the Barefoot Bar, located on the beach, offers burgers, fish, pizza, and salads.

In Whalers Village, 2435 Kaanapali Pkwy. Ⓒ 808/667-6636. www.hulagrill.com. Reservations recommended for dinner. Lunch and Barefoot Bar menus $8–$18; dinner main courses $18–$34. AE, DC, DISC, MC, V. Grill daily 11am–3pm and 5–9:30pm. Barefoot Bar daily 11am–10:30pm.

INEXPENSIVE

CJ's Deli and Diner *R* ⓥⓐⓛⓤⓔ AMERICAN/DELI   If you are staying in Kaanapali, this restaurant is within walking distance of your resort; if you're not staying in Kaanapali, it's worth the drive to sample the "comfort food" (as they call it) at this hip, happening eatery with prices so low you won't believe you're still on Maui (most items are under $12). A huge billboard menu hangs from the yellow-and-gold textured wall, and highly polished wooden floors give the roadside eatery a homey feeling. You can eat in or take out (you can even get a "chef-to-go" to come to your accommodations and cook for you), the atmosphere is friendly, and there's even a computer with high-speed Internet connection to keep the techies humming. Huge, delicious breakfasts start at 7am (check out the $4.95 early-bird special of two eggs, bacon or sausage, rice, and coffee) and is served until 11am. They have a wide selection of egg dishes, plus pancakes and waffles, and don't forget the tempting delights from the bakery. Lunch ranges from deli sandwiches, burgers, and hot sandwiches to pot roast, ribs, and fish dishes. If you are on your way to Hana or up to the top of Haleakala, stop by and get a box lunch. CJ's even has a menu for the kids.

Kaanapali Fairway Shops, 2580 Keka'a Dr. (just off Honoapiilani Hwy.), Kaanapali Resort. Ⓒ 808/667-0968. Breakfast items $3–$9.50; lunch $7–$12; and Hana Lunch Box and Air Travel Lunch Box $12 each. AE, MC, V. Daily 7am–8pm.

HONOKOWAI, KAHANA & NAPILI

Note: You'll find the following restaurants on the "Where to Stay & Dine from Honokowai to Kapalua" map on p. 49.

EXPENSIVE

Roy's Kahana Bar & Grill 🎇🎇 EURO-ASIAN   Despite the lack of dramatic view and an upstairs location in a shopping mall, Roy's remains crowded and extremely popular for one reason: fabulous food. It bustles with young, hip, impeccably trained servers delivering wasabi-pistachio crusted ahi steak, hibachi-grilled salmon (with Japanese-style citrus *ponzu*), Asian-jade-pesto-steamed kampachi, and glazed honey mustard short ribs. You could make a meal of the creative appetizers, such as Roy's original Hawaiian blackened ahi, crab cakes, seared shrimp sticks, crispy shrimp and pork lumpia, or the Kula baby spinach salad. Large picture windows open up Roy's Kahana but don't quell the noise, another tireless trait long ago established by Roy's Restaurant in Honolulu, the flagship of Yamaguchi's burgeoning empire.

In the Kahana Gateway Shopping Center, 4405 Honoapiilani Hwy. ℂ **808/ 669-6999.** www.roysrestaurant.com. Reservations strongly recommended. Main courses $27–$37. AE, DC, DISC, MC, V. Daily 5:30–10pm.

MODERATE

Maui Brewing Company and Fish & Game Rotisserie SEAFOOD/STEAK   This restaurant consists of a bar, retail section, and tables. The small retail section sells fresh seafood, and the sit-down menu covers basic tastes: salads (Caesar, Oriental chicken with won tons), fish and chips, fresh-fish sandwiches, cheeseburgers, and beer—lots of it. At dinner count on heavier meats and the fresh catch of the day (ahi, mahimahi, ono), with rotisserie items such as grilled chicken, steaks, and duck. The late-night menu includes shrimp, cheese fries, and quesadillas.

In the Kahana Gateway Shopping Center, 4405 Honoapiilani Hwy. ℂ **808/ 669-3474.** www.mauibrewingco.com. Reservations recommended for dinner. Main courses $8–$14 lunch, $12–$36 dinner. AE, DC, DISC, MC, V. Daily 11am–10pm; late-night menu 10:30pm–1am. During football season (Sept–Jan) brunch Sun 7:30am–3pm.

INEXPENSIVE

Maui Tacos MEXICAN   Mark Ellman's Maui Tacos chain has grown faster than you can say "Haleakala." Ellman put gourmet Mexican on paper plates and on the island's culinary map long before the island became known as Hawaii's center for salsa and chimichangas. Barely more than a takeout counter with a few tables, this and the six other Maui Tacos in Hawaii (five on Maui alone) are popular with hungry surfers, discerning diners, burrito buffs, and Hollywood glitterati like Sharon Stone, whose picture adorns a wall or two. Choices include excellent fresh-fish tacos (garlicky and flavorful), chimichangas, and mouth-breaking compositions such as the Hookipa (a personal favorite): a "surf burrito" of fresh fish, black beans, and salsa. The green-spinach burrito contains four kinds of beans, rice, and potatoes—it's a knockout, requiring a siesta afterward. Expect good food but not very fast service.

In Napili Plaza, 5095 Napili Hau St. © 808/665-0222. www.mauitacos.com. Items range from $1.75–$7.95. AE, DISC, MC, V. Daily 9am–9pm. Also in Lahaina Sq., Lahaina, © 808/661-8883; Kamaole Beach Center, Kihei, © 808/879-5005; Kaahumanu Center, Kahului, © 808/871-7726; Piilani Village Shopping Center, Kihei, © 808/875-9340.

Pizza Paradiso Italian Caffe PIZZA/ITALIAN Order at the counter (pastas, gourmet pizza whole or by the slice, salads, and desserts) and find a seat at one of the few tables. The pasta sauces— marinara, pescatore, Alfredo, Florentine, and pesto, with options and add-ons—are as popular as the pizzas (which took best pizza in the 2005 *Maui News* Reader Poll) and panini sandwiches. The Massimo, a pesto sauce with artichoke hearts, sun-dried tomatoes, and capers, comes with a choice of chicken, shrimp, or clams, and is so good it was a Taste of Lahaina winner in 1999. Recent new additions to the menu include gyros, souvlaki, hummus, and cheesesteak sandwiches. Take out or dine in, this is a hot spot in the neighborhood, with free delivery.

In the Honokowai Marketplace, 3350 Lower Honoapiilani Rd. © 808/667-2929. www.pizzaparadiso.com. Pastas $9.95–$11; pizzas $14–$28. DISC, MC, V. Daily 11am–10pm.

KAPALUA

Note: You'll find the following restaurants on the "Where to Stay & Dine from Honokowai to Kapalua" map on p. 49.

EXPENSIVE

Pineapple Grill Kapalua 🌟🌟🌟 PACIFIC ISLAND If you had only 1 night to eat on the island of Maui, I would send you here. Up-and-coming young chef Ryan Luckey (a local Lahaina boy) has taken the helm and is winning high praises from restaurant reviewers and the local residents who flock here nightly. My picks on this creative menu would be pistachio-and-wasabi-pea-crusted ahi steak (with coconut-scented rice, Hamakua mushrooms, and wasabi ginger butter), sake-soy grilled mahimahi (in a ginger-carrot emulsion), or the wonderful Maui-style seafood paella (with a hint of Portuguese sausage and Kula herbs). An excellent list of wine pairings by the glass are available. Save room for dessert: Maui gold-pineapple upside-down cake (with Whaler dark rum sauce and Maui-made Roselani gourmet mac-nut ice cream). There are also lots of tasty sandwiches and salads at lunch, and a continental-style breakfast in the morning. Plus, it's all served in a very Maui-like atmosphere, overlooking the rolling hills of the Kapalua Golf Course out to the Pacific Ocean.

200 Kapalua Dr. ⓒ **808/669-9600**. www.pineapplekapalua.com. Dinner reservations recommended. Lunch entrees $7–$17; dinner entrees $25–$35. AE, MC, V. Daily 8am–10pm.

Plantation House Restaurant ⓡⓡ SEAFOOD/HAWAIIAN-MEDITERRANEAN With its teak tables, fireplace, and open sides, Plantation House gets stellar marks for atmosphere. The 360-degree view from high among the resort's pine-studded hills takes in Molokai and Lanai, the ocean, the rolling fairways and greens, the northwestern flanks of the West Maui Mountains, and the daily sunset spectacular. Readers of the *Maui News* have deemed this the island's "Best Ambience"—a big honor on an island of wonderful views. It's the best place for breakfast in west Maui, hands down, and one of my top choices for dinner. Marvelous starters include polenta and scampi-style shrimp, crab cakes, and Kula and Mediterranean salads. The menu changes constantly but may include fresh fish prepared several ways—among them, Mediterranean (on roasted Maui onions with couscous), Venice (panko-pressed with a golden raisin and pine-nut butter), Maui (pistachio-crusted), Plantation (with sautéed crab and lemon beurre blanc), and Italy (pepper-dusted with olives and caper-berry salsa). Plus numerous vegetarian entrees and wonderful Australian lamb, New Zealand lobster, and a Tuscan style rib-eye steak you'll long remember.

2000 Plantation Club Dr. (at Kapalua Plantation Golf Course). ⓒ **808/669-6299**. www.theplantationhouse.com. Reservations recommended. Main courses $24–$32. AE, DC, MC, V. Daily 8am–3pm and 5:30–10pm.

MODERATE

Sansei Seafood Restaurant & Sushi Bar ⓡⓡ PACIFIC RIM Perpetual award-winner Sansei offers an extensive menu of Japanese and East-West delicacies. Part fusion, part Hawaii Regional Cuisine, Sansei is tirelessly creative, with a menu that scores higher with adventurous palates than with purists (although there are endless traditional choices as well). Choices include panko-crusted ahi sashimi, sashimi trio, ahi carpaccio, noodle dishes, lobster, Asian shrimp cakes, traditional Japanese tempura, and sauces that surprise, in creative combinations such as ginger-lime chile butter and cilantro pesto. But there's simpler fare as well, such as shrimp tem-pura, noodles, and wok-tossed upcountry vegetables. Don't-miss desserts include Granny Smith apple tart and tempura-fried ice cream with chocolate sauce. There's karaoke Thursday and Friday nights from 10pm to 1am. *Money-saving tip:* Eat early—all food is 25% off between 5:30 and 6pm.

600 Office Rd. ✆ **808/669-6286.** www.sanseihawaii.com. Reservations recom-mended. Main courses $16–$43. AE, DISC, MC, V. Daily 5:30–10pm. Also at Kihei Town Center, Kihei, ✆ **808/879-0004.**

Vino Italian Tapas & Wine Bar ⭐ *Finds* ITALIAN   Two Japan-ese guys, D. K. Kodama (chef and owner of Sansei Seafood Restau-rant & Sushi Bar, reviewed above) and Chuck Furuya (Hawaii's only master sommelier) teamed up to create this culinary adventure for foodies. Vino opened in August 2003 to big, big accolades. This exquisite restaurant overlooks the rolling hills of the Kapalua Golf Course. Always wanting to be on the cutting edge, the duo rebranded the restaurant in December 2004 to Vino Italian Tapas & Wine Bar. The new menu features more than two dozen tapas (small plates), ranging from the signature asparagus Milanese (just $7) to slow butter-poached Kona lobster ($20). Plus they have retained the most popular large-plate dishes, like fresh mahimahi with artichokes and grape tomatoes on capellini, crusted pan-fried veal stuffed with prosciutto, and *osso buco* with spinach risotto.

Kapalua Village Course Golf Club House, Kapalua Resort. ✆ **808/661-VINO.** Reser-vations recommended. Tapas $6–$20; large plates $19–$38. AE, DISC, MC, V. Daily 11am–2pm and 5–9:30pm.

3 South Maui

You'll find the following restaurants on the "Where to Stay & Dine in South Maui" map on p. 55.

KIHEI/MAALAEA
EXPENSIVE
Five Palms ⭐ PACIFIC RIM   This is the best lunch spot in Kihei—open-air, with tables a few feet from the beach and up-close-and-personal views of Kahoolawe and Molokini. They feature a menu of breakfast and lunch items served from 8am to 2:30pm, so if you're jet-lagged and your stomach isn't on Hawaiian time, you can get a crab omelet at 2 in the afternoon or a juicy Kobe beef ham-burger at 8 in the morning. At dinner, with the torches lit on the beach and the main dining room open, the ambience is romantic, but still casual. Just-caught fish is the star of the dinner menu.

In the Mana Kai Resort, 2960 S. Kihei Rd., Kihei. © 808/879-2607. www.fivepalms restaurant.com. Reservations recommended for dinner. Breakfast and lunch $7.95–$19; dinner $28–$45. AE, DC, MC, V. Daily 8am–2:30pm and 5–9:30pm, with pupu menu daily 2:45–6pm.

The Waterfront at Maalaea 🦀🦀 SEAFOOD The family-owned Waterfront has won many prestigious awards for wine excellence, service, and seafood, but its biggest boost is word of mouth. Loyal diners rave about the friendly staff and seafood, fresh off the boat in nearby Maalaea Harbor and prepared with care. The bay and harbor view is one you'll never forget, especially at sunset. You have nine choices of preparations for the several varieties of fresh Hawaiian fish, ranging from *en papillote* (baked in buttered parchment) to Southwestern (smoked chile and cilantro butter) to Cajun spiced and Island-style (sautéed, broiled, poached, or baked and paired with tiger prawns). Other choices: Kula onion soup, an excellent Caesar salad, the signature lobster chowder, and grilled eggplant layered with Maui onions, tomatoes, and spinach, served with red-pepper coulis and feta ravioli. Like the seafood, it's superb.

50 Hauoli St., Maalaea Harbor. © 808/244-9028. www.waterfrontrestaurant.net. Reservations recommended. Main courses $19–$41. AE, DC, DISC, MC, V. Daily 5pm–closing; last seating at 8:30pm.

MODERATE

Café O'Lei Kihei 🦀🦀 STEAK/SEAFOOD Chefs Michael and Dana Pastula have had a host of Café O'Lei restaurants on Maui (Makawao, Lahaina, Maalaea, Napili), and I've loved every one of them. Their latest (in addition to the Ma'alaea Grill, reviewed below) is in an out-of-the-way location, in an open and airy room with floor-to-ceiling windows and hardwood floors; in the middle is a big circular bar and, on one side, an exhibition kitchen. The atmosphere is relaxing and inviting. The food is, as usual, not only outstanding, but a real bargain. You can't beat lunch with fresh fish, rice, and salad for under $12 (but it's no secret—arrive early or book in advance). Dinners range from fresh fish to prime rib; mac-nut-crusted chicken breast to roast duck; and even a mushroom-asparagus-pine-nut linguine for the vegetarians. Save room for pineapple upside-down cake or a fudge brownie sundae.

2439 S. Kihei Rd., Kihei. © 808/891-1368. Reservations recommended. Lunch entrees $7–$13; dinner entrees $15–$35. AE, DC, DISC, MC, V. Tues–Sun 10:30am–10pm.

Ma'alaea Grill 🦀 ECLECTIC This relaxing restaurant, with hardwood floors, bamboo dividers, and high ceilings, has one of the best views of the Pacific Ocean in Maalaea. There's a great lanai for sitting outside, but it's rarely used because the near-constant winds in Maalaea are wickedly strong. The lunch menu includes a yummy Asian salad (oriental veggies and Chinese noodles over organic baby greens with a sesame vinaigrette) for $9, mac-nut-crusted ono with a ginger butter sauce for $12, and a range of burgers. At dinner enjoy a terrific selection of fresh fish (prepared numerous ways), chicken, beef, and pasta—come before sunset if you can. The restaurant once again is under the helm of Michael and Dana Pastula (who also own Café O'Lei in Kihei, see above), whose philosophy is "good food without hurting your pocketbook."

300 Maalaea Rd., Maalaea Harbor Village. ℂ **808/243-2206.** Lunch entrees $7–$13; dinner entrees $15–$35. AE, DC, DISC, MC, V. Tues–Sun 10:30am–9pm; Mon 10:30am–3pm.

Stella Blues Cafe ✿ AMERICAN   Stella Blues gets going at breakfast and continues through to dinner with something for everyone—vegetarians, kids, pasta and sandwich lovers, hefty steak eaters, and sensible diners who go for the inexpensive fresh Maui greens salad. Grateful Dead posters line the walls, and a covey of gleaming motorcycles is invariably parked outside. It's loud and lively, irreverent and unpretentious. Sandwiches are the highlight, ranging from Tofu Extraordinaire to egg salad on a croissant to garden burgers and grilled chicken. Tofu wraps and mountain-size Cobb salads are popular, as are large coffee shakes with mounds of whipped cream. Daily specials include fresh seafood. All the home-style meals are made from scratch, down to the pesto mayonnaise and herb bread. At dinner selections are geared toward good-value family dining, from affordable full dinners to pastas and burgers.

Azeka II Shopping Center, 1279 S. Kihei Rd., Kihei. ℂ **808/874-3779.** Main courses $8–$26. AE, DC, DISC, MC, V. Daily 7:30am–10pm.

Tastings Wine Bar & Grill ✿✿ *Finds* AMERICAN   Hidden in a nondescript minimall (across the street from the Foodland in Kihei) lies a jewel of culinary creativity. Run by dynamic duo chef Derek McCarthy and his wife, Sandy Kim, this tiny bistro offers interesting, delicious "island-inspired American cuisine," at excellent prices. I highly recommend the five-course menu with terrific wine pairings for $49. The regular menu includes such items as lettuce-wrapped prawn bundles with shaved carrots, cashews, cilantro, and mint for just $12, or spiced ahi seared rare ($14), or boat scallops on truffled cauliflower purée with a watercress salad ($15). The most expensive item on the menu is torchon of foie gras with grilled pineapple and *lilikoi* honey for $19. Don't leave without dessert: warm banana mac-nut bread with bananas Foster ice cream or bittersweet chocolate torte with hazelnut butter and caramelized bananas. Make reservations; this place is tiny and it's becoming popular.

Kihei Kalama Village, 1912 S. Kihei Rd. ℰ 808/879-8711. Reservations highly recommended. Main courses $12–$19. 5-course meal with wine pairings $49. MC, V. Tues–Sun 5–10pm.

INEXPENSIVE

Peggy Sue's AMERICAN   Just for a moment, forget that diet and take a leap. It's Peggy Sue's to the rescue! This 1950s-style diner has oodles of charm and is a swell place to spring for the best chocolate malt on the island. You'll also find sodas, shakes, floats, egg creams, milkshakes, and 14 flavors of made-on-Maui Roselani-brand gourmet ice cream. Old-fashioned soda-shop stools, an ELVIS PRESLEY BOULEVARD sign, and jukeboxes on every Formica table serve as a backdrop for the famous burgers (and garden burgers), brushed with teriyaki sauce and served with all the goodies. The fries are great, too.

In Azeka Place II, 1279 S. Kihei Rd., Kihei. ℰ 808/875-8944. Burgers $8.45–$11; plate lunches $6.95–$16. AE, DISC, MC, V. Sun–Thurs 11am–9pm; Fri–Sat 11am–10pm.

Shaka Sandwich & Pizza PIZZA   How many "best pizzas" are there on Maui? It depends which shore you're on, the west or the south. This south-shore old-timer recently moved to a new (and much larger) location, but the award-winning pizzas, New York–style heroes, Philly cheese steaks, calzones, salads, and homemade garlic bread haven't changed. Shaka uses fresh Maui produce, long-simmered sauces, and homemade Italian bread. Choose thin or Sicilian thick crust with gourmet toppings: Maui onions, spinach, anchovies, jalapeños, and a spate of other vegetables. Try the white pizza; with the perfectly balanced flavors of olive oil, garlic, and cheese, you won't even miss the tomato sauce. My favorite, the spinach pizza (with olive oil, spinach, garlic, and mozzarella), is a real treat.

1770 S. Kihei Rd., Kihei. ℰ 808/874-0331. Sandwiches $6.35–$15; pizzas $17–$26. MC, V. Sun–Thurs 10:30am–9pm; Fri–Sat 10:30am–10pm.

WAILEA
VERY EXPENSIVE

Longhi's ℱ ITALIAN   The open-air room, coupled with restaurateur Bob Longhi's trademark black-and-white checkered floor, provides a great way to start the day. Breakfasts here are something you want to wake up to: perfect baguettes, fresh-baked cinnamon rolls (one is enough for two people), and eggs Benedict or Florentine with hollandaise. Lunch is either an Italian banquet (ahi torino, prawns amaretto, and a wide variety of pastas) or fresh salads and sandwiches. Dinner (unfortunately the ocean view is now blocked by yet another high-rise) is where Longhi shines, with a long list of fresh-made pasta dishes, seafood platters, and beef and chicken dishes (filet mignon with basil or veal scaloppine). Leave room for the daily dessert specials.

The Shops at Wailea, 3750 Wailea Alanui Dr., Wailea. *C* **808/891-8883.** www.longhi-maui.com. Reservations recommended for dinner. Breakfast $8.50–$20; lunch $8.50–$33; dinner $28–$100. AE, DC, DISC, MC, V. Mon–Fri 8am–10pm; Sat–Sun 7:30am–10pm.

Nick's Fishmarket Maui ⟨R⟩ SEAFOOD   Here's the place to bring your sweetie to enjoy the moon rise and the sweet smell of the stephanotis growing in on the terrace. Fans love this classic seafood restaurant that sticks to the tried-and-true. The few detractors complain that the food is too old-style (ca. 1970s). Most agree that there is a high degree of professionalism in service and preparation, and it's hard to beat the fantasy setting on the south Maui shoreline. The Greek Maui Wowie salad gets my vote as one of the top salads in Hawaii. The menu features great fresh fish like opakapaka (one of their signature dishes), seared opah, and Hawaiian spiny lobster. There are ample choices for the nonfish-eaters as well, including rack of lamb, roasted chicken, and dry-aged New York steak.

In the Fairmont Kea Lani Hotel, 4100 Wailea Alanui. *C* **808/879-7224.** www.tristar restaurants.com. Reservations recommended. Main courses $30–$60; prix-fixe dinners $55–$85. AE, DC, DISC, MC, V. Daily 5:30–10pm; bar until 11pm.

Spago ⟨RR⟩ HAWAIIAN/CALIFORNIA/PACIFIC REGIONAL California meets Hawaii in this contemporary-designed eatery featuring fresh, local Hawaii ingredients prepared under the culinary watch of master chef Wolfgang Puck. The room, formerly Seasons Dining Room, has been stunningly transformed into a sleek modern layout using stone and wood in the open-air setting overlooking the Pacific Ocean. The cuisine lives up to Puck's reputation of using traditional Hawaiian dishes with his own brand of cutting-edge innovations. The menu features Hawaiian hapu'upu'u steamed in ti leaves; pineapple Thai red curry with onaga, mahi, and shrimp; grilled Chinois-style lamb chops; and caramelized pork chops with pineapple and papaya. The wine and beverage list is well thought out and extensive. Make reservations as soon as you land on the island (if not before)—this place is popular. And bring plenty of cash, or your platinum card.

Four Seasons Resort Maui, 3900 Wailea Alanui Dr., Wailea. ℂ 808/879-2999.
www.fourseasons.com/maui. Reservations required. Main courses $37–$59. AE,
DC, DISC, MC, V. Daily 5:30–9:30pm; bar with pupu daily 5–11pm.

EXPENSIVE

Ferraro's at Seaside ℱ ITALIAN   This was a master stroke for
Four Seasons: authentic Italian fare in a casual outdoor tropical setting, with a drop-dead gorgeous view of the ocean and the West Maui
Mountains. Ferraro's is not inexpensive, but the food is first-rate.
Lunch in the open-air restaurant features fabulous salads (my pick is
the seared Hawaiian tuna niçoise salad), sandwiches (from a chicken
pita to a grilled sirloin burger), and some Hawaiian classics (try the
sesame-crusted salmon). At dinner the romantic setting, with the
sound of the ocean waves, makes for a memorable evening. The fish
selection is noteworthy: grilled ahi with a crispy basil risotto roll, can-
died bell peppers, goat cheese, and a pine-nut dressing, or pan-fried
mahi with basil gnocchi. Make room for dessert—my favorite is the
roasted Maui pineapple cobbler with buttermilk rum ice cream.

In the Four Seasons Resort Maui at Wailea, 3900 Wailea Alanui Dr. ℂ **808/874-8000**. Reservations recommended. Lunch $15–$22; dinner courses $25–$46. AE,
DC, DISC, MC, V. Daily 11:30am–9pm.

SeaWatch ℱ ISLAND CUISINE   Under the same ownership as
Kapalua's Plantation House Restaurant (p. 89), SeaWatch is a good
choice from morning to evening, and it's one of the more affordable
stops in tony Wailea. You'll dine on the terrace or in a high-ceilinged
room, on a menu that carries the tee-off-to-19th-hole crowd with
ease. From breakfast on, it's a celebration of island bounty: crab-cake
eggs Benedict or smoked salmon Benedict is a great way to start your
day. Lunch has a range of sandwiches (from a mango barbecue kalua
pork sandwich to the traditional burgers to fresh-fish sandwiches), salads, and entrees (wok-stir-fried vegetables with grilled basil chicken to
blackened fresh catch). Dinner, with that fabulous ocean view, offers
five different ways to prepare the fish of the day, plus roasted New
Zealand lamb, muscovy duck, and free-range chicken breast.

100 Wailea Golf Club Dr. ℂ **808/875-8080**. www.seawatchrestaurant.com. Reservations recommended for dinner. Breakfast $7–$12; lunch $8.50–$15; dinner main
courses $28–$34. AE, DC, MC, V. Daily 8am–10pm.

MODERATE

Caffe Ciao ℱ ITALIAN   There are two parts to this charming
trattoria: the deli, with a takeout section, and the cafe, with tables
under the trees, next to the bar. Rare and wonderful wines, such as
Vine Cliff, are sold in the deli, along with ultraluxe rose soaps and

other bath products, assorted pastas, pizzas, roasted potatoes, vegetable panini, vegetable lasagna, abundant salads, and an appealing selection of microwavable and takeout goodies. On the terrace under the trees, the tables are cheerfully accented with Italian herbs growing in cachepots. *A fave:* the linguine pomodoro, with fresh tomatoes, spinach-tomato sauce, and a dollop of mascarpone. Unfortunately, lunch is only served in summer and from mid-December to mid-March, when most of the tourists are around.

In the Fairmont Kea Lani Hotel, 4100 Wailea Alanui. © **808/875-4100.** Reservations recommended. Main courses $13–$20 lunch, $17–$36 dinner; pizzas $17–$19. AE, DC, DISC, MC, V. Lunch (seasonally) daily noon–3pm; dinner daily 5:30–10pm. Bar daily 11am–10pm.

Joe's Bar & Grill ☞☞ AMERICAN GRILL   The 270-degree view spans the golf course, tennis courts, ocean, and Haleakala—a worthy setting for Beverly Gannon's style of American home cooking with a regional twist. The hearty staples include excellent mashed potatoes, lobster, fresh fish, and filet mignon, but the meatloaf (a whole loaf, like Mom used to make) upstages them all. The Tuscan white-bean soup is superb, and the tenderloin, with roasted portobellos, mashed potatoes with whole garlic, and a pinot noir demi-glace, is American home cooking at its best. Daily specials could be grilled ahi with white truffle–Yukon gold mashed potatoes or sautéed mahimahi with shrimp bisque and sautéed spinach. If chocolate cake is on the menu, you should definitely spring for it.

In the Wailea Tennis Club, 131 Wailea Ike Place. © **808/875-7767.** Reservations recommended. Main courses $26–$34. AE, DC, DISC, MC, V. Daily 5:30–9pm.

MAKENA

Prince Court ☞☞ CONTEMPORARY ISLAND   Half of the Sunday brunch experience here is the head-turning view of Makena Beach, the Molokini islet, and Kahoolawe island. The other half is the fabled Sunday buffet, bountiful and sumptuous, spread over several tables: pasta, omelets, cheeses, pastries, sashimi, crab legs, smoked salmon, fresh Maui produce, and a smashing array of ethnic and Continental foods, plus a few surprises, including assorted dim sum, Thai-style beef curry, specialty pastas, and not-to-be-missed desserts. The dinner menu changes regularly but might include a rack of lamb, vegetable risotto, coquilles St. Jacques, or veal scaloppine ala Marsala. On a recent visit we dined on blackened ahi, pulehu teriyaki short ribs, and Asian seafood noodles. Don't miss the Friday-night seafood and prime-rib buffet, with one of the largest selections of seafood on ice (fresh sashimi, shrimp, Hawaiian poke, and oysters), a roast-beef carving station, tons of salads (with a Caesar salad bar), and a range of other entrees (fresh fish, grilled chicken, and more).

In the Maui Prince Hotel, 5400 Makena Alanui. ✆ 808/874-1111. Reservations recommended. Main courses $27–$45; Fri prime rib and seafood buffet $45 ($25 children, children 5 and under eat free); Sun brunch $42. AE, MC, V. Sun 9am–1pm (with last seating at noon); Fri–Wed 6–9pm (call for seating times).

4 Upcountry Maui

HALIIMAILE (ON THE WAY TO UPCOUNTRY MAUI)

Haliimaile General Store ✿✿✿ HAWAII REGIONAL/AMER-ICAN   For more than 2 decades, Bev Gannon, one of the original Hawaii Regional Cuisine chefs, has been going strong at her foodie haven in the pineapple fields. You'll dine at tables set on old wood floors under high ceilings (sound ricochets fiercely here), in a peach-colored room emblazoned with works by local artists. The food, a blend of eclectic American with ethnic touches, puts an innovative spin on Hawaii Regional Cuisine. Even the fresh-catch sandwich on the lunch menu is anything but prosaic. Sip the *lilikoi* lemonade and nibble the sashimi napoleon or the house salad—island greens with mandarin oranges, onions, toasted walnuts, and blue-cheese crumble—all are notable items on a menu that bridges Hawaii with Gannon's Texas roots.

Haliimaile Rd. ✆ 808/572-2666. www.haliimailegeneralstore.com. Reservations recommended. Lunch $8–$22; dinner $22–$39. AE, DC, MC, V. Mon–Fri 11am–2:30pm; daily 5:30–9:30pm.

MAKAWAO & PUKALANI

Casanova Italian Restaurant ✿ ITALIAN   Look for the tiny veranda with a few stools, always full, in front of a deli at Makawao's busiest intersection—that's the most visible part of the Casanova restaurant and lounge. Makawao's nightlife center contains a stage, dance floor, restaurant, and bar—and food to love and remember. This is pasta heaven; try the spaghetti *fra diavolo* or the spinach gnocchi in a fresh tomato-Gorgonzola sauce. Other choices include a huge pizza selection, grilled lamb chops in an Italian mushroom marinade, lots more pasta dishes, and luscious desserts. My personal picks on a stellar menu: garlic spinach topped with Parmesan and pine nuts, and tiramisu, the best on the island.

1188 Makawao Ave. ✆ 808/572-0220. www.casanovamaui.com. Reservations recommended for dinner. Main courses $22–$28; 12-in. pizzas $12–$20; pasta

$12–$18. AE, DC, DISC, MC, V. Mon–Sat 11:30am–2pm and 5:30–9:30pm; Sun 5:30–9pm. Dancing Wed–Sat 9:45pm–1am. Lounge daily 5:30pm–12:30am. Deli Mon–Sat 7:30am–6pm; Sun 8:30am–6pm.

KULA (AT THE BASE OF HALEAKALA NATIONAL PARK)
EXPENSIVE

Kula Lodge ⍟ HAWAII REGIONAL/AMERICAN   Don't let the dinner prices scare you: The Kula Lodge is equally enjoyable, if not more so, at breakfast and lunch, when the prices are lower and the views through the picture windows have an eye-popping intensity. The million-dollar vista spans the flanks of Haleakala, rolling 3,200 feet down to central Maui, the ocean, and the West Maui Mountains. The Kula Lodge has always been known for its breakfasts: fabulous eggs Benedict, including a vegetarian version with Kula onions, shiitake mushrooms, and scallions; legendary banana–mac-nut pancakes; and a highly recommended tofu scramble with green onions, Kula vegetables, and garlic chives. If possible, go for sunset cocktails and watch the colors change into deep end-of-day hues. When darkness descends, a roaring fire and lodge atmosphere add to the coziness of the room. The dinner menu features "small plates" of Thai summer rolls, seared ahi, and other starters. Sesame-seared ono leads the seafood attractions, but there's also pasta, rack of lamb, filet mignon, and free-range chicken breast.

Haleakala Hwy. (Hwy. 377). ℂ **808/878-2517.** Reservations recommended for dinner. Breakfast $7.50–$16; lunch $11–$18; dinner main courses $14–$29. AE, DC, DISC, MC, V. Daily 6:30am–9pm.

INEXPENSIVE

Grandma's Coffee House COFFEEHOUSE/AMERICAN Alfred Franco's grandmother started what is now a five-generation coffee business back in 1918, when she was 16 years old. Today this tiny wooden coffeehouse, still fueled by homegrown Haleakala coffee beans, is the quintessential roadside oasis. Grandma's offers espresso, hot and cold coffees, home-baked pastries, inexpensive pasta, sandwiches (including sensational avocado and garden burgers), homemade soups, fresh juices, and local plate-lunch specials that change daily. The lemon squares and the pumpkin bread are standouts.

At the end of Hwy. 37, Keokea (about 6 miles before the Tedeschi Vineyards in Ulupalakua). ℂ **808/878-2140.** Most items less than $8.95. AE, DC, MC, V. Daily 7am–5pm.

Kula Sandalwoods Restaurant ⊘ AMERICAN   Chef Eleanor Loui, a graduate of the Culinary Institute of America, makes hollandaise sauce every morning from fresh upcountry egg yolks, sweet butter, and Meyer lemons, which her family grows in the yard above the restaurant. This is Kula cuisine, with produce from the backyard and everything made from scratch, including French toast with home-baked Portuguese sweet bread; hotcakes or Belgian waffles with fresh fruit; open-faced country omelets; hamburgers drenched in a special cheese sauce made with grated sharp cheddar; a killer kalua pork sandwich; and an outstanding veggie burger. The grilled chicken breast sandwich is marvelous, served with soup of the day and Kula mixed greens. Dine in the gazebo or on the terrace, with dazzling views in all directions, including, in the spring, a yard dusted with lavender jacaranda flowers and a hillside ablaze with fields of orange akulikuli blossoms.

15427 Haleakala Hwy. (Hwy. 377). ℗ **808/878-3523.** Breakfast $6.95–$12; lunch $7.25–$12; Sun brunch $6.95–$12. MC, V. Mon–Sat 6:30am–3pm; Sun brunch 6:30am–noon.

5 East Maui: On the Road to Hana

PAIA
MODERATE

Jacques North Shore ⊘⊘ *Value* SEAFOOD/SUSHI   Jacques is difficult to pin down: Some have called it a hipper, cheaper version of the upscale Mama's Fish House (see review below) just down the road, others depict it as an atypical Maui dining experience with excellent food and great prices. The clientele tends to be trendy, hard-body windsurfers; blonde, tan surfers; and chic north-shore residents. The decor is patio dining under a big circus tent. My top picks: North Shore pumpkin fish (fish, bananas, and oranges served with a ginger pumpkin sauce and miso butter), Greek pasta (roasted bell peppers, roasted garlic, and feta cheese over orecchiette pasta), or one of the fabulous vegetarian entrees like the vegetable curry (with tofu, bananas, and oranges). The sushi bar (closed Sun–Mon) whips out a mean spicy ahi roll and a died-and-gone-to-heaven California roll.

120 Hana Hwy. ℗ **808/579-8844.** Reservations not accepted. Main courses $11–$27. AE, DC, DISC, MC, V. Daily 5–10pm; sushi bar Tues–Sat 5–10pm.

Milagros Food Company ⊘ SOUTHWESTERN/SEAFOOD Milagros has gained a following with its great home-style cooking and upbeat atmosphere. I love Paia's tie-dyes, beads, and hippie flavor, and this is the front-row seat for it all. Sit outdoors and watch the parade of Willie Nelson look-alikes ambling by as you tuck into the ahi creation of the evening, a combination of Southwestern and Pacific Rim styles and flavors accompanied by fresh veggies and Kula greens. Grilled ahi burrito, Mexican red enchiladas, seafood enchiladas, New York strip steak, shrimp pasta, and even Chesapeake Bay crab cakes. For breakfast, I recommend the spinach omelet or the huevos rancheros. Lunch ranges from ahi burger to honey and macnut grilled salmon salad. Watch for happy hour, with cheap and fabulous margaritas.

Hana Hwy. and Baldwin Ave. ℂ **808/579-8755.** Breakfast $6–$9; lunch $7–$12; dinner $14–$25. AE, MC, V. Daily 8am–11pm.

Moana Bakery & Cafe 🍴🍴 LOCAL/EUROPEAN   Moana gets high marks for its stylish concrete floors, high ceilings, booths and cafe tables, and fabulous food. Don Ritchey, formerly a chef at Haliimaile General Store, has created the perfect Paia eatery, a casual bakery-cafe that highlights his stellar skills. All the bases are covered: saimin, omelets, wraps, pancakes, and fresh-baked goods in the morning; soups, sandwiches, pasta, and satisfying salads for lunch; and for dinner, varied selections with Asian and European influences and fresh island ingredients. The lemon-grass-grilled prawns with green papaya salad are an explosion of flavors and textures, the roasted vegetable napoleon is gourmet fare, and the Thai red curry with coconut milk, served over vegetables, seafood, or tofu, comes atop jasmine rice with crisp rice noodles and fresh sprouts to cool the fire. Ritchey's Thai-style curries are richly spiced and intense. I also vouch for his special gift with fish: The nori-sesame-crusted mahimahi with miso garlic tapioca pearls is cooked, like the curry, to perfection. There's live jazz most Friday nights.

71 Baldwin Ave. ℂ **808/579-9999.** Reservations recommended for dinner. Breakfast $7–$14; lunch $6–$13; dinner main courses $7–$32. MC, V. Tues–Sun 8am–9pm; Mon 8am–2:30pm.

INEXPENSIVE

Cafe des Amis 🍴🍴 *Finds* CREPES/MEDITERRANEAN/ INDIAN   This tiny eatery is a hidden delight: healthy and tasty breakfasts, lunches, and dinners that are easy on the wallet. Crepes are the star here, and they are popular: spinach with feta cheese, shrimp curry with coconut milk, and dozens more choices, including breakfast crepes and dessert crepes (like banana and chocolate or strawberries and cream). Equally popular are the Greek salads and smoothies. Dinners feature authentic Indian curries, such as a vegetable curry with spinach, carrots, cauliflower, and potato with Tamil spices and tomato; all curries come with rice, mango chutney, and tomato chutney. The cafe also serves the best coffee in Paia.

42 Baldwin Ave. ✆ 808/579-6323. Breakfast crepes $8–$9; lunch crepes $7.25–$9; dinner entrees $11–$15. MC, V. Daily 8:30am–8:30pm.

Paia Fish Market SEAFOOD This really is a fish market, with fresh fish to take home and cooked seafood, salads, pastas, fajitas, and quesadillas to take out or enjoy at the few picnic tables inside the restaurant. It has an appealing and budget-friendly selection: Cajun-style fresh catch, fresh-fish specials (usually ahi or salmon), fresh-fish tacos and quesadillas, and seafood and chicken pastas. You can also order hamburgers, cheeseburgers, fish and chips (or shrimp and chips), and wonderful lunch and dinner plates that are cheap and tasty. Peppering the walls are photos of the number-one sport here, windsurfing.

110 Hana Hwy. ✆ 808/579-8030. Lunch and dinner plates $8–$22. DISC, MC, V. Daily 11am–9:30pm.

HAIKU

Colleen's at the Cannery 𝕮𝕮𝕮 *Finds* ECLECTIC Way, way, way off the beaten path lies this fabulous find in the rural Haiku Cannery Marketplace. Once through the doors, you'd swear you'd drop down in the middle of a hot, chic boutique restaurant in SoHo in Manhattan (only when you look around at the patrons they are pure Haiku upcountry residents). It's worth the drive to enjoy Colleen's fabulous culinary creations, like a wild-mushroom ravioli with sautéed portobello mushrooms, tomatoes, herbs, and a roasted pepper coulis for $14 (not New York City prices) or pan-seared ahi for $15, or filet mignon with a side salad for $16. Colleen also serves up smaller meals, such as burgers and fish and chips. Breakfast includes mouthwatering bakery products such as French toast ($7.75) with Colleen's own homemade bread or the wonderful omelets ($9). Lunch stars baguette sandwiches, wraps, salads, and burgers and fries. I only wish they would take reservations.

Haiku Cannery Marketplace, 810 Haiku Rd. ✆ 808/575-9211. www.colleen sinhaiku.com. Reservations not accepted. Breakfast $5.75–$9; lunch $7–$15; dinner entrees $14–$24. MC, V. Daily 6am–10pm.

ELSEWHERE ON THE ROAD TO HANA
VERY EXPENSIVE

Mama's Fish House 𝕮𝕮𝕮 SEAFOOD Okay, it's expensive—maybe the most expensive seafood house on Maui—but if you love fish, this is the place for you. The restaurant's entrance, a cove with windsurfers, tide pools, white sand, and a canoe resting under palm trees, is a South Seas fantasy worthy of Gauguin. The interior features curved lauhala-lined ceilings, walls of split bamboo, lavish arrangements of tropical blooms, and picture windows to let in the view. With servers wearing Polynesian prints and flowers behind their ears, and the setting sun casting a rosy glow on everything, Mama's mood is hard to beat. The fish is fresh (the fishermen are even credited by name on the menu) and prepared either Hawaiian-style, with tropical fruit, or baked in a crust of macadamia nuts and vanilla beans, or in a number of dishes involving ferns, seaweed, Maui onions, and roasted kukui nut. My favorite menu item is mahimahi laulau with luau leaves (taro greens) and Maui onions, baked in ti leaves and served with kalua pig and Hanalei poi. You can get deepwater ahi seared with coconut and lime, or ono "caught by Keith Nakamura along the 40-fathom ledge near Hana" in Hana ginger teriyaki with mac nuts and crisp Maui onion. Other special touches include the use of Molokai sweet potato, organic lettuces, Haiku bananas, and fresh coconut, which evoke the mood and tastes of old Hawaii.

799 Poho Place, just off the Hana Hwy., Kuau. (©) **808/579-8488.** Reservations recommended for lunch, required for dinner. Main courses $32–$48 lunch, $35–$55 dinner. AE, DC, DISC, MC, V. Daily 11am to last seating at 9pm (light menu 2:30–4:30pm).

INEXPENSIVE

Nahiku Coffee Shop, Smoked Fish Stand, and Ti Gallery ✹

(Finds SMOKED KABOBS   What a delight to stumble across this trio of comforts on the long drive to Hana! The small coffee shop purveys locally made baked goods, several flavors of Maui-grown coffee, banana breads made in the neighborhood, organic tropical fruit smoothies, and the Original and Best Coconut Candy made by Hana character Jungle Johnny. Next door, the Ti Gallery sells locally made Hawaiian arts and crafts, such as pottery and koa wood vessels.

The barbecue smoker, though, is my favorite part of the operation. It puts out superb smoked and grilled fish, fresh and locally caught, sending seductive aromas out into the moist Nahiku air. These are not jerkylike smoked meats: The process keeps the kabobs moist while retaining the smoke flavor. The breadfruit—sliced, wrapped in banana leaf, and baked—can be bland and starchy (like a baked potato), but it's a stroke of genius to give visitors a taste of this important Polynesian staple. The teriyaki-based marinade, made by the owner, adds a special touch to the fish (ono, ahi, marlin). One of the biggest sellers is the kalua pig sandwich. Also a hit are the Island-style, two-hand tacos of fish, beef, and chicken, served with about six condiments, including cheese, jalapeños, and salsa. When available, fresh corn on the cob from Kipahulu is served and is grabbed up apace. There are a few roadside picnic tables, or you can take your lunch to go for a beachside picnic in Hana.

Hana Hwy., ½ mile past mile marker 28. No phone. Kabobs $3 each. No credit cards. Coffee shop daily 9am–5:30pm; fish stand Fri–Wed 10am–5pm; gallery daily 10am–5pm.

6 At the End of the Road in East Maui: Hana

EXPENSIVE

Hotel Hana-Maui &&& LOCAL/ECLECTIC   Not even Passport Resorts' executive chef, John Cox, who is in charge of developing the daily menu changes, can put his finger on the delicious type of cuisine served in the open, airy dining room. "I call it cuisine inspired by eastern Maui," he says, pointing to the ingredients-driven menu: the fresh fish caught by local fishermen, the produce brought in by nearby farmers, the fruits that are in season. The result is true Hawaiian food, grown right on the island. Breakfast features an omelet with local Maui onions and a Hana fern salad, almond-crusted French toast, or local papaya with yogurt and homemade granola. Lunch ranges from Maui Cattle Company burgers to just-caught fish sandwiches. Dinner, which changes daily, can include just-picked lettuce for salads (Kula-grown baby romaine with Gruyère crostini and sherry-thyme vinaigrette, or baby salad greens with Kula citrus, local radishes, and Kalamata olives), a range of soups (such as a chilled Kula cucumber soup), and entrees such as seared rare Hana-caught ahi with smoked bacon, forest mushrooms, and wilted greens, or oven-roasted chicken breast with crispy polenta, Nihiku bush beans, and mole sauce. Try the three- or four-course tasting menu, or even better, the Chef's Choice.

Hana Hwy. © 808/248-8211. Reservations recommended for dinner Fri–Sat. Entrees $13–$18 breakfast, $10–$21 lunch, $26–$36 dinner; tasting menu $55 for 3 courses, $65 for 4 courses; $75 for Chef's Choice. AE, DISC, MC, V. Daily 7:30–10:30am, 11:30am–2:30pm, and 6–9pm. Fri buffet and Hawaiian show 6:30–7:30pm ($50).

4

Fun On & Off the Beach

This is why you've come to Maui—the sun, the sand, and the surf. In this chapter, I'll tell you about the best beaches, from where to soak up the rays to where to plunge beneath the waves. I've covered a range of ocean activities on Maui, as well as my favorite places and outfitters for these marine adventures. Also in this chapter are things to do on dry land, including the best spots for hiking and camping and the greatest golf courses.

1 Beaches

Hawaii's beaches belong to the people. All beaches, even those in front of exclusive resorts, are public property, and you are welcome to visit. Hawaii state law requires all resorts and hotels to offer public right-of-way access to the beach, along with public parking. For snorkel gear, boogie boards, and other ocean toys, head to one of **Snorkel Bob's** (www.snorkelbob.com) four locations: 1217 Front St., Lahaina (© **808/661-4421**); Napili Village, 5425-C Lower Honoapiilani Hwy., Napili (© **808/669-9603**); in North Kihei at Azeka Place II, 1279 S. Kihei Rd. #310 (© **808/875-6188**); and in South Kihei/Wailea at Kamaole Beach Center, 2411 S. Kihei Rd. (© **808/879-7449**). All locations are open daily from 8am to 5pm. If you're island hopping, you can rent from a Snorkel Bob's location on one island and return to a branch on another.

WEST MAUI
D. T. FLEMING BEACH PARK ✸✸
This quiet, out-of-the-way beach cove, named after the man who started the commercial growing of pineapples on the Valley Isle, is a great place to take the family. The crescent-shaped beach, located north of the Ritz-Carlton hotel, starts at the 16th hole of the Kapalua golf course (Makaluapuna Point) and rolls around to the sea cliffs at the other side. Ironwood trees provide shade on the land side. Offshore, a shallow sandbar extends to the edge of the surf. The waters are generally good for swimming and snorkeling; sometimes, off on the right side near the sea cliffs, the waves build

enough for body boarders and surfers to get a few good rides in. This park has lots of facilities: restrooms, showers, picnic tables, barbecue grills, and a paved parking lot.

KAANAPALI BEACH ☆☆

Four-mile-long Kaanapali is one of Maui's best beaches, with grainy gold sand as far as the eye can see. The beach parallels the sea channel through most of its length, and a paved beach walk links hotels and condos, open-air restaurants, and Whalers Village shopping center. Because Kaanapali is so long, and because most hotels have adjacent swimming pools, the beach is crowded only in pockets—there's plenty of room to find seclusion. Summertime swimming is excellent.

There's fabulous snorkeling around **Black Rock,** in front of the Sheraton. The water is clear, calm, and populated with clouds of tropical fish. You might even spot a turtle or two.

Facilities include outdoor showers; you can use the restrooms at the hotel pools. Various beach-activity vendors line up in front of the hotels, offering nearly every type of water activity and equipment.

Parking is a problem, though. There are two public entrances: At the south end, turn off Honoapiilani Highway into the Kaanapali Resort, and pay for parking there, or continue on Honoapiilani Highway, turn off at the last Kaanapali exit at the stoplight near the Maui Kaanapali Villas, and park next to the beach signs indicating public access (this is a little tricky to find and limited to only a few cars, so to save time, you might want to just head to the Sheraton or Whalers Village and plunk down your money).

KAPALUA BEACH ☆☆☆

The beach cove that fronts the former Kapalua Bay hotel (now in the process of being replaced by condos) is the stuff of dreams: a golden crescent bordered by two palm-studded points. The sandy bottom slopes gently to deep water at the bay mouth; the water is so clear that you can see where the gold sands turn to green and then deep blue. Protected from strong winds and currents by the lava-rock promontories, Kapalua's calm waters are great for snorkelers and swimmers of all ages and abilities, and the bay is big enough to paddle a kayak around without getting into the more challenging channel that separates Maui from Molokai. Waves come in just right for riding. Fish hang out by the rocks, making it great for snorkeling.

The sandy beach isn't so wide that you'll burn your feet getting in or out of the water, and the inland side is edged by a shady path and cool lawns. Facilities include outdoor showers, restrooms, lifeguards, a rental shack, and plenty of shade.

Parking is limited to about 30 spaces in a small lot off Lower Honoapiilani Road, by Napili Kai Beach Club, so arrive early.

SOUTH MAUI
KAMAOLE III BEACH PARK 𝒜

Three beach parks—Kamaole I, II, and III—stand like golden jewels in the front yard of the funky seaside town of Kihei, which is exploding with suburban sprawl. The beaches are the best things about Kihei. All three are popular with local residents and visitors because they're easily accessible. On weekends they're jampacked with fishermen, picnickers, swimmers, and snorkelers.

The most popular is Kamaole III, or "Kam-3," as locals say. The biggest of the three beaches, with wide pockets of golden sand, it's the only one with a playground for children and a grassy lawn that meets the sand. Swimming is safe here, but scattered lava rocks are toe stubbers at the water line, and parents should watch to make sure that kids don't venture too far out, because the bottom slopes off quickly. Both the north and south shores are rocky fingers with a surge big enough to attract fish and snorkelers, and the winter waves attract bodysurfers. Kam-3 is also a wonderful place to watch the sunset. Facilities include restrooms, showers, picnic tables, barbecue grills, and lifeguards. There's also plenty of parking on South Kihei Road, across from the Maui Parkshore condos.

WAILEA BEACH 𝒜𝒜

Wailea is the best golden-sand crescent on Maui's sunbaked southwestern coast. One of five beaches within Wailea Resort, Wailea is big, wide, and protected on both sides by black-lava points. It's the front yard of the Four Seasons Wailea and the Grand Wailea Resort Hotel & Spa. From the beach, the view out to sea is magnificent, framed by neighboring Kahoolawe and Lanai and the tiny crescent of Molokini, probably the most popular snorkel spot in these parts. The clear waters tumble to shore in waves just the right size for gentle riding, with or without a board. From shore, you can see Pacific humpback whales in season (Dec–Apr) and unreal sunsets nightly. Facilities include restrooms, outdoor showers, and limited free parking at the blue SHORELINE ACCESS sign, on Wailea Alanui Drive, the main drag of this resort.

ULUA BEACH 𝒜

One of the most popular beaches in Wailea, Ulua is a long, wide, crescent-shaped gold-sand beach between two rocky points. When the ocean is calm, Ulua offers Wailea's best snorkeling; when it's rough, the waves are excellent for bodysurfers. The ocean bottom is shallow and gently slopes down to deeper waters, making swimming generally safe. The beach is usually occupied by guests of nearby resorts; in high season (Christmas–Mar and June–Aug), it's carpeted with beach towels. Facilities include showers and restrooms. A variety of equipment is available for rent at the nearby Wailea Ocean Activity Center. To find Ulua, look for the blue SHORELINE ACCESS sign on South Kihei Road, north of the Wailea Elua condos. There's a tiny parking lot nearby.

MALUAKA BEACH (MAKENA BEACH) 🐠🐠

On the southern end of Maui's resort coast, development falls off dramatically, leaving a wild, dry countryside of green kiawe trees. The Maui Prince sits in isolated splendor, sharing Makena Resort's 1,800 acres with only a couple of first-rate golf courses and a necklace of perfect beaches. The strand nearest the hotel is Maluaka Beach, often called Makena, notable for its beauty and its views of Molokini Crater, the offshore islet, and Kahoolawe, the so-called "target" island. It's a short, wide, palm-fringed crescent of golden, grainy sand set between two black-lava points and bounded by big sand dunes topped by a grassy knoll. Swimming in this mostly calm bay is considered the best on Makena Bay, which is bordered on the south by Puu Olai cinder cone and historic Keawala'i Congregational Church. Facilities include restrooms, showers, a landscaped park, lifeguards, and roadside parking. Along Makena Alanui, look for the SHORELINE ACCESS sign near the hotel, turn right, and head down to the shore.

ONELOA BEACH (BIG BEACH) 🐠🐠

Oneloa, which means "long sand" in Hawaiian, is one of the most popular beaches on Maui. Locals call it Big Beach—it's 3,300 feet long and more than 100 feet wide. Mauians come here to swim, fish, sunbathe, surf, and enjoy the view of Kahoolawe and Lanai. Snorkeling is good around the north end at the foot of Puu Olai, a 360-foot cinder cone. During storms, however, big waves lash the shore and a strong rip current sweeps the sharp drop-off, posing a danger for inexperienced open-ocean swimmers. There are no facilities except portable toilets, but there's plenty of parking. To get here, drive past the Maui Prince Hotel to the second dirt road, which leads through a kiawe thicket to the beach.

On the other side of Puu Olai is **Little Beach,** a small pocket beach where assorted nudists work on their all-over tans, to the chagrin of uptight authorities, who take a dim view of public nudity. You can get a nasty sunburn and a lewd-conduct ticket, too.

EAST MAUI
HOOKIPA BEACH PARK *&*

Two miles past Paia on the Hana Highway, you'll find one of the most famous windsurfing sites in the world. Due to its constant winds and endless waves, Hookipa attracts top windsurfers and wave jumpers from around the globe. Surfers and fishermen also enjoy this small, gold-sand beach at the foot of a grassy cliff, which provides a natural amphitheater for spectators. Except when international competitions are being held, weekdays are the best time to watch the daredevils fly over the waves. When the water is flat, snorkelers and divers explore the reef. Facilities include restrooms, showers, pavilions, picnic tables, barbecue grills, and a parking lot.

WAIANAPANAPA STATE PARK *&*

Four miles before Hana, off the Hana Highway, is this beach park, which takes its name from the legend of the Waianapanapa Cave. Chief Kaakea, a jealous and cruel man, suspected his wife, Popoalaea, of having an affair. Popoalaea left her husband and hid herself in a chamber of the Waianapanapa Cave. A few days later, when Kaakea was passing by the cave, the shadow of a servant gave away Popoalaea's hiding place, and Kaakea killed her. During certain times of the year, the water in the tide pool turns red as a tribute to Popoalaea, commemorating her death. (Scientists claim, however, that the change in color is due to the presence of small red shrimp.)

Waianapanapa State Park's 120 acres have 12 cabins (see chapter 2), a caretaker's residence, a beach park, picnic tables, barbecue grills, restrooms, showers, a parking lot, a shoreline hiking trail, and a black-sand beach (it's actually small black pebbles). This is a wonderful area for both shoreline hikes (mosquitoes are plentiful, so bring insect repellent) and picnicking. Swimming is generally unsafe due to powerful rip currents and strong waves breaking offshore, which roll into the beach unchecked. Waianapanapa is crowded on weekends; weekdays are generally a better bet.

HAMOA BEACH *&&*

This half-moon-shaped, gray-sand beach (a mix of coral and lava) in a truly tropical setting is a favorite among sunbathers seeking rest and refuge. The Hotel Hana-Maui maintains the beach and acts as though it's private, which it isn't—so just march down the lava-rock steps and grab a spot on the sand. James Michener said of Hamoa,

"Paradoxically, the only beach I have ever seen that looks like the South Pacific was in the North Pacific—Hamoa Beach . . . a beach so perfectly formed that I wonder at its comparative obscurity." The 100-foot-wide beach is three football fields long and sits below 30-foot black-lava sea cliffs. Hamoa is often swept by powerful rip currents. Surf breaks offshore and rolls ashore, making this a popular surfing and bodysurfing area. The calm left side is best for snorkeling in summer. The hotel has numerous facilities for guests; there's an outdoor shower and restrooms for nonguests. Parking is limited. Look for the Hamoa Beach turnoff from Hana Highway.

2 Watersports

BOATING & SAILING

Later in this section, you can find information on snorkel cruises to Molokini under "Snorkeling," fishing charters under "Sport Fishing," and trips that combine snorkeling with whale-watching under "Whale-Watching Cruises."

Scotch Mist Sailing Charters This 50-foot Santa Cruz sailboat offers 2-hour sailing adventures. Prices include snorkel gear, juice, fresh pineapple spears, Maui chips, beer, wine, and soda.

Lahaina Harbor, slip 2. (℗ **808/661-0386**. www.scotchmistsailingcharters.com. Sail trips $45 adults, $25 children ages 5–12; sunset sail $45.

OCEAN KAYAKING

One of Maui's best kayak routes is along the **Kihei Coast,** where there's easy access to calm water. Early mornings are always best, because the wind comes up around 11am, making seas choppy and paddling difficult.

For beginners, my favorite kayak-tour operator is **Makena Kayak Tours** ℱ (℗ **877/879-8426** or 808/879-8426; www.makenakayaks. com). Professional guide Dino Ventura leads a 2½-hour trip from Makena Landing for $55 and loves taking first-timers over the secluded coral reefs and into remote coves. Prices include refreshments and snorkel and kayak equipment. Check the website for discounts.

South Pacific Kayaks, 2439 S. Kihei Rd., Kihei (℗ **800/776-2326** or 808/875-4848; www.mauikayak.com), is Maui's oldest kayak-tour company. Its expert guides lead ocean-kayak trips that include lessons, a guided tour, and snorkeling. Tours run from 2½ to 5 hours and range in price from $65 to $139.

In Hana, **Hana-Maui Sea Sports** (℗ **808/248-7711;** www. hana-maui-seasports.com) runs 2-hour tours of Hana's coastline on wide, stable "no roll" kayaks, with snorkeling, for $89.

SCUBA DIVING

Some people come to Maui for the sole purpose of plunging into the tropical Pacific and exploring the underwater world. You can see the great variety of tropical marine life (more than 100 endemic species found nowhere else on the planet), explore sea caves, and swim with sea turtles and monk seals in the clear tropical waters off the island. I recommend going early in the morning; trade winds often rough up the seas in the afternoon.

Unsure about scuba diving? Take an introductory dive: Most operators offer no-experience-necessary dives, ranging from $95 to $125.

Everyone dives **Molokini**, a marine-life park and one of Hawaii's top dive spots. This crescent-shaped crater has three tiers of diving: a 35-foot plateau inside the crater basin (used by beginning divers and snorkelers), a wall sloping to 70 feet just beyond the inside plateau, and a sheer wall on the outside and backside of the crater that plunges 350 feet. This underwater park is very popular thanks to calm, clear, protected waters and an abundance of marine life, from manta rays to yellow butterfly fish.

For personalized diving, **Ed Robinson's Diving Adventures** ✆ (© **800/635-1273** or 808/879-3584; www.mauiscuba.com) is the only Maui company rated one of *Scuba Diver* magazine's top five best dive operators for 7 years straight. Two-tank dives are $126 ($137 with equipment); his dive boats depart from Kihei Boat Ramp.

If Ed is booked, call **Mike Severns Diving** (© **808/879-6596**; www.mikeseversnsdiving.com), for small (maximum 12 people, divided into two groups of six), personal diving tours on a 38-foot Munson/Hammerhead boat with freshwater shower. Two-tank dives are $125 if you have your own equipment or $140 with rental.

Stop by any location of **Maui Dive Shop** ✆ (www.maui diveshop.com), Maui's largest diving retailer, with everything from rentals to scuba-diving instruction to dive-boat charters, for a free copy of the 24-page *Maui Dive Guide* (you can also order a copy online). Inside are maps of and details on the 20 best shoreline and offshore dives and snorkel sites, each ranked for beginner, intermediate, or advanced snorkelers/divers. Maui Dive Shop has branches at Azeka Place II Shopping Center, 1455 S. Kihei Rd., Kihei (© **808/879-3388**); Kamaole Shopping Center, 2463 S. Kihei Rd., Suite A-15, Kamaole (© **808/879-1533**); Shops at Wailea, 3750 Wailea Alanui Rd., Suite B-29, Wailea (© **808/875-9904**); Lahaina Cannery Mall, 1221 Honoapiilani Hwy., Suite B-2, Lahaina

(© **808/661-5388**); and in the Honokowai Marketplace, 118 Lower
Honoapiilani Hwy., Honokowai (© **808/661-6166**). Other locations include Whalers Village, 2435 Kaanapali Pkwy., Suite N, Kaanapali (© **808/661-5117**), Kaanapali Fairway Shops (© **808/551-
9663**), Maalaea Village (© **808/244-5514**), and Kahana Gateway,
4405 Honoapiilani Hwy., Suite 204, Kahana (© **808/669-3800**).

SNORKELING

Snorkeling is the main attraction in Maui—and almost anyone can
do it. All you need are a mask, a snorkel, fins, and some basic swimming skills. In many places all you have to do is wade into the water
and look down. Most resorts and excursion boats offer instruction for
first-time snorkelers, but it's plenty easy to figure it out for yourself.

Some snorkel tips: Always go with a buddy. Look up every once
in a while to see where you are and check for boat traffic. Don't
touch anything; not only can you damage coral, but camouflaged
fish and shells with poisonous spines might surprise you. Always
check with a dive shop, lifeguards, and others on the beach about
conditions in the area in which you plan to snorkel. If you're not a
good swimmer, wear a life jacket or other flotation device, which
you can rent at most places offering watersports gear.

Snorkel Bob's ⋆ (www.snorkelbob.com) will rent you everything
you need; see the introduction to this section for locations. Also see
"Scuba Diving" (see above) for Maui Dive Shop's free booklet on
great snorkeling sites.

When the whales aren't around, **Capt. Steve's Rafting Excursions** (© **808/667-5565;** www.captainsteves.com) offers 7-hour
snorkel trips from Mala Wharf in Lahaina to the waters around
Lanai (you don't actually land on the island). Rates of $150 for
adults and $115 for children 12 and under include breakfast, lunch,
snorkel gear, and wet suits.

Maui's best snorkeling beaches include **Kapalua Beach; Black
Rock,** at Kaanapali Beach, in front of the Sheraton; along the Kihei
coastline, especially at **Kamaole III Beach Park;** and along the
Wailea coastline, particularly at **Ulua Beach.** Mornings are best
because local winds don't kick in until around noon. **Olowalu** has
great snorkeling around the **14-mile marker,** where there is a tur-
tle-cleaning station about 150 to 225 feet out from shore. Turtles
line up here to have cleaner wrasses pick off small parasites.

Ahihi-Kinau Natural Preserve, on Maui's rugged south coast, is
another terrific place. It requires more effort to reach it, but it's
worth it because it's home to Maui's tropical marine life at its best.

After you snorkel, check out La Pérouse Bay on the south side of Cape Kinau, where the French admiral La Pérouse became the first European to set foot on Maui. A lava-rock pyramid known as Pérouse Monument marks the spot. To get here, drive south of Makena past Puu Olai to Ahihi Bay, where the road turns to gravel and sometimes seems like it'll disappear under the waves. At Cape Kinau, there are three four-wheel-drive trails that lead across the lava flow; take the shortest one, nearest La Pérouse Bay. If you have a standard car, drive as far as you can, park, and walk the remainder of the way.

SNORKEL CRUISES TO MOLOKINI

Like a crescent moon fallen from the sky, the crater of **Molokini** ℛ sits almost midway between Maui and the uninhabited island of Kahoolawe. Tilted so that only the thin rim of its southern side shows above water in a perfect semicircle, Molokini stands like a scoop against the tide, and it serves, on its concave side, as a natural sanctuary for tropical fish and snorkelers, who commute daily in a fleet of dive boats to this marine-life preserve. Note that in high season, Molokini can be extremely crowded.

Maui Classic Charters ℛℛ   Maui Classic Charters offers morning and afternoon **snorkel-sail cruises to Molokini** on *Four Winds II,* a 55-foot, glass-bottom catamaran, for $84 adults ($49 children 3–12 years) for the morning sail and $42 adults ($30 children) in the afternoon. *Four Winds* trips include a continental breakfast; a barbecue lunch; complimentary beer, wine, and soda; complimentary snorkeling gear and instruction; and sport fishing.

   Those looking for speed should book a trip on the fast, state-of-the-art catamaran *Maui Magic.* The company offers a 5-hour snorkel journey to both Molokini and La Pérouse for $99 for adults and $79 for children ages 5 to 12, including a continental breakfast; barbecue lunch; beer, wine, and soda; snorkel gear; and instruction. During **whale season** (Dec 22–Apr 22), the *Four Winds* has a whale-watch trip, a 3½-hour trip with beverages is $42 for adults and $30 for children ages 3 to 12.

Maalaea Harbor, slip 55 and slip 80. ℂ **800/736-5740** or 808/879-8188. www. mauicharters.com. Prices vary depending on cruise.

Pacific Whale Foundation   This not-for-profit foundation supports its whale research by offering **whale-watch cruises** and **snorkel tours,** some to Molokini and Lanai. It operates a 65-foot power catamaran called *Ocean Spirit,* a 50-foot sailing catamaran called *Manute'a,* and a fleet of other boats. There are 15 daily trips from which to choose, offered from December through May, out of both Lahaina and Maalaea harbors.

101 N. Kihei Rd., Kihei. ℂ **800/942-5311** or 808/879-8811. www.pacificwhale.org. Trips from $20 adults, $17 children ages 7–12, free for ages 6 and under; snorkeling cruises from $80 adults, children $30.

Pride of Maui   For a high-speed, action-packed snorkel-sail experience, consider the *Pride of Maui.* These 5½-hour **snorkel cruises** take in not only **Molokini** but also Turtle Bay and Makena for more snorkeling; the cost is $90 for ages 13 and up and $56 for children ages 3 to 12. Continental breakfast, barbecue lunch, gear, and instruction are included. They also have an afternoon Molokini cruise ($42 for ages 13 and up and $27 for children ages 3–12, plus an optional lunch for an additional $7), an evening sunset cruise ($50 for ages 13 and up and $26 for children ages 3–12), and, during whale season, a whale-watching cruise ($26 for ages 13 and up and $17 for children ages 3–12).

Maalaea Harbor. ℂ **877/TO-PRIDE** or 808/875-0955. www.prideofmaui.com. Prices vary; see above.

Trilogy ⊛⊛⊛ (Kids   Trilogy offers my favorite **snorkel-sail trips.** The half-day trip to Molokini leaves from Maalaea Harbor and costs $110 for adults, half price for kids ages 3 to 12, including breakfast and a barbecue lunch. There's also a late-morning half-day snorkel-sail off Kaanapali Beach for the same price.

These are the most expensive sail-snorkel cruises on Maui, but they're worth every penny. The crews are fun and knowledgeable, and the boats comfortable and well equipped. Note, however, that you will be required to wear a flotation device no matter how good your swimming skills are; if this bothers you, go with another outfitter.

ℂ **888/MAUI-800** or 808/TRILOGY. www.sailtrilogy.com. Prices and departure points vary with cruise.

SPORT FISHING

Marlin (as big as 1,200 lb.), tuna, ono, and mahimahi await the baited hook in Maui's coastal and channel waters. No license is required; just book a sport-fishing vessel out of Lahaina or Maalaea harbors. Most charter boats that troll for big-game fish carry a maximum of six passengers. You can walk the docks, inspect boats, and talk to captains and crews, or book through an activities desk or one of the outfitters recommended below.

Shop around: Prices vary widely according to the boat, the crowd, and the captain. A shared boat for a half-day of fishing starts at $100; a shared full day of fishing starts at around $250. A half-day exclusive (you get the entire boat) starts at $600; a full-day exclusive starts at $900. Also, many boat captains tag and release marlin or keep the fish for themselves (sorry, that's Hawaii style). If you want to eat your mahimahi for dinner or have your marlin mounted, tell the captain before you go.

The best way to book a sport-fishing charter is through the experts; the best booking desk in the state is **Sportfish Hawaii** 𝕽 (ⓒ **877/388-1376** or 808/396-2607; www.sportfishhawaii.com), which not only books boats on Maui but on all islands. These fishing vessels have been inspected and must meet rigorous criteria to guarantee that you will have a great time. Prices range from $895 to $1,000 for a full-day exclusive charter (you, plus five friends, get the entire boat to yourself); it's $599 to $750 for a half-day exclusive.

SUBMARINE DIVES

Plunging 100 feet below the surface of the sea in a state-of-the-art, high-tech submarine is a great way to experience Maui's magnificent underwater world, especially if you're not a swimmer. **Atlantis Submarines** 𝕽, 658 Front St., Lahaina (ⓒ **800/548-6262** or 808/ 667-2224; www.goatlantis.com), offers trips out of Lahaina Harbor every hour on the hour from 9am to 2pm at a cost of $84 for adults and $42 for children under 12 (children must be at least 3 ft. tall). Allow 2 hours for this underwater adventure. This is not a good choice if you're claustrophobic.

SURFING

The ancient Hawaiian sport of *hee nalu* (wave sliding) is probably the sport most people picture when they think of the islands. If you'd like to give it a shot, just sign up at any one of the recommended surfing schools listed below.

Tide and Kiva Rivers, two local boys who have been surfing since they could walk, operate **Rivers to the Sea** (ⓒ **808/280-8795** or 808/280-6236; www.riverstothesea.com), one of the best surfing schools on Maui. Rates are $75 each for a 2-hour class for a group of three or more, $200 for a couple for a 2-hour class, and $160 for a 2-hour private lesson. All lessons include equipment and instruction.

Well-known surfer Nancy Emerson can also teach you how to surf at the **Nancy Emerson School of Surfing,** 358 Papa Place, Suite F, Kahului (ⓒ **808/244-SURF** or 808/662-4445; fax 808/662-4443;

www.surfclinics.com). Nancy has been surfing since 1961 and has even been a stunt performer for various movies, including *Waterworld*. It's $75 per person for a 2-hour group lesson; private 2-hour classes are $175.

In Hana, **Hana-Maui Sea Sports** (© **808/248-7711;** www. hana-maui-seasports.com) has 2-hour long-board lessons taught by a certified ocean lifeguard for $89.

WHALE-WATCHING

Every winter pods of Pacific humpback whales make the 3,000-mile swim from the chilly waters of Alaska to bask in Maui's summery shallows, fluking, spy hopping, spouting, and having an all-around swell time.

The humpback is the star of the annual whale-watching season, which usually begins in December or January and lasts until April or sometimes May. Adults grow to be about 45 feet long and weigh a hefty 40 tons. Humpbacks are officially an endangered species: In 1997 some of the waters around the state were designated the Hawaiian Islands Humpback Whale National Marine Sanctuary, the country's only federal single-species sanctuary.

WHALE-WATCHING FROM SHORE

Between mid-December and April, you can just look out to sea. There's no best time of day for whale-watching, but the whales seem to appear when the sea is glassy and the wind calm. Once you see one, keep watching in the same vicinity—they might stay down for 20 minutes. Bring a book—and binoculars, if you can. Some good whale-watching points on Maui are:

McGregor Point   On the way to Lahaina, there's a scenic lookout at mile marker 9 (just before you get to the Lahaina Tunnel).

Wailea Beach Marriott Resort & Spa   On the Wailea coastal walk, stop at this resort to look through the telescope installed by the Hawaiian Islands Humpback Whale National Marine Sanctuary.

Olowalu Reef   Along the straight part of Honoapiilani Highway, between McGregor Point and Olowalu, you'll often spot whales leaping out of the water.

Puu Olai   It's a tough climb up this coastal landmark near the Maui Prince Hotel, but you're likely to be well rewarded: This is the island's best spot for offshore whale-watching. On the 360-foot cinder cone overlooking Makena Beach, you'll be at the right elevation to see Pacific humpbacks as they dodge Molokini and cruise up Alalakeiki Channel between Maui and Kahoolawe.

WHALE-WATCHING CRUISES

For a closer look, take a whale-watching cruise. The **Pacific Whale Foundation,** 101 N. Kihei Rd., Kihei (🕿 **800/942-5311** or 808/879-8811; www.pacificwhale.org), is a nonprofit foundation in Kihei that supports its whale research by offering cruises and snorkel tours, some to Molokini and Lanai. It operates a 65-foot power catamaran called the *Ocean Spirit,* a 50-foot sailing catamaran called the *Manute'a,* and a sea kayak. There are 15 daily trips from which to choose, and the rates for a 2-hour whale-watching cruise start at $20 for adults, $17 for children. Cruises are offered from December through May, out of both Lahaina and Maalaea harbors.

If you want to combine ocean activities, then a snorkel or dive cruise to Molokini, the sunken crater off Maui's south coast, might be just the ticket. You can see whales on the way there, at no extra charge. See "Scuba Diving" and "Boating & Sailing" earlier in this section.

WHALE-WATCHING BY KAYAK & RAFT

Seeing a humpback whale from an ocean kayak or raft is awesome. **Capt. Steve's Rafting Excursions** (🕿 808/667-5565; www.captain steves.com) offers 2-hour whale-watching excursions out of Lahaina Harbor for $49 for adults, $39 for children 12 and under. *Tip:* Save $10 by booking the "Early Bird" adventure, which leaves at 7:30am.

WINDSURFING

Maui has Hawaii's best windsurfing beaches. In winter, windsurfers from around the world flock to the town of **Paia** to ride the waves. **Hookipa Beach** is the site of several world-championship contests. **Kanaha,** west of Kahului Airport, also has dependable winds. When the winds turn northerly, **Kihei** is the spot to be: Some days you can spot whales in the distance behind the windsurfers. The northern end of Kihei is best: **Ohukai Park,** the first beach as you enter South Kihei Road from the northern end, has not only good winds but parking, a long strip of grass to assemble your gear, and good access to the water. Experienced windsurfers here are found in front of the **Maui Sunset** condo, 1032 S. Kihei Rd., near Waipuilani Street (a block north of McDonald's), which has great windsurfing conditions but a very shallow reef (not good for beginners).

Hawaiian Island Surf and Sport, 415 Dairy Rd., Kahului (🕿 **800/231-6958** or 808/871-4981; www.hawaiianisland.com), offers lessons (from $79), rentals, and repairs. Other shops that offer rentals and lessons are **Hawaiian Sailboarding Techniques,** 425 Koloa St., Kahului (🕿 **800/968-5423** or 808/871-5423; www.hst windsurfing.com), with 2½-hour lessons from $79, and **Maui**

Windsurf Co., 22 Hana Hwy., Kahului (© **800/872-0999** or 808/877-4816; www.maui-windsurf.com), which has complete equipment rental (board, sail, rig harness, and roof rack) from $45 and 1- or 2-hour lessons ranging from $75.

For daily reports on wind and surf conditions, call the **Wind and Surf Report** at © **808/877-3611.**

3 Hiking

In the past 3 decades, Maui has grown from a rural island to a fast-paced resort destination, but its natural beauty largely remains; there are still many places that can be explored only on foot. Those interested in seeing the backcountry—complete with virgin waterfalls, remote wilderness trails, and quiet meditative settings—should head for Haleakala's upcountry or the tropical Hana coast.

For more information on Maui hiking trails and to obtain free maps, contact **Haleakala National Park,** P.O. Box 369, Makawao, HI 96768 (© **808/572-4400;** www.nps.gov/hale), and the **State Division of Forestry and Wildlife,** 54 S. High St., Wailuku, HI 96793 (© **808/984-8100;** www.hawaii.gov). For information on Maui County Parks, contact **Maui County Parks and Recreation,** 1580-C Kaahumanu Ave., Wailuku, HI 96793 (© **808/243-7380;** www.mauimapp.com).

TIPS ON SAFE HIKING   Water might be everywhere in Hawaii, but it more than likely isn't safe to drink. Most stream water must be treated because cattle, pigs, and goats have probably contaminated the water upstream. The Department of Health continually warns campers of bacterium leptospirosis, which is found in freshwater streams throughout the state and enters the body through breaks in the skin or through the mucous membranes. It produces flulike symptoms and can be fatal. Make sure that your drinking water is safe by vigorously boiling it, or if boiling is not an option, use tablets with hydroperiodide; portable water filters will not screen out bacterium leptospirosis.

Remember, the island is not crime-free: Never leave your valuables (wallet, airline ticket, and so on) unprotected. Some more do's and don'ts: Do bury personal waste away from streams. Don't eat unknown fruit. Do carry your trash out. And don't forget there is very little twilight in Maui when the sun sets—it gets dark quickly.

GUIDED HIKES   If you'd like a knowledgeable guide to accompany you on a hike, call **Maui Hiking Safaris** ✦ (© **888/445-3963** or 808/573-0168; www.mauihikingsafaris.com), **Hike Maui** ✦

> ⎛*Moments* **A Different Viewpoint: Zipping**
> **over the Forest Canopy**
>
> For those looking for a different perspective on Haleakala,
> try **Skyline Eco-Adventures' Zipline Haleakala Tour** (P.O.
> Box 880518, Pukalani, HI 96788; ℂ **808/878-8400;**
> www.skylinehawaii.com), which blends a short hike
> through a eucalyptus forest with four "zipline" crossings.
> During the zipline crossing, you'll be outfitted with a seat
> harness and connected to a cable, and then launched from
> a 70-foot-high platform to "zip" along the cable sus-
> pended over the slopes of Haleakala. From this viewpoint,
> you fly over treetops, valleys, gulches, and waterfalls at 10
> to 35 mph. These bird's-eye tours operate daily and take
> riders from ages 12 and up, weighing between 80 and 300
> pounds. The trip costs $79 ($67 if you book online).

(ℂ **808/879-5270;** fax 808/893-2515; www.hikemaui.com), or
Maui Eco-Adventures (ℂ **877/661-7720** or 808/661-7720; www.
ecomaui.com). For a hike through the verdant Kahakuloa Valley,
call **Ekahi Tours** (ℂ **888/292-2422** or 808/877-9775; www.ekahi.
com). For information on hikes given by the **Hawaii Sierra Club**
on Maui, call ℂ **808/573-4147** (www.hi.sierraclub.org).

HALEAKALA NATIONAL PARK 𝒢𝒢𝒢
For complete coverage of the national park, see "House of the Sun:
Haleakala National Park" in chapter 5.

DAY HIKES FROM THE MAIN ENTRANCE
Anyone can take a .5-mile walk down the **Hosmer Grove Nature
Trail** 𝒢, or you can start down **Sliding Sands Trail** for a mile or two
to get a hint of what lies ahead. Even this short hike can be exhaust-
ing at the high altitude. A good day hike is **Halemauu Trail** to
Holua Cabin and back, an 8-mile, half-day trip. A 20-minute orientation presentation is given daily in the Summit Building at 9:30,
10:30, and 11:30am. The park rangers offer two **guided hikes.** The
2-hour, 2-mile **Cinder Desert Hike** takes place Tuesday and Friday
at 10am and starts from the Sliding Sands Trailhead at the end of
the Haleakala Visitor Center parking lot. The 3-hour, 3-mile

Waikamoi Cloud Forest Hike leaves every Monday and Thursday at 9am; it starts at the Hosmer Grove, just inside the park entrance, and traverses through the Nature Conservancy's Waikamoi Preserve. *Always call in advance:* The hikes and briefing sessions may be canceled, so check first. For details, call the park at ℂ **808/572-4400** or visit www.nps.gov/hale.

THE EAST MAUI SECTION OF THE PARK AT KIPAHULU (NEAR HANA)

APPROACHING KIPAHULU FROM HANA   If you drive to Kipahulu, you'll have to approach it from the Hana Highway—it's not accessible from the summit. Always check in at the ranger station before you begin your hike; the staff can inform you of current conditions and share their wonderful stories about the history, culture, flora, and fauna of the area. The entry fee is $10 a car, the same as for the summit atop Haleakala.

There are two hikes you can take here. The first is a short, easy .5-mile loop along the **Kaloa Point Trail** (Kaloa Point is a windy bluff overlooking **Oheo Gulch**), which leads toward the ocean along pools and waterfalls and back to the ranger station. The clearly marked path leaves the parking area and rambles along the flat, grassy peninsula. Along the way you'll see the remnants of an ancient fishing shrine, a house site, and a lauhala-thatched building depicting an earlier time. The pools are above and below the bridge; the best for swimming are usually above the bridge.

The second hike is for the more hardy. Although just a 4-mile round-trip, the trail is steep and you'll want to stop and swim in the pools, so allow 3 hours. You'll be climbing over rocks and up steep trails, so wear hiking boots. Take water, snacks, swim gear, and insect repellent. Always be on the lookout for flash-flood conditions. This walk will pass two magnificent waterfalls, the 181-foot **Makahiku Falls** and the even bigger 400-foot **Waimoku Falls** 𝕱. The trail starts at the ranger station, where you'll walk uphill for .5 mile to a fence overlook at the thundering Makahiku Falls. If you're tired, you can turn around here; true adventurers should press on. Behind the lookout the well-worn trail picks up again and goes directly to a pool on the top of the Makahiku Falls. The pool is safe to swim in as long as the waters aren't rising; if they are, get out and head back to the ranger station. The rest of the trail takes you through a meadow and bamboo forest to Waimoku Falls.

GUIDED HIKES   The rangers at Kipahulu conduct a 1-mile hike to the **Bamboo Forest** ⊛ at 9am daily; .5-mile hikes or orientation talks are given at noon, 1:30, 2:30, and 3:30pm daily; and a 4-mile round-trip hike to **Waimoku Falls** takes place on Saturday at 9:30am. All programs and hikes begin at the ranger station. Again, always call in advance to make sure the hike will take place that day by contacting the **Kipahulu Ranger Station,** Haleakala National Park, HI 96713 (✆ **808/248-7375;** www.nps.gov/hale).

SKYLINE TRAIL, POLIPOLI SPRINGS STATE RECREATION AREA ⊛

This is some hike—strenuous but worth every step. It's 8 miles, all downhill, with a dazzling 100-mile view of the islands dotting the blue Pacific, plus the West Maui Mountains, which seem like a separate island.

The trail is located just outside Haleakala National Park at Polipoli Springs National Recreation Area; however, you access it by going through the national park to the summit. The Skyline Trail starts just beyond the Puu Ulaula summit building on the south side of Science City and follows the southwest rift zone of Haleakala from its lunarlike cinder cones to a cool redwood grove. The trail drops 3,800 feet on a 4-hour hike to the recreation area in the 12,000-acre Kahikinui Forest Reserve. If you'd rather drive, you'll need a four-wheel-drive vehicle to access the trail.

POLIPOLI STATE PARK ⊛

You'll find one of the most unusual hiking experiences in the state at Polipoli State Park, part of the 21,000-acre Kula and Kahikinui Forest Reserve on the slope of Haleakala. At Polipoli it's hard to believe that you're in Hawaii. First of all, it's cold, even in summer, because the loop is up at 5,300 to 6,200 feet. Second, this former forest of native koa, ohia, and mamane trees, which was overlogged in the 1800s, was reforested in the 1930s with introduced species: pine, Monterey cypress, ash, sugi, red alder, redwood, and several varieties of eucalyptus.

The **Polipoli Loop** ⊛ is an easy 5-mile hike that takes about 3 hours; dress warmly for it. To get here, take the Haleakala Highway (Hwy. 37) to Keokea and turn right onto Highway 337; after less than ½ mile, turn on Waipoli Road, which climbs swiftly. After 10 miles Waipoli Road ends at the Polipoli State Park campground. The well-marked trail head is next to the parking lot, near a stand of Monterey cypress; the tree-lined trail offers the best view of the island.

The Polipoli Loop is really a network of three trails: Haleakala Ridge, Plum Trail, and Redwood Trail. After ½ mile of meandering through groves of eucalyptus, blackwood, swamp mahogany, and hybrid cypress, you'll join the Haleakala Ridge Trail, which, about a mile into the trail, joins with the Plum Trail (named for the plums that ripen June–July). It passes through massive redwoods and by an old Conservation Corps bunkhouse and a run-down cabin before joining up with the Redwood Trail, which climbs through Mexican pine, tropical ash, Port Orford cedar, and—of course—redwood.

HANA-WAIANAPANAPA COAST TRAIL &

This is an easy, 6-mile hike that takes you back in time. Allow 4 hours to walk along this relatively flat trail, which parallels the sea, along lava cliffs and a forest of lauhala trees. The best time of day is in either the early morning or the late evening, when the light on the lava and surf makes for great photos. Midday is the worst time; not only is it hot (lava intensifies the heat), but there's no shade or potable water available. There's no formal trail head; join the route at any point along the Waianapanapa Campground and go in either direction.

Along the trail you'll see remains of an ancient *heiau* (temple), stands of lauhala trees, caves, a blowhole, and a remarkable plant, *naupaka,* that flourishes along the beach. Upon close inspection you'll see that the *naupaka* has only half-blossoms; according to Hawaiian legend, a similar plant living in the mountains has the other half of the blossoms. One ancient explanation is that the two plants represent never-to-be-reunited lovers: As the story goes, the two lovers bickered so much that the gods, fed up with their incessant quarreling, banished one lover to the mountain and the other to the sea.

WAIHEE RIDGE &

This strenuous 3- to 4-mile hike, with a 1,500-foot climb, offers spectacular views of the valleys of the West Maui Mountains. Allow 3 to 4 hours for the round-trip hike. Pack a lunch, carry water, and pick a dry day, as this area is very wet. There's a picnic table at the summit with great views.

To get here from Wailuku, turn north on Market Street, which becomes the Kahekili Highway (Hwy. 340) and passes through Waihee. Go just over 2½ miles from the Waihee Elementary School and look for the turnoff to the Boy Scouts' Camp Maluhia on the left. Turn into the camp and drive nearly a mile to the trail head on the jeep road. About ⅓ mile in, there will be another gate, marking the entrance to the West Maui Forest Reserve. A foot trail, kept in good shape by the State Department of Land and Natural Resources, begins here. The trail climbs to the top of the ridge, offering great views of the various valleys. The trail is marked by a number of switchbacks and can be extremely muddy and wet. In some areas it's so steep that you have to grab onto the trees and bushes for support. The trail takes you through a swampy area, and then up to **Lanilili Peak,** where a picnic table and magnificent views await.

4 Great Golf

Golfers new to Maui should know that it's windy here, especially between 10am and 2pm, when winds of 10 to 15 mph are the norm. Play two to three clubs up or down to compensate for the wind factor. I also recommend bringing extra balls—the rough is thicker here and the wind will pick your ball up and drop it in very unappealing places (like water hazards).

If your heart is set on playing on a resort course, book at least a week in advance. For the ardent golfer on a tight budget: Play in the afternoon, when discounted twilight rates are in effect. There's no guarantee you'll get 18 holes in, especially in winter when it's dark by 6pm, but you'll have an opportunity to experience these world-famous courses at half the usual fee.

For last-minute and discount tee times, call **Stand-by Golf** (© **888/645-BOOK** or 808/874-0600; www.stand-bygolf.com) between 7am and 9pm. Stand-by offers discounted (up to 50% off greens fees), guaranteed tee times for same-day or next-day golfing.

Golf Club Rentals (© **808/665-0800;** www.mauiclubrentals. com) has custom-built clubs for men, women, and juniors (both right- and left-handed), which can be delivered island-wide; the rates are just $20 to $25 a day.

WEST MAUI

Kaanapali Courses 🏌 Both courses at Kaanapali offer a challenge to all golfers, from high handicappers to near-pros. The par-72, 6,305-yard **North Course** is a true Robert Trent Jones, Sr., design: an abundance of wide bunkers; several long, stretched-out tees; and the largest, most contoured greens on Maui. The par-72, 6,250-yard **South Course** is an Arthur Jack Snyder design; although shorter than the North Course, it requires more accuracy on the narrow, hilly fairways.

Off Hwy. 30, Kaanapali. ✆ **808/661-3691**. www.kaanapali-golf.com. Greens fees: $205 (North Course), $175 (South Course); Kaanapali guests pay $170 (North), $130 (South); twilight rates $110 (North), $85 (South) for everyone. At the 1st stoplight in Kaanapali, turn onto Kaanapali Pkwy.; the 1st building on your right is the clubhouse.

Kapalua Resort Courses ☆☆☆ The views from these three championship courses are worth the greens fees alone. The par-72, 6,761-yard **Bay Course** (✆ **808/669-8820**) was designed by Arnold Palmer and Ed Seay. This course is a bit forgiving, with its wide fairways; the greens, however, are difficult to read. The par-71, 6,632-yard **Village Course** (✆ **808/669-8830**), another Palmer/Seay design, is the most scenic of the three courses. The **Plantation Course** (✆ **808/669-8877**), site of the Mercedes Championships, is a Ben Crenshaw/Bill Coore design. This par-73, 6,547-yard course, set on a rolling hillside, is excellent for developing your low shots and precise chipping.

Off Hwy. 30, Kapalua. ✆ **877/KAPALUA (527-2582)**. www.kapaluamaui.com. Greens fees: Village Course $185 ($130 for hotel guests), twilight rate $85; Bay Course $200 ($140 for guests), twilight rate $90; Plantation Course $250 ($160 for guests), twilight rate $100.

SOUTH MAUI

Elleair Maui Golf Club (formerly Silversword Golf Club) Sitting in the foothills of Haleakala, just high enough to afford spectacular ocean vistas from every hole, this is a course for golfers who love the views as much as the fairways and greens. It's very forgiving. *Just one caveat:* Go in the morning. Not only is it cooler, but, more important, it's also less windy.

1345 Piilani Hwy. (near Lipoa St. turnoff), Kihei. ✆ **808/874-0777**. www.golf-maui.com. Greens fees: $120; twilight rate $90.

Makena Courses ☆☆ Here you'll find 36 holes of "Mr. Hawaii Golf"—Robert Trent Jones, Jr.—at its best. Add to that spectacular views: Molokini islet looms in the background, humpback whales gambol offshore in winter, and the tropical sunsets are spectacular. The par-72, 6,876-yard **South Course** has a couple of holes you'll never forget. The view from the par-4 15th hole, which shoots from an elevated tee 183 yards downhill to the Pacific, is magnificent. The 16th hole has a two-tiered green that's blind from the tee 383 yards away (that is, if you make it past the gully off the fairway). The par-72, 6,823-yard **North Course** is more difficult and more spectacular. The 13th hole, located partway up the mountain, has a view that makes most golfers stop and stare. The next hole is even more memorable: a 200-foot drop between tee and green.

On Makena Alanui Dr., just past the Maui Prince Hotel. © **808/879-3344.** www.maui.net/~makena. Greens fees: $185 ($110–$115 for Makena Resort guests), twilight rate $115–$125 ($95–$100 for guests); guest rates vary seasonally, with higher rates in the winter.

Wailea Courses 🏌️🏌️   There are three courses from which to choose at Wailea. The **Blue Course,** a par-72, 6,758-yard course designed by Arthur Jack Snyder and dotted with bunkers and water hazards, is for duffers and pros alike. The wide fairways appeal to beginners, while the undulating terrain makes it a course everyone can enjoy. A little more difficult is the par-72, 7,078-yard championship **Gold Course,** with narrow fairways, several tricky dogleg holes, and the classic Robert Trent Jones, Jr., challenges: natural hazards like lava-rock walls. The **Emerald Course,** also designed by Robert Trent Jones, Jr., is Wailea's newest, with tropical landscaping and a player-friendly design.

Wailea Alanui Dr. (off Wailea Iki Dr.), Wailea. © **888/328-MAUI** or 808/875-7450. www.waileagolf.com. Greens fees: Blue Course $135–$185 ($135–$155 resort guests), twilight $115–$125 everyone; Gold Course $200 ($175 resort guests); Emerald Course $200 ($175 resort guests) no twilight rates.

UPCOUNTRY MAUI

Pukalani Country Club   This cool, par-72, 6,962-yard course at 1,100 feet offers a break from the resorts' high greens fees, and it's really fun to play. The 3rd hole offers golfers two different options: a tough (especially into the wind) iron shot from the tee, across a gully (yuck!) to the green; or a shot down the side of the gully across a second green into sand traps below. (Most people choose to shoot down the side of the gully; it's actually easier than shooting across a ravine.) High handicappers will love this course, and more experienced players can make it more challenging by playing from the back tees.

360 Pukalani St., Pukalani. © **808/572-1314.** www.pukalanigolf.com. Greens fees, including cart: $68 for 18 holes before 11am; $63 11am–2pm; $45 after 2pm; 9 holes $35. Take the Hana Hwy. (Hwy. 36) to Haleakala Hwy. (Hwy. 37) to the Pukalani exit; turn right onto Pukalani St. and go 2 blocks.

5 Biking, Horseback Riding & Tennis

BIKING

Cruising down Haleakala, from the lunarlike landscape at the top, past flower farms, pineapple fields, and eucalyptus groves, is quite an experience—and you don't have to be an expert cyclist to do it. This is a safe, comfortable bicycle trip, although it requires some stamina in the colder, wetter months between November and March. Wear layers of warm clothing, because there may be a 30° change in temperature from the top of the mountain to the ocean. Generally, tour groups will not take riders under 12, but younger children can ride along in the van that accompanies the groups, as can pregnant women. The trip usually costs between $100 and $140, which includes hotel pickup, transport to the top, bicycle and safety equipment, and meals.

Maui's oldest downhill company is **Maui Downhill** ⚜ (© **800/535-BIKE** or 808/871-2155; www.mauidownhill.com), which offers a sunrise safari bike tour, including continental breakfast and brunch, starting at $125 (book online and save $21). If it's all booked up, try **Maui Mountain Cruisers** (© **800/232-6284** or 808/871-6014; www.mauimountaincruisers.com), which has sunrise trips for $144 and midday trips for $110. **Mountain Riders Bike Tours** (© **800/706-7700** or 808/242-9739; www.mountainriders.com) offers sunrise rides for $155 (book online for $125) and midday trips for $120. All rates include hotel pickup, transport to the top, bicycle, safety equipment, and meals.

If you want to avoid the crowd and go down the mountain at your own pace, call **Haleakala Bike Company** (© **888/922-2453;** www.bikemaui.com). They will outfit you with the latest gear and take you up Haleakala. *Note:* Not all tours go to the summit. If you want to start your bike ride at the summit, be sure to confirm. The cheapest trip starts at around the 6,500-foot level (about two-thirds up the mountain). After making sure you are secure on the bike, they will let you ride down by yourself at your own pace. Trips range from $60 to $105; they also have bicycle rentals to tour other parts of Maui on your own (from $30 a day).

If you want to venture out on your own, **Maui Sunriders Bike Company,** 71 Baldwin Ave., Paia (© **866/500-BIKE;** www.mauibikeride.com) rents bikes from $26.

For information on bikeways and maps, get a copy of the *Maui County Bicycle Map,* which has information on road suitability, climate, trade winds, mileage, elevation changes, bike shops, safety tips, and various bicycling routes. The map is available at bike shops all over the island. A great book for mountain bikers who want to venture out on their own is John Alford's *Mountain Biking the Hawaiian Islands,* published by Ohana Publishing (www.bikehawaii.com).

HORSEBACK RIDING

Maui offers spectacular adventure rides through rugged ranchlands, into tropical forests, and to remote swimming holes. One of my favorites is **Piiholo Ranch** in Makawao (© 866/572-5544 or 808/357-5544; www.piiholo.com). If you're out in Hana, don't pass up the **Maui Stables** ®®, in Kipahulu (a mile past Oheo Gulch) (© **808/248-7799;** www.mauistables.com). For those horse lovers who are looking for the ultimate, check out Frank Levinson's **"Maui Horse Whisperer Experience"** (© **808/572-6211;** www.maui horses.com), which includes a seminar on the language of the horse.

If you'd like to ride down into Haleakala's crater, contact **Pony Express Tours** ® (© **808/667-2200** or 808/878-6698; www.pony expresstours.com), which offers a variety of rides down to the crater floor and back up.

I also recommend riding with **Mendes Ranch & Trail Rides** ®, 3530 Kahekili Hwy., 4 miles past Wailuku (© **808/244-7320;** www.mendesranch.com) on the 300-acre Mendes Ranch.

TENNIS

Maui has excellent public tennis courts; all are free and available from daylight to sunset (a few are even lit for night play until 10pm). The courts are available on a first-come, first-served basis; when someone's waiting, limit your play to 45 minutes. For a complete list of public courts, call **Maui County Parks and Recreation** (© **808/243-7230**). Because most public courts require a wait and are not conveniently located near the major resort areas, most visitors pay a fee to play at their own hotels. The exceptions to that rule are in Kihei (which has courts in Kalama Park on S. Kihei Rd. and in Waipualani Park on W. Waipualani Rd., behind the Maui Sunset Condo), in Lahaina (courts are in Malu'uou o lele Park, at Front and Shaw sts.), and in Hana (courts are in Hana Park, on the Hana Hwy.). Private tennis courts are available at most resorts and hotels on the island. The **Kapalua Tennis Garden and Village Tennis Center,** Kapalua Resort (© **808/669-5677;** www.kapaluamaui.com), is home to the Kapalua Open, which features the largest purse in the state, on Labor Day weekend. Court rentals are $14 per person for resort guests and $18 per person for nonguests. The staff will match you up with a partner if you need one. In Wailea try the **Wailea Tennis Club,** 131 Wailea Iki Place (© **808/879-1958;** www.waileatennis.com), with 11 Plex-ipave courts. Court fees are $15 per player.

5

Seeing the Sights

There is far more to the Valley Isle than just sun, sand, and surf. Get out and see for yourself the otherworldly interior of a 10,000-foot volcanic crater, watch endangered sea turtles make their way to nesting sites in a wildlife sanctuary, wander back in time to the days when whalers and missionaries fought for the soul of Lahaina, and feel the energy of a thundering waterfall cascade into a serene mountain pool.

1 Central Maui

Central Maui isn't exactly tourist central; this is where real people live. You'll most likely land here and head directly to the beach. However, there are a few sights worth checking out if you need a respite from the sun and surf.

KAHULUI

Under the airport flight path, next to Maui's busiest intersection and across from Costco in Kahului's new business park, is the most unlikely place: **Kanaha Wildlife Sanctuary,** Haleakala Highway Extension and Hana Highway (© **808/984-8100**). In the parking area off Haleakala Highway Extension (behind the mall, across the Hana Hwy. from Cutter Automotive), you'll find a 150-foot trail that meanders along the shore to a shade shelter and lookout. Watch for the sign proclaiming this the permanent home of the endangered black-neck Hawaiian stilt, whose population is now down to about 1,000 to 1,500. Naturalists say this is a good place to see endangered Hawaiian Koloa ducks, stilts, coots, and other migrating shorebirds. For a quieter, more natural-looking wildlife preserve, try the **Kealia Pond National Wildlife Preserve** in Kihei (p. 136).

WAILUKU

This historic gateway to Iao Valley (see below) is worth a visit for some terrific shopping (see chapter 6), and a brief stop at the **Bailey House Museum** ★, 2375-A Main St. (© **808/244-3326;**

Moments **Flying High: Helicopter Rides**

Only a helicopter can bring you face-to-face with remote sites like Maui's little-known Wall of Tears, near the summit of Puu Kukui in the West Maui Mountains. You'll glide through canyons etched with 1,000-foot waterfalls and over dense rainforests; you'll climb to 10,000 feet, high enough to glimpse the summit of Haleakala, and fly by the dramatic vistas at Molokai.

Among the many helicopter-tour operators on Maui, the best is **Blue Hawaiian Helicopters** ★★, at Kahului Airport (© **800/745-BLUE** or 808/871-8844; www.bluehawaiian.com), with prices ranging from **$159 to $323** depending on the length of your flight.

www.mauimuseum.org). Missionary and sugar planter Edward Bailey's 1833 home is a treasure-trove of Hawaiiana. Inside you'll find an eclectic collection, from precontact artifacts like scary temple images, dog-tooth necklaces, and a rare lei made of tree-snail shells to latter-day relics like Duke Kahanamoku's 1919 redwood surfboard. Open Monday to Saturday from 10am to 4pm; admission $5 adults, $1 children (age 7–12).

IAO VALLEY

A couple of miles north of Wailuku, where the little plantation houses stop and the road climbs ever higher, Maui's true nature begins to reveal itself. The transition between suburban sprawl and raw nature is so abrupt that most people who drive up into the valley don't realize they're suddenly in a rainforest. The walls of the canyon begin to close around them, and a 2,250-foot-high needle-like rock pricks gray clouds scudding across the blue sky. The air is moist and cool, and the shade a welcome comfort. This is Iao Valley, an eroded volcanic caldera in the West Maui Mountains whose great nature, history, and beauty have been enjoyed by millions of people from around the world for more than a century.

Iao ("Supreme Light") Valley, is 10 miles long and encompasses 4,000 acres. The head of the Iao Valley is a broad circular amphitheater where four major streams converge into Iao Stream. At the back of the amphitheater is rain-drenched Puu Kukui, the West Maui

Mountains' highest point. No other Hawaiian valley lets you go from seacoast to rainforest so easily. This peaceful valley, full of tropical plants, rainbows, waterfalls, swimming holes, and hiking trails, is a place of solitude, reflection, and escape for residents and visitors alike. From Wailuku, take Main Street, and then turn right on Iao Valley Road to the entrance to the state park. The park is open daily from 7am to 7pm.

For information, contact the **Division of State Parks,** 54 S. High St., Room 101, Wailuku, HI 96793 (© **808/984-8109;** www.state.hi.us/dlnr). The **Hawaii Nature Center** ♠, 875 Iao Valley Rd. (© **808/244-6500;** www.hawaiinaturecenter.org), home of the Iao Valley Nature Center, features hands-on, interactive exhibits and displays relating the story of Hawaiian natural history; it's an important stop for all who want to explore Iao Valley. Hours are daily from 10am to 4pm. Admission is $6 for adults, $4 for children 4 to 12, and free for children under 4. They also feature a Rainforest Walk (children must be at least 5 years old) for $30 adults and $20 kids (the fee to the museum is included in this price); reserve in advance and wear closed-toed shoes (no sandals).

You can take the loop trail into the massive Iao Valley green amphitheater for free. The public walkway crosses the bridge of Iao Stream and continues along the stream itself. The .35-mile paved loop is an easy walk—you can even take your grandmother on this one. A leisurely stroll will allow you to enjoy lovely views of the Iao Needle and the lush vegetation. Others often proceed beyond the state park border and take two trails deeper into the valley, but the trails enter private land, and NO TRESPASSING signs are posted.

The feature known as **Iao Needle** is an erosional remnant composed of basalt dikes. The phallic rock juts an impressive 2,250 feet above sea level. Youngsters play in **Iao Stream,** a peaceful brook that belies its bloody history. In 1790 King Kamehameha the Great and his men engaged in the bloody battle of Iao Valley to gain control of Maui. When the battle ended, so many bodies blocked Iao Stream that the battle site was named Kepaniwai, or "damming of the waters." An architectural heritage park of Hawaiian, Japanese, Chinese, Filipino, and New England–style houses stands in harmony by Iao Stream at **Kepaniwai Heritage Garden.** This is a good picnic spot, with plenty of picnic tables and benches. You can see ferns, banana trees, and other native and exotic plants in the **Iao Valley Botanic Garden** along the stream.

2 Lahaina & West Maui

HISTORIC LAHAINA

Located between the West Maui Mountains and the deep azure ocean offshore, Lahaina stands out as one of the few places in Hawaii that has managed to preserve its 19th-century heritage while still accommodating 21st-century guests. This is no quiet seaside village, but a vibrant, cutting-edge kind of place, filled with a sense of history—but definitely with its mind on the future.

Baldwin Home Museum ⟡   The oldest house in Lahaina, this coral-and-rock structure was built in 1834 by Rev. Dwight Baldwin, a doctor with the fourth company of American missionaries to sail to Hawaii. After 17 years of service, Baldwin was granted 2,600 acres in Kapalua for farming and grazing. His ranch manager experimented with what Hawaiians called *hala-kahiki,* or pineapple, on a 4-acre plot. The rest is history. The house looks as if Baldwin has just stepped out for a minute to tend to a sick neighbor.

Next door is the **Masters' Reading Room,** Maui's oldest building. This became visiting sea captains' favorite hangout once the missionaries closed down all of Lahaina's grog shops and banned prostitution. By 1844, once hotels and bars started reopening, it lost its appeal. It's now the headquarters of the **Lahaina Restoration Foundation** (✆ **808/661-3262**), a plucky band of historians who try to keep this town alive and antique at the same time. Stop in and pick up a self-guided walking-tour map of Lahaina's historic sites.

120 Dickenson St. (at Front St.). ✆ **808/661-3262.** www.lahainarestoration.org. Admission $3 adults, $2 seniors, $5 families. Daily 10am–4:30pm.

Banyan Tree *Kids*   Of all the banyan trees in Hawaii, this is the greatest—so big that you can't get it in your camera's viewfinder. It was only 8 feet tall when it was planted in 1873 by Maui sheriff William O. Smith to mark the 50th anniversary of Lahaina's first Christian mission. Now it's more than 50 feet tall, has 12 major trunks, and shades ⅔ acre in Courthouse Square.

At the Courthouse Building, 649 Wharf St.

Hale Pai   When the missionaries arrived in Hawaii to spread the word of God, they found the Hawaiians had no written language. They quickly rectified the situation by converting the Hawaiian sounds into a written language. They then built the first printing press in order to print educational materials that would assist them on their mission. Hale Pai was the printing house for the

Lahainaluna Seminary, the oldest American school west of the Rockies. Today Lahainaluna is the public high school for the children of west Maui.

Lahainaluna High School Campus, 980 Lahainaluna Rd. (at the top of the mountain). ℂ **808/661-3262.** www.lahainarestoration.org/halepai. Free admission. Mon–Fri by appointment only.

Lahaina Jodo Mission This site has long been held sacred. The Hawaiians called it Puunoa Point, which means "the hill freed from taboo." Once a small village named *Mala* (garden), this peaceful place was a haven for Japanese immigrants, who came to Hawaii in 1868 as laborers for the sugar-cane plantations. They eventually built a small wooden temple to worship here. In 1968, on the 100th anniversary of Japanese presence in Hawaii, a Great Buddha statue (some 12 ft. high and weighing 3½ tons) was brought here from Japan. The immaculate grounds also contain a replica of the original wooden temple and a 90-foot-tall pagoda.

12 Ala Moana St. (off Front St., near the Mala Wharf). ℂ **808/661-4304.** Free admission. Daily during daylight hours.

Maluuluolele Park *(Kids)* At first glance this Front Street park appears to be only a hot, dry, dusty softball field. But under home plate is the edge of Mokuula, where a royal compound once stood more than 100 years ago. Here, Prince Kauikeaouli, who ascended the throne as King Kamehameha III when he was only 10, lived with the love of his life, his sister Princess Nahienaena. Missionaries took a dim view of incest, which was acceptable to Hawaiian nobles in order to preserve the royal bloodlines. Torn between love for her brother and the new Christian morality, Nahienaena grew despondent and died at the age of 21. King Kamehameha III, who reigned for 29 years—longer than any other Hawaiian monarch—presided over Hawaii as it went from kingdom to constitutional monarchy, and absolute power over the islands began to transfer from island nobles to missionaries, merchants, and sugar planters. Kamehameha died in 1854 at the age of 39. In 1918 his royal compound was demolished and covered with dirt to create a public park. The baseball team from Lahainaluna School now plays games on the site of this royal place, still considered sacred to many Hawaiians.

Front and Shaw sts.

Wo Hing Temple *(★)* The Chinese were among the various immigrants brought to Hawaii to work in the sugar-cane fields. In 1909 several Chinese workers formed the Wo Hing society, a chapter of

Lahaina

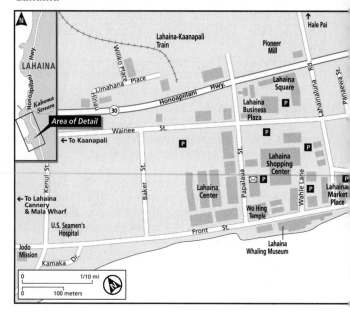

the Chee Kun Tong society, which dates from the 17th century. In 1912 they built this social hall for the Chinese community. Completely restored, the Wo Hing Temple contains displays and artifacts on the history of the Chinese in Lahaina. Next door in the old cookhouse is a theater with movies of Hawaii taken by Thomas Edison in 1898 and 1903.

Front St. (between Wahie Lane and Papalaua St.). © 808/661-3262. Admission by donation. Daily 10am–4pm.

A WHALE OF A PLACE IN KAANAPALI

Heading north from Lahaina, the next resort area you'll come to is Kaanapali, which boasts a gorgeous stretch of beach. If you haven't seen a real whale yet, go to **Whalers Village,** 2435 Kaanapali Pkwy., a shopping center that has adopted the whale as its mascot. You can't miss it: A huge, almost life-size metal sculpture of a mother whale and two nursing calves greets you. A few more steps and you're met by the looming, bleached-white bony skeleton of a 40-foot sperm whale. It's pretty impressive.

On the second floor of the mall is the **Whale Center of the Pacific** (© 808/661-5992), a museum celebrating the "Golden Era

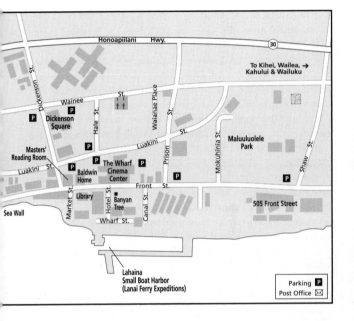

Parking 🅿
Post Office ✉

of Whaling" (1825–60). Harpoons and scrimshaw are on display; the museum has even re-created the cramped quarters of a whaler's seagoing vessel. Open during mall hours, daily from 9:30am to 10pm; admission is free.

THE SCENIC ROUTE FROM WEST MAUI TO CENTRAL OR UPCOUNTRY MAUI: THE KAHEKILI HIGHWAY

The usual road from west Maui to Wailuku is the Honoapiilani Highway (Hwy. 30), which runs along the coast and then turns inland at Maalaea. But those in search of a back-to-nature driving experience should go the other way, along the **Kahekili Highway (Hwy. 340)** 𝔊. (*Highway* is a bit of a euphemism for this paved but somewhat precarious narrow road; check your rental-car agreement before you head out—some don't allow cars on this road. If it is raining or has been raining, skip this road due to mud and rock slides.) It was named after the great chief Kahekili, who built houses from the skulls of his enemies.

You'll start out on the Honoapiilani Highway (Hwy. 30), which becomes the Kahekili Highway (Hwy. 340) after Honokohau, at the northernmost tip of the island. Around this point are **Honolua Bay** 𝔊 and **Mokuleia Bay** ✿, which have been designated as Marine Life Conservation Areas (the taking of fish, shells, or anything else is prohibited).

From this point, the quality of the road deteriorates, and you may share the way with roosters, goats, cows, and dogs. The narrow road weaves along for the next 20 miles, following an ancient Hawaiian coastal footpath and showing you the true wild nature of Maui. These are photo opportunities from heaven: steep ravines, rolling pastoral hills, tumbling waterfalls, exploding blowholes, crashing surf, jagged lava coastlines, and a tiny Hawaiian village straight off a postcard.

Just before mile marker 20, look for a small turnoff on the **mauka** (*mow*-kah, meaning toward the mountain) side of the road (just before the guardrail starts). Park here and walk across the road, and on your left you'll see a spouting **blowhole.** In winter this is an excellent spot to look for whales.

About 3 miles farther along the road, you'll come to a wide turnoff providing a great photo op: a view of the jagged coastline down to the crashing surf.

Less than half a mile farther along, just before mile marker 16, look for the POHAKU KANI sign, marking the huge, 6×6-foot bell-shaped stone. To "ring" the bell, look on the side facing Kahakuloa for the deep indentations, and strike the stone with another rock.

Along the route, nestled in a crevice between two steep hills, is the picturesque village of **Kahakuloa** ✿ ("the tall hau tree"), with a dozen weather-worn houses, a church with a red-tile roof, and vivid green taro patches. From the northern side of the village, you can look back at the great view of Kahakuloa, the dark boulder beach, and the 636-foot Kahakuloa Head rising in the background.

At various points along the drive are artists' studios nestled into the cliffs and hills. One noteworthy stop is the **Kaukini Gallery,** which features work by more than two dozen local artists, with lots of gifts and crafts to buy in all price ranges. (You may also want to stop here to use one of the few restrooms along the drive.)

When you're approaching Wailuku, stop at the **Halekii and Pihanakalani Heiau,** which visitors rarely see. To get here from Wailuku, turn north from Main Street onto Market Street. Turn right onto Mill Street and follow it until it ends; then make a left on Lower Main Street. Follow Lower Main until it ends at Waiehu Beach Road (Hwy. 340), and turn left. Turn left on Kuhio Street and again at the first left onto Hea Place, and drive through the gates and look for the Hawaii Visitors Bureau marker.

These two *heiau,* built in 1240 from stones carried up from the Iao Stream below, sit on a hill with a commanding view of central Maui and Haleakala. Kahekili, the last chief of Maui, lived here. After the bloody battle at Iao Stream, Kamehameha I reportedly came to the temple here to pay homage to the war god, Ku, with a human sacrifice. *Halekii* (House of Images) is made of stone walls with a flat grassy top, whereas *Pihanakalani* (gathering place of supernatural beings) is a pyramid-shaped mount of stones. If you sit quietly nearby (never walk on any *heiau*—it's considered disrespectful), you'll see that the view alone explains why this spot was chosen.

3 South Maui

MAALAEA

At the bend in the Honoapiilani Highway (Hwy. 30), Maalaea Bay runs along the south side of the isthmus between the West Maui Mountains and Haleakala. This is the windiest area on Maui: Trade winds blowing between the two mountains are funneled across the isthmus, and by the time they reach Maalaea, gusts of 25 to 30 mph are not uncommon.

This creates ideal conditions for **windsurfers** out in Maalaea Bay. Surfers are also seen just outside the small boat harbor in Maalaea, which has one of the fastest breaks in the state.

Maui Ocean Center *kk* *(Kids)*   This 5-acre facility houses the largest aquarium in Hawaii and features one of Hawaii's largest predators: the tiger shark. Exhibits are geared toward the residents of Hawaii's ocean waters. As you walk past the three dozen or so tanks and numerous exhibits, you'll slowly descend from the "beach" to the deepest part of the ocean, without ever getting wet. Start at the surge pool, where you'll see shallow-water marine life like spiny urchins and cauliflower coral, then move on to the reef tanks, turtle pool, "touch" pool (with starfish and urchins), and eagle-ray pool before reaching the star of the show: the 100-foot-long, 600,000-gallon main tank featuring tiger, gray, and white-tip sharks, as well as tuna, surgeonfish, triggerfish, and numerous other tropicals. A walkway goes right through the tank, so you'll be surrounded on three sides by marine creatures. A very cool place, and well worth the time. Some new additions are a hammerhead exhibit and the Shark Dive Maui Program—if you're a certified scuba diver, you can plunge into the aquarium with sharks, stingrays, and tropical fish while friends and family watch safely from the other side of the glass. ***Helpful hint:*** Buy your tickets online to avoid the long admission lines.

Maalaea Harbor Village, 192 Maalaea Rd. (the triangle between Honoapiilani Hwy. and Maalaea Rd.) (€) **808/270-7000.** www.mauioceancenter.com. Admission $23 adults, $19 seniors, $16 children 3–12. Daily 9am–5pm (until 6pm July–Aug).

KIHEI

Capt. George Vancouver landed at Kihei in 1778, when it was only a collection of fishermen's grass shacks on the hot, dry, dusty coast (hard to believe, eh?). A **totem pole** stands today where he's believed to have landed, across from the Maui Lu Resort, 575 S. Kihei Rd. Vancouver sailed on to what later became British Columbia, where a great international city and harbor now bear his name.

West of the junction of Piilani Highway (Hwy. 31) and Mokulele Highway (Hwy. 350) is **Kealia Pond National Wildlife Preserve** (€) **808/875-1582**), a 700-acre U.S. Fish and Wildlife wetland preserve where endangered Hawaiian stilts, coots, and ducks hang out and splash. These ponds work two ways: as bird preserves and as sedimentation basins that keep the coral reefs from silting from runoff. You can take a self-guided tour along a boardwalk dotted with interpretive signs and shade shelters, through sand dunes, and around ponds to Maalaea Harbor. The boardwalk starts at the outlet of Kealia Pond on the ocean side of North Kihei Road (near mile marker 2 on Piilani Hwy.). Among the Hawaiian water birds seen here are the black-crowned high heron, Hawaiian coot, Hawaiian duck, and Hawaiian stilt. There are also shorebirds like sanderling, Pacific golden plover, ruddy turnstone, and wandering tattler. From July to December the hawksbill turtle comes ashore here to lay her eggs. *Tip:* If you're bypassing Kihei, take the Piilani Highway (Hwy. 31), which parallels strip-mall-laden South Kihei Road, and avoid the hassle of stoplights and traffic.

WAILEA

The dividing line between arid Kihei and artificially green Wailea is distinct. Wailea once had the same kiawe-strewn, dusty landscape as Kihei until Alexander & Baldwin Inc. (of sugar-cane fame) began developing a resort here in the 1970s (after piping water from the other side of the island to the desert terrain of Wailea). Today the manicured 1,450 acres of this affluent resort stand out like an oasis along the normally dry leeward coast.

The best way to explore this golden resort coast is to rise with the sun and head for Wailea's 1.5-mile **coastal nature trail** (ℝ), stretching between the Fairmont Kea Lani Hotel and the green grass of the Wailea Marriott. It's a great morning walk, a serpentine path that meanders uphill and down past native plants, old Hawaiian habitats, and a billion dollars' worth of luxury hotels. You can pick up the trail at any of the resorts or from clearly marked SHORELINE ACCESS points along the coast. The best times to go are early morning or sunset; by midmorning it gets crowded with joggers and later with beachgoers. As the path crosses several bold black-lava points, it affords vistas of islands and ocean. Benches allow you to pause and contemplate the view across Alalakeiki Channel, where you might see **whales** in season.

MAKENA

A few miles south of Wailea, the manicured coast changes over to the wilderness of *Makena* (abundance). In the 1800s cattle were driven down the slope from upland ranches and loaded onto boats that waited to take them to market. Now **Makena Landing** ⚓ is a beach park with boat-launching facilities, showers, toilets, and pic-nic tables. It's great for snorkeling and for launching kayaks bound for Pérouse Bay and Ahihi-Kinau preserve.

From the landing, go south on Makena Road; on the right is **Keawali Congregational Church** ⚓ (© **808/879-5557**), built in 1855 with walls 3 feet thick. Surrounded by ti leaves, which by Hawaiian custom provides protection, and built of lava rock with coral used as mortar, this Protestant church sits on its own cove with a gold-sand beach. It always attracts a Sunday crowd for its 9:30am Hawaiian-language service. Take some time to wander through the cemetery; you'll see some tombstones with a ceramic picture of the deceased on them, which is an old custom.

A little farther south on the coast is **La Pérouse Monument** ⚓, a pyramid of lava rocks that marks the spot where French explorer Admiral Comte de La Pérouse set foot on Maui in 1786. The first Westerner to "discover" the island, La Pérouse described the "burn-ing climate" of the leeward coast, observed several fishing villages near Kihei, and sailed on into oblivion, never to be seen again; some believe he may have been eaten by cannibals in what is now Vanu-atu. To get here, drive south past Puu Olai to Ahihi Bay, where the road turns to gravel. Go another 2 miles along the coast to La Pérouse Bay; the monument sits amid a clearing at the end of the dirt road.

The rocky coastline and sometimes rough seas contribute to the lack of appeal for water activities here; **hiking** opportunities, how-ever, are excellent. Bring plenty of water and sun protection, and wear hiking boots that can withstand walking on lava. From La Pérouse Bay, you can pick up the old King's Highway trail, which at one time circled the island. Walk along the sandy beach at La Pérouse and look for the trail indentation in the lava, which leads down to the lighthouse at the tip of Cape Hanamanioa, about a .75-mile round-trip. Or you can continue on the trail as it climbs up the hill for 2 miles, then ventures back toward the ocean, where there are quite a few old Hawaiian home foundations and rocky/coral beaches.

4 House of the Sun: Haleakala National Park ★★★

At once forbidding and compelling, **Haleakala National Park** is Maui's main natural attraction (*Haleakala* means house of the sun). More than 1.3 million people a year ascend the 10,023-foot-high mountain to peer down into the crater of the world's largest dormant volcano. (Haleakala is officially considered to be "active, but not currently erupting," even though it has not rumbled or spewed lava since 1790.) That hole would hold Manhattan: 3,000 feet deep, 7½ miles long by 2½ miles wide, and encompassing 19 square miles.

The Hawaiians recognized the mountain as a sacred site. Ancient chants tell of Pele, the volcano goddess, and one of her siblings doing battle on the crater floor where *Kawilinau* (Bottomless Pit) now stands. Commoners in ancient Hawaii didn't spend much time here, though. The only people allowed into this sacred area were the Kahuna, who took their apprentices to live for periods of time in this intensely spiritual place. Today New Agers also revere Haleakala as one of the earth's powerful energy points, and even the U.S. Air Force has a not-very-well-explained presence here.

But there's more to do here than simply stare into a big black hole: Just going up the mountain is an experience in itself. Where else on the planet can you climb from sea level to 10,000 feet in just 37 miles, or a 2-hour drive? The snaky road passes through big, puffy, cumulus clouds to offer magnificent views of the isthmus of Maui, the West Maui Mountains, and the Pacific Ocean.

Many drive up to the summit in predawn darkness to watch the **sun rise** over Haleakala. Writer Mark Twain called it "the sublimest spectacle" of his life. Others take a trail ride inside the bleak lunar landscape of the wilderness inside the crater or coast down the 37-mile road from the summit on a bicycle with special brakes (see "Biking" and "Horseback Riding" in chapter 4). Hardy adventurers hike and camp inside the crater's wilderness (see "Hiking" in chapter 4). Those bound for the interior bring their survival gear because the terrain is raw, rugged, and punishing. However, if you choose to experience Haleakala National Park, it will prove memorable—guaranteed.

JUST THE FACTS

Haleakala National Park extends from the summit of Mount Haleakala into the crater, down the volcano's southeast flank to Maui's eastern coast, beyond Hana. There are actually two separate and distinct destinations within the park: **Haleakala Summit** 𝄞 and the **Kipahulu** 𝄞 coast. The summit gets all the publicity, but Kipahulu draws crowds, too—it's lush, green, and tropical, and home to Oheo Gulch (also known as Seven Sacred Pools). No road links the summit and the coast; you have to approach them separately, and you need at least a day to see each place.

WHEN TO GO   At the 10,023-foot summit, weather changes fast. With wind chill, temperatures can be below freezing any time of year. Summers can be dry and warm, winters wet, windy, and cold. Before you go, get current weather conditions from the park (✆ **808/572-4400**) or the **National Weather Service** (✆ **808/ 871-5054**).

From sunrise to noon, the light is weak, but the view is usually free of clouds. The best time for photos is in the afternoon, when the sun lights the crater and clouds are few. Go on full-moon nights for spectacular viewing. However, even when the forecast is promising, the weather at Haleakala can change in an instant—be prepared.

ACCESS POINTS   **Haleakala Summit** is 37 miles, or about a 2-hour drive, from Kahului. To get here, take Highway 37 to Highway 377 to Highway 378. For details on the drive, see "The Drive to the Summit," below. Pukalani is the last town for water, food, and gas.

The **Kipahulu** section of the national park is on Maui's east end near Hana, 60 miles from Kahului on Highway 36 (the Hana Hwy.). Due to traffic and rough road conditions, plan on 4 hours for the drive from Kahului (see "Driving the Road to Hana," below). Hana is the only nearby town for services, water, gas, food, and overnight lodging; some facilities may not be open after dark.

At both entrances to the park, the admission fee is $5 per person or $10 per car, good for a week of unlimited entry.

INFORMATION, VISITOR CENTERS & RANGER PRO-GRAMS   For information before you go, contact **Haleakala National Park,** P.O. Box 369, Makawao, HI 96768 (✆ **808/ 572-4400;** www.nps.gov/hale).

One mile from the park entrance, at 7,000 feet, is **Haleakala National Park Headquarters** (☎ **808/572-4400**), open daily from 7am to 4pm. You can pick up information on park programs and activities, get camping permits, and occasionally see a nene (Hawaiian goose)—one or more are often here to greet visitors. Restrooms, a pay phone, and drinking water are available.

The **Haleakala Visitor Center,** open daily from sunrise to 3pm, is near the summit, 11 miles from the park entrance. It offers a panoramic view of the volcanic landscape, with photos identifying the various features, and exhibits that explain its history, ecology, geology, and volcanology. Park staff members are often on hand to answer questions. The only facilities are restrooms and water.

Rangers offer excellent, informative, and free **naturalist talks** at 9:30, 10:30, and 11:30am daily in the summit building. For information on **hiking** (including guided hikes), see "Hiking" in chapter 4.

THE DRIVE TO THE SUMMIT

If you look on a Maui map, almost in the middle of the part that resembles a torso, there's a black wiggly line that looks like this: WWWWW. That's **Highway 378,** also known as **Haleakala Crater Road**—one of the fastest-ascending roads in the world. This grand corniche has at least 33 switchbacks; passes through numerous climate zones; goes under, in, and out of clouds; takes you past rare silversword plants and endangered Hawaiian geese sailing through the clear, thin air; and offers a view that extends for more than 100 miles.

Going to the summit takes about 2 hours from Kahului. No matter where you start out, you'll follow Highway 37 (Haleakala Hwy.) to Pukalani, where you'll pick up Highway 377 (which is also Haleakala Hwy.), which you take to Highway 378. Along the way, expect fog, rain, and wind. You might encounter stray cattle and downhill bicyclists. Fill up your gas tank before you go—the only gas available is 27 miles below the summit at Pukalani. There are no facilities beyond the ranger stations, so bring your own food and water.

Remember, you're entering a high-altitude wilderness area. Some people get dizzy due to the lack of oxygen; you might also suffer lightheadedness, shortness of breath, nausea, or worse: severe headaches, flatulence, and dehydration. People with asthma, pregnant women, heavy smokers, and those with heart conditions should be especially careful in the rarefied air. Bring water and a jacket or a blanket, especially if you go up for sunrise. Or you might want to go up to the summit for sunset, which is also spectacular.

As you go up the slopes, the temperature drops about 3° every 1,000 feet, so the temperature at the top can be 30° cooler than it was at sea level. Come prepared with sweaters, jackets, and rain gear.

At the **park entrance,** you'll pay an entrance fee of $10 per car (or $2 for a bicycle). About a mile from the entrance is **Park Head-quarters,** where an endangered **nene,** or Hawaiian goose, might greet you with its unique call. With its black face, buff cheeks, and partially webbed feet, the gray-brown bird looks like a small Canada goose with zebra stripes; it brays out "nay-nay" (thus its name), doesn't migrate, and prefers lava beds to lakes. The unusual goose clings to a precarious existence on these alpine slopes. Vast popula-tions of more than 25,000 once inhabited Hawaii, but hunters, pigs, feral cats and dogs, and mongooses preyed on the nene; cou-pled with habitat destruction, these predators nearly caused its extinction. By 1951 there were only 30 left. Now protected as Hawaii's state bird, the wild nene on Haleakala number fewer than 250—and the species remains endangered.

Beyond headquarters are **two scenic overlooks** on the way to the summit. **Leleiwi Overlook** ✖ is just beyond mile marker 17. From the parking area, a short trail leads you to a panoramic view of the lunarlike crater. Two miles farther along is **Kalahaku Overlook** ✖, the best place to see a rare **silversword.** You can turn into this over-look only when you are descending from the top. The silversword is the punk of the plant world; its silvery bayonets display tiny purple bouquets—like a spacey artichoke with attitude. Silverswords grow only in Hawaii, take from 4 to 50 years to bloom, and then, usually between May and October, send up a 1- to 6-foot stalk with a pur-ple bouquet of sunflower-like blooms. They're now very rare, so don't even think about taking one home.

Continue on, and you'll quickly reach the **Haleakala Visitor Center** ✖, which offers spectacular views. You'll feel as if you're at the edge of the earth. But don't turn around here: The actual sum-mit's a little farther on, at **Puu Ulaula Overlook** ✖ (also known as Red Hill), the volcano's highest point. If you do go up for sunrise, the building at Puu Ulaula Overlook, a triangle of glass that serves as a windbreak, is the best viewing spot. After sunrise you can see all the way across Alenuihaha Channel to the often snowcapped sum-mit of Mauna Kea on the Big Island.

MAKING YOUR DESCENT   Put your car in low gear so you don't destroy your brakes by riding them the whole way down.

5 More in Upcountry Maui

On the slopes of Haleakala, cowboys, planters, and other country people make their homes in serene, neighborly communities like **Makawao** and **Kula,** a world away from the bustling beach resorts. Even if you can't spare a day or two in the cool upcountry air, there are some sights that are worth a look on your way to or from the crater. Shoppers and gallery hoppers especially might want to make the effort; see chapter 6 for details.

Kula Botanical Garden ✿   You can take a self-guided, informative, leisurely stroll through more than 700 native and exotic plants—including three unique collections of orchids, proteas, and bromeliads—at this 5-acre garden. It offers a good overview of Hawaii's exotic flora in one small, cool place.

Hwy. 377, south of Haleakala Crater Rd. (Hwy. 378), ½ mile from Hwy. 37. ✆ 808/878-1715. Admission $5 adults, $1 children 6–12. Daily 9am–4pm.

Tedeschi Vineyards and Winery ✿   On the southern shoulder of Haleakala is **Ulupalakua Ranch,** a 20,000-acre spread once owned by legendary sea captain James Makee, celebrated in the Hawaiian song and dance "Hula O Makee." Wounded in a Honolulu waterfront brawl in 1843, Makee moved to Maui and bought Ulupalakua. He renamed it Rose Ranch, planted sugar as a cash crop, and grew rich. Still in operation, the ranch is now home to Maui's only winery, established in 1974 by Napa vintner Emil Tedeschi, who began growing California and European grapes here and producing serious still and sparkling wines, plus a silly wine made of pineapple juice. The rustic grounds are the perfect place for a picnic. Pack a basket before you go and enjoy it with a bottle of Tedeschi wine.

Across from the winery are the remains of the three smokestacks of the **Makee Sugar Mill,** built in 1878. This is home to Maui artist Reems Mitchell, who carved the mannequins on the front porch of the Ulupalakua Ranch Store: a Filipino with his fighting cock, a cowboy, a farmhand, and a sea captain, all representing the people of Maui's history.

Off Hwy. 37 (Kula Hwy.). ✆ 808/878-6058. www.mauiwine.com. Daily 9am–5pm. Free tastings; tours given 10:30am–1:30pm.

6 Driving the Road to Hana ★★★

Top down, sunscreen on, radio tuned to a little Hawaiian music on a Maui morning: It's time to head out to Hana along the Hana

Highway (Hwy. 36), a wiggle of a road that runs along Maui's northeastern shore. The drive takes at least 3 hours, but plan to take all day. Going to Hana is about the journey, not the destination.

In all of Hawaii, no road is more celebrated than this one. It winds for 50 miles past taro patches, magnificent seascapes, waterfall pools, botanical gardens, and verdant rainforests, and it ends at one of Hawaii's most beautiful tropical places.

The outside world discovered the little village of Hana in 1926, when the narrow coastal road, carved by pickax-wielding convicts, opened. The mud-and-gravel road, often subject to landslides and washouts, was paved in 1962, when tourist traffic began to increase; today more than 1,000 cars traverse the road each day, according to storekeeper Harry Hasegawa. That equals about 500,000 people a year on this road, which is way too many. Go at the wrong time and you'll be stuck in a bumper-to-bumper rental-car parade—peak traffic hours are midmorning and midafternoon year-round, especially on weekends.

In the rush to "do" Hana in a day, most visitors spin around town in 10 minutes flat and wonder what all the fuss is about. It takes time to take in Hana, play in the waterfalls, sniff the tropical flowers, hike to bamboo forests, and marvel at the spectacular scenery; stay overnight if you can. However, if you really must do the Hana Highway in a day, go just before sunrise and return after sunset.

THE JOURNEY BEGINS IN PAIA   Before you even start out, fill up your gas tank. Gas in Paia is very expensive (even by Maui standards), and it's the last place for gas until you get to Hana, some 42 miles, 54 bridges, and 600 hairpin turns down the road.

The former plantation village of Paia was once a thriving sugar-mill town. The mill is still here, but the population shifted to Kahului in the 1950s when subdivisions opened there, leaving Paia to shrivel up and die. But the town refused to give up and has proven its ability to adapt to the times. Now chic eateries and trendy shops stand next door to the mom-and-pop establishments that have been serving generations of Paia customers.

Plan to be here early, around 7am, when **Charley's** ⍟, 142 Hana Hwy. (⟨🕻 **808/579-9453**), opens. Enjoy a big, hearty breakfast for a reasonable price.

After you leave Paia, just before the bend in the road, you'll pass the Kuau Mart on your left; a small general store, it's the only reminder of the once-thriving sugar plantation community of **Kuau.** The road then bends into an S-turn; in the middle of the S

The Road to Hana

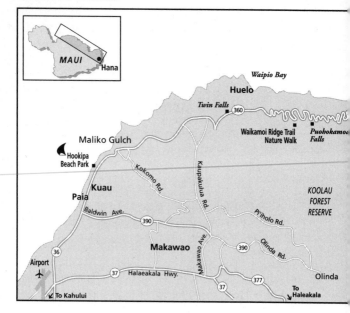

is the entrance to **Mama's Fish House,** marked by a restored boat with Mama's logo on the side. Just past the truck on the ocean side is the entrance to Mama's parking lot and adjacent small sandy cove in front of the restaurant. It's not good for swimming—ocean access is over very slippery rocks into strong surf—but the beach is a great place to sit and soak up some sun.

WINDSURFING MECCA A mile from Mama's, just before mile marker 9, is a place known around the world as one of the greatest windsurfing spots on the planet, **Hookipa Beach Park** ✿. *Hookipa* (hospitality) is where the top-ranked windsurfers come to test themselves against the forces of nature: thunderous surf and forceful wind. World-championship contests are held here, but on nearly every windy afternoon (the board surfers have the waves in the morning), you can watch dozens of windsurfers twirling and dancing in the wind like colorful butterflies. To watch the windsurfers, go past the park and turn left at the entrance on the far side of the beach. You can either park on the high grassy bluff or drive down to the sandy beach and park alongside the pavilion. The park also has restrooms, a shower, picnic tables, and a barbecue area.

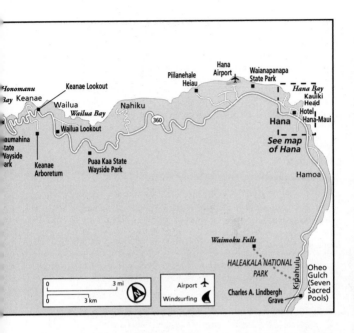

INTO THE COUNTRY   Past Hookipa Beach the road winds down into *Maliko* **(Budding) Gulch** at mile marker 10. At the bottom of the gulch, look for the road on your right, which will take you out to **Maliko Bay.** Take the first right, which goes under the bridge and past a rodeo arena (scene of competitions by the Maliko Roping Club in summer) and on to the rocky beach. There are no facilities here except a boat-launch ramp. In the 1940s Maliko had a thriving community at the mouth of the bay, but its residents rebuilt farther inland after a strong tidal wave wiped it out. The bay may not look that special, but if the surf is up, it's a great place to watch the waves.

Back on the Hana Highway, as you leave Maliko Gulch, around mile marker 11, you'll pass through the rural area of **Haiku,** with banana patches, cane grass blowing in the wind, and forests of guava trees, avocados, kukui trees, palms, and Christmas berry. Just before mile marker 15 is the **Maui-Grown Market and Deli** (© **808/572-1693**), a good stop for drinks or snacks for the ride.

A GREAT PLUNGE ALONG THE WAY   A dip in a waterfall pool is everybody's tropical-island fantasy. A great place to stop is

Twin Falls 𝕏, at mile marker 2. Just before the wide, concrete bridge, pull over on the mountain side and park. There is a NO TRES-PASSING sign on the gate. Although you will see several cars parked in the area and a steady line of people going up to the falls, be aware that this is private property and trespassing is illegal in Hawaii. If you decide that you want to "risk it," you will walk about 3 to 5 minutes to the waterfall and pool, or continue on another 10 to 15 minutes to the second, larger waterfall and pool (don't go in if it has been raining).

HIDDEN HUELO   Just before mile marker 4 on a blind curve, look for a double row of mailboxes on the left-hand side by the pay phone. Down the road lies a hidden Hawaii of an earlier time, where an indescribable sense of serenity prevails. Hemmed in by Waipo and Hoalua bays is the remote community of **Huelo** 𝕏, which means "tail end, last." This fertile area once supported a pop-ulation of 75,000; today only a few hundred live among the scat-tered homes here, where a handful of B&Bs and exquisite vacation rentals cater to a trickle of travelers (see chapter 2).

The only reason Huelo is even marked is the historic 1853 **Kaulanapueo Church.** Reminiscent of New England architecture, this coral-and-cement church, topped with a plantation-green steeple and a gray tin roof, is still in use, although services are held just once or twice a month. It still has the same austere, stark inte-rior of 1853: straight-backed benches, a no-nonsense platform for the minister, and no distractions on the walls to tempt you from paying attention to the sermon. Next to the church is a small grave-yard, a personal history of this village in concrete and stone.

KOOLAU FOREST RESERVE   After Huelo, the vegetation seems lusher, as though Mother Nature had poured Miracle-Gro on everything. This is the edge of the **Koolau Forest Reserve.** *Koolau* means "windward," and this certainly is one of the greatest examples of a lush windward area: The coastline here gets about 60 to 80 inches of rain a year, as well as runoff from the 200 to 300 inches that falls farther up the mountain. Here you'll see trees laden with guavas, as well as mangoes, java plums, and avocados the size of soft-balls. The spiny, long-leafed plants are *hala* trees, which the Hawai-ians used for weaving baskets, mats, and even canoe sails.

From here on out, there's a waterfall (and one-lane bridge) around nearly every turn in the road, so drive slowly and be pre-pared to stop and yield to oncoming cars.

DANGEROUS CURVES   About ½ mile after mile marker 6, there's a sharp U-curve in the road, going uphill. The road is practically one-lane here, with a brick wall on one side and virtually no maneuvering room. Sound your horn at the start of the U-curve to let approaching cars know you're coming. Take this curve, as well as the few more coming up in the next several miles, very slowly.

Just before mile marker 7 is a forest of waving **bamboo.** The sight is so spectacular that drivers are often tempted to take their eyes off the road. Be very cautious. Wait until just after mile marker 7, at the **Kaaiea Bridge** (literally "breath-taking view") and stream below, to pull over and take a closer look at the hand-hewn stone walls. Then turn around to see the vista of bamboo.

A GREAT FAMILY HIKE   At mile marker 9 there's a small state wayside area with restrooms, picnic tables, and a barbecue area. The sign says KOOLAU FOREST RESERVE, but the real attraction here is the **Waikamoi Ridge Trail** ♔, an easy .75-mile loop. The start of the trail is just behind the QUIET TREES AT WORK sign. The well-marked trail (Waikamoi means "waters of the king") meanders through eucalyptus, ferns, and *hala* trees.

SAFETY WARNING   I used to recommend another waterfall, **Puohokamoa Falls** ("suddenly awakening"), at mile marker 11, but not anymore. Unfortunately, what once was a great thing has been overrun by hordes of not-so-polite tourists. You will see cars parking on the already dangerous, barely two-lane Hana Highway a half a mile before the waterfall. Slow down after the 10-mile marker. As you get close to the 11-mile marker, the road becomes a congested one-lane road due to visitors parking on this narrow highway. Don't add to the congestion by trying to park: There are plenty of other great waterfalls; just drive slowly and safely through this area.

CAN'T-MISS PHOTO OPS   Just past mile marker 12 is the **Kaumahina State Wayside Park** ♔ (*kaumahina* means literally "moon rise"). This is not only a good pit stop (restrooms are available) and a wonderful place for a picnic (with tables and a barbecue area), but also a great vista point. The view of the rugged coastline makes an excellent shot—you can see all the way down to the jutting Keanae Peninsula.

Another mile and a couple of bends in the road, and you'll enter the Honomanu Valley, with its beautiful bay. To get to the **Honomanu Bay County Beach Park** ♔, look for the turnoff on your left, just after mile marker 14, located at a point in the road where you begin your ascent up the other side of the valley. The rutted dirt-and-cinder road takes you down to the rocky black-sand beach. There are no facilities here. Because of the strong rip currents offshore, swimming is best in the stream inland from the ocean. You'll consider the drive down worthwhile as you stand on the beach, well away from the ocean, and turn to look back on the steep cliffs covered with vegetation.

MAUI'S BOTANICAL WORLD   Farther along the winding road, between mile markers 16 and 17, is a cluster of bunkhouses composing the YMCA Camp Keanae. A quarter-mile down is the **Keanae Arboretum** 𝕲𝕲, where the region's botany is divided into three parts: native forest, introduced forest, and traditional Hawaiian plants, food, and medicine. You can swim in the pools of Piinaau Stream, or press on along a mile-long trail into Keanae Valley, where a lovely tropical rainforest waits at the end (see "Hiking" in chapter 4).

KEANAE PENINSULA   The old Hawaiian village of **Keanae** 𝕲𝕲 stands out against the Pacific like a place time forgot. Here, on an old lava flow graced by an 1860 stone church and swaying palms, is one of the last coastal enclaves of native Hawaiians. They still grow taro in patches and pound it into poi, the staple of the old Hawaiian diet. And they still pluck opihi (limpet) from tide pools along the jagged coast and cast throw-nets at schools of fish. The turnoff to the Keanae Peninsula is on the left, just after the arboretum.

ANOTHER PHOTO OP: KEANAE LOOKOUT   Just past mile marker 17 is a wide spot on the ocean side of the road, where you can see the entire Keanae Peninsula's checkerboard pattern of green taro fields and its ocean boundary etched in black lava. Keanae was the result of a postscript eruption of Haleakala, which flowed through the Koolau Gap and down Keanae Valley and added this geological punctuation to the rugged coastline.

WAIANAPANAPA STATE PARK 𝕲𝕲   At mile marker 32, just on the outskirts of Hana, shiny black-sand Waianapanapa Beach appears like a vivid dream, with bright-green jungle foliage on three sides and cobalt-blue water lapping at its feet. The 120-acre park on an ancient *aa* lava flow includes sea cliffs, lava tubes, arches, and the beach, plus 12 cabins, tent camping, picnic pavilions, restrooms, showers, drinking water, and hiking trails. If you're interested in staying here, see chapter 2; also see "Beaches" and "Hiking" in chapter 4.

7 The End of the Road: Heavenly Hana ⭐⭐

Green, tropical Hana is a destination all its own, a small coastal village that's probably what you came to Maui in search of. Here you'll
find a rainforest dotted with cascading waterfalls and sparkling blue
pools, skirted by red- and black-sand beaches.

Beautiful Hana enjoys more than 90 inches of rain a year—more
than enough to keep the scenery lush. Banyans, bamboo, breadfruit
trees—everything seems larger than life in this small town, especially the flowers, such as wild ginger and plumeria.

The last unspoiled Hawaiian town on Maui is, oddly enough, the
home of Maui's first resort, which opened in 1946. Paul Fagan,
owner of the San Francisco Seals baseball team, bought an old inn
and turned it into the **Hotel Hana-Maui,** which gave Hana its first
taste of tourism.

As you enter Hana, the road splits about a half-mile past mile
marker 33, at the police station. Both roads will take you to Hana,
but the lower road, Uakea Road, is more scenic. Just before you
get to Hana Bay, you'll see the old wood-frame **Hana District
Police Station and Courthouse.** Next door is the **Hana Cultural
Center and Museum** ⭐, on Uakea Road (✆ **808/248-8622;**
http://hookele.com/hccm), usually open daily from 10am to 4pm.
This small building has an excellent collection of Hawaiian quilts,
artifacts, books, and photos. Also on the grounds are Kauhala O
Hana, composed of four *hale* (houses) for living, meeting, cooking, and canoe building or canoe storage.

Cater-cornered from the cultural center is the entrance to **Hana
Bay** ⭐. You can drive right down to the pier and park. There are
restrooms, showers, picnic tables, barbecue areas, and even a snack
bar here. The 386-foot, red-faced cinder cone beside the bay is
Kauiki Hill, the scene of numerous fierce battles in ancient Hawaii
and the birthplace of Queen Kaahumanu in 1768. A short, 5-
minute walk will take you to the spot. Look for the trail along the
hill on the wharf side, and follow the path through the ironwood
trees; the lighthouse on the point will come into view, and you'll see
pocket beaches of red cinder below. Grab onto the ironwood trees
for support because the trail has eroded in some areas. This is a perfect place for a secluded picnic, or you can continue on the path out
to the lighthouse. To get to the lighthouse, which sits on a small
island, watch the water for about 10 minutes to get a sense of how
often and from which direction the waves are coming. Between

wave sets, either swim or wade in the shallow, sandy bottom channel or hop across the rocks to the island.

To get to the center of town, leave Hana Bay, cross Uakea Road, and drive up Keawa Place; turn left on Hana Highway, and on the corner will be the **Hotel Hana-Maui,** the now-luxurious hotel established by Paul Fagan in 1946. On the green hills above Hotel Hana-Maui stands a 30-foot-high white cross made of lava rock. Citizens erected the cross in memory of Paul Fagan, who founded the Hana Ranch as well as the hotel and helped keep the town alive. The hike up to **Fagan's Cross** provides a gorgeous view of the Hana coast, especially at sunset, when Fagan himself liked to climb this hill. Ask the hotel for details on this hike.

Back on the Hana Highway, just past Hauoli Road, is the majestic **Wananalua Congregation Church.** It's on the National Historic Register not only because of its age (it was built in 1838–42 from coral stones) but also because of its location, atop an old Hawaiian *heiau.*

Just past the church, on the right side of the Hana Highway, is the turnoff to the **Hana Ranch Center,** the commercial center for Hana, with a post office, bank, general store, the Hana Ranch Stables, and a restaurant and snack bar. But the real shopping experience is across the Hana Highway at the **Hasegawa General Store** ✦, a Maui institution (p. 169), which carries oodles of merchandise from soda and fine French wines to fishing line to name-brand clothing, plus everything you need for a picnic or a gourmet meal. This is also the place to find out what's going on in Hana: The bulletin board at the entrance has fliers and handwritten notes advertising everything from fundraising activities to classes to community-wide events.

If you need gas before heading back, fill up at the **Chevron Service Station** on the right side of the Hana Highway as you leave town. *Warning:* The price of gas here will take your breath away.

OUTDOOR ACTIVITIES

Hana is one of the best areas on Maui for ocean activities and also boasts a wealth of nature hikes, remote places to explore on horseback, and waterfalls to discover.

BEACHES & OCEAN ACTIVITIES

Call **Hana-Maui Sea Sports** (✆ **808/248-7711;** www.hana-maui-seasports.com) if you'd like to snorkel or kayak, or venture out on your own at one of my favorite beaches:

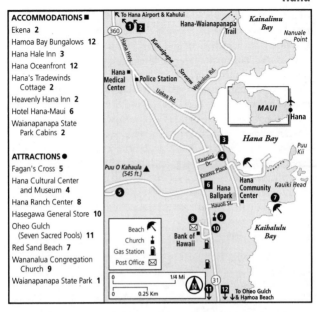

ACCOMMODATIONS ■

Ekena **2**

Hamoa Bay Bungalows **12**

Hana Hale Inn **3**

Hana Oceanfront **12**

Hana's Tradewinds
Cottage **2**

Heavenly Hana Inn **2**

Hotel Hana-Maui **6**

Waianapanapa State
Park Cabins **2**

ATTRACTIONS ●

Fagan's Cross **5**

Hana Cultural Center
and Museum **4**

Hana Ranch Center **8**

Hasegawa General Store **10**

Oheo Gulch
(Seven Sacred Pools) **11**

Red Sand Beach **7**

Wananalua Congregation
Church **9**

Waianapanapa State Park **1**

HANA   The waters in the Hana Bay are calm most of the time and great for swimming. There's excellent snorkeling and diving by the lighthouse. Strong currents can run through here, so don't venture farther than the lighthouse. See the info on Hana Bay, above, for more details on the facilities and hikes here.

RED SAND BEACH   The Hawaiian name for this beach is *Kaihalulu* (roaring sea) Beach. It's truly a sight to see. The beach is on the ocean side of Kauiki Hill, just south of Hana Bay, in a wild, natural setting on a pocket cove, where the volcanic cinder cone lost its seaward wall to erosion and spilled red cinders everywhere to create the red sands. Before you put on your bathing suit, there are three things to know about this beach: You have to trespass to get here (which is against the law); due to recent heavy rains, there have been several serious injuries on the muddy, slippery terrain (enter at your own risk, it can be extremely dangerous); and nudity (also illegal in Hawaii—arrests have been made) is common here.

If you are determined to go, ask for permission at the Hotel Hana-Maui. And ask about conditions on the trail (which drops several stories down to the ocean rocks). To reach the beach, put on solid walking shoes (no flip-flops) and walk south on Uakea Road, past Haoli Street and the Hotel Hana-Maui, to the parking lot for the hotel's Sea Ranch Cottages. Turn left and cross the open field next to the Hana Community Center. Look for the dirt trail and follow it to the huge ironwood tree, where you turn right (do not go ahead to the old Japanese cemetery). Use the ironwood trees to maintain your balance as you follow the ever-eroding cinder foot-path a short distance along the shoreline, down the narrow cliff trail (do not attempt this if it's wet). The trail suddenly turns the corner, and into view comes the burnt-red beach, set off by the turquoise waters, black lava, and vivid green ironwood trees.

The lava outcropping protects the bay and makes it safe for swim-ming. Snorkeling is excellent, and there's a natural whirlpool area on the Hana Bay side of the cove. Stay away from the surge area where the ocean enters the cove.

HAMOA BEACH 🦀🦀   For one of Hana's best beaches—great for swimming, boogie boarding, and sunbathing—continue another ½ mile down the Haneoo Road loop to Hamoa Beach. There is easy access from the road down to the sandy beach, and facilities include a small restroom and an outdoor shower. The large pavilion and beach accessories are for Hotel Hana-Maui guests.

HIKING

Hana is woven with hiking trails along the shoreline, through the rainforest, and up in the mountains. See "Hiking" in chapter 4 for a discussion of hiking in Waianapanapa.

Another excellent hike that takes you back in time is through Kahanu Garden and to **Piilanihale Heiau** 🦀🦀, one of the largest ancient Hawaiian temples in the state. Turn toward the ocean on Ulaino Road, by mile marker 31. Drive down the paved road (which turns into a dirt road but is still drivable) to the first stream (about 1½ miles). If the stream is flooded, turn around and go back. If you can forge the stream, cross it and park on the right side of the road by the huge breadfruit trees. The trees are part of the 122-acre **Kahanu Garden** 🦀🦀 (© 808/248-8912), owned and operated by the National Tropical Botanical Garden (www.ntbg.org), which also has two gardens on Kauai. Open Monday through Friday from 10am to 2pm, admission is $10 for self-guided tours. Allow at least an hour and a half to explore the gardens and *heiau*.

The 122 acres encompass plant collections from the Pacific Islands, concentrating on plants of value to the people of Polynesia, Micronesia, and Melanesia. Kahanu Garden contains the largest known collection of breadfruit cultivars from more than 17 Pacific Island groups and Indonesia, the Philippines, and the Seychelles.

The real draw here is the **Piilanihale Heiau (House of Piilani,** one of Maui's greatest chiefs). Believed to be the largest in the state, it measures 340 feet by 415 feet, and it was built in a unique terrace design not seen anywhere else in Hawaii. The walls are some 50 feet tall and 8 to 10 feet thick. Historians believe that Piilani's two sons and his grandson built the mammoth temple, which was dedicated to war, sometime in the 1500s.

TROPICAL HALEAKALA: OHEO GULCH AT KIPAHULU &&

If you're thinking about heading out to the so-called Seven Sacred Pools, out past Hana at the Kipahulu end of Haleakala National Park, let's clear this up right now: There are more than seven pools—about 24, actually—and *all* water in Hawaii is considered sacred. Folks here call the attraction by its rightful name, **Oheo Gulch,** and visitors sometimes refer to it as Kipahulu, which is actually the name of the area where Oheo Gulch is located. No matter what you call it, it's a beautiful sight. The dazzling series of waterfall pools and cataracts cascading into the sea is so popular that it now has its own roadside parking lot.

Even though Oheo is part of Haleakala National Park, you cannot drive here from the summit. To drive to Oheo, head for Hana, some 60 miles from Kahului on the Hana Highway (Hwy. 36). Oheo is about 30 to 50 minutes beyond Hana, along Highway 31. The Highway 31 bridge passes over pools near the ocean; the other pools, plus magnificent 400-foot Waimoku Falls, are reachable via an often-muddy, but rewarding, hour-long uphill hike (see "Hiking" in chapter 4). Expect showers on the Kipahulu coast. The admission fee is $5 per person or $10 per car.

The **Kipahulu Ranger Station** (℗ **808/248-7375**) is staffed from 9am to 5pm daily. Restrooms are available, but there's no drinking water. Kipahulu rangers offer safety information, exhibits, books, and a variety of walks and hikes year-round; check at the station for current activities.

There are a number of hikes in the park, and tent camping is allowed. See "Hiking" in chapter 4 for details.

Check with the Haleakala Park rangers before hiking up to or swimming in the pools, and always keep one eye on the water in the streams; the sky can be sunny near the coast, but floodwaters from Kipahulu Valley can cause the pools to rise 4 feet in less than 10 minutes.

6

Shops & Galleries

Maui is a shopaholic's dream as well as an arts center, with a large number of resident artists who show their works in dozens of galleries and countless gift shops. Maui is also the queen of specialty products, an agricultural cornucopia that includes Kula onions, upcountry protea, Kaanapali coffee, and many other tasty treats that are shipped worldwide.

As with any popular visitor destination, you'll have to wade through bad art and mountains of trinkets, particularly in Lahaina and Kihei, where touristy boutiques line the streets between rare pockets of treasures. If you shop in south or west Maui, expect to pay resort prices, clear down to a bottle of Evian or sunscreen.

Central Maui is home to some first-rate boutiques. Watch Wailuku, which is poised for a resurgence. The town has its own antiques alleys, Sig Zane Designs has brought a delightful infusion of creative and cultural energy, and a major promenade on Main Street is in the works. The Kaahumanu Center, in neighboring Kahului, is becoming more fashionable by the month.

Upcountry, Makawao's boutiques are worth seeking out, despite some attitude and high prices. The charm of shopping on Maui has always rested in the small, independent shops and galleries that crop up in surprising places.

1 Central Maui

KAHULUI

Kahului's best shopping is concentrated in two places. Almost all of the shops listed below are at one of the following centers:

The once rough-around-the-edges **Maui Mall,** 70 E. Kaahumanu Ave. (© **808/877-7559**), has been renovated and is bigger and better, not only retaining some of my favorite stores but also adding a 12-screen movie megaplex that features current releases as well as art-house films. The mall is still a place of everyday good things, from **Longs Drugs** to **Star Market** to **Tasaka Guri Guri,** the decades-old purveyor of inimitable icy treats, neither ice cream nor shave ice but something in between.

Queen Kaahumanu Center, 275 Kaahumanu Ave. (© **808/ 877-3369**), 5 minutes from the Kahului Airport on Highway 32, offers more than 100 shops, restaurants, and theaters. Its second-floor Plantation District offers home furnishings and gift shops. Kaahumanu covers all the bases, from arts and crafts to a **Foodland Supermarket** and everything in between: a thriving food court; the island's best beauty supply, **Lisa's Beauty Supply & Salon** (© **808/ 877-6463**), and its sister store for cosmetics, **Madison Avenue Day Spa and Boutique** (© **808/873-0880**); mall standards like **Sun-glass Hut, Radio Shack,** and **Local Motion** (surf and beachwear); and standard department stores like **Macy's** and **Sears** and great specialty shops like **Sharper Image.**

Cost Less Imports   Natural fibers are ubiquitous in this corner of the Maui Mall. Household accessories include lauhala, bamboo blinds, grassy floor and window coverings, shoji-style lamps, burlap yardage, baskets, Balinese cushions, Asian imports, *noreng* (Japanese folk curtains), and made-on-Maui soaps and handicrafts. A good source of tropical and Asian home decor. In the Maui Mall. © **808/877-0300.**

Maui County Store   Attention T-shirt collectors: Here's your chance to get official Maui County Police and Fire logo T-shirts and other Maui County logo shirts, plus logo wear from the University of Hawaii and other made-in-Maui items. This fundraising store (it helps the police and fire departments) is staffed by students from Maui Community College learning retail sales. Prices are great, money goes to a good cause, the students get to learn a trade, and you get to take home excellent souvenirs from your Maui vacation. Maui Mall, 70 Kaahumanu Ave., Kahului. © **808/877-6669.**

Maui Swap Meet   After Thanksgiving and throughout December, the number of booths at this popular swap meet nearly explodes into the hundreds, and the activity reaches fever pitch. The colorful Maui specialties include vegetables from Kula and Keanae, fresh taro, plants, proteas, crafts, household items, homemade ethnic foods, and baked goods. Every Saturday from 7am to noon, vendors spread out their wares in booths and under tarps, in a festival-like atmosphere that is pure Maui with a touch of kitsch. Between the cheap Balinese imports and New Age crystals and incense, you may find some vintage John Kelly prints and 1930s collectibles. Admission is 50¢, and if you go early while the vendors are setting up, no one will turn you away. The Swap Meet currently is located on S. Puunene Ave. (next to the Kahului Post Office), but in the spring of 2008, it will move to the back lot behind Maui Community College, Kahului Beach and Weihnepo roads. Call for more info. © 808/877-3100.

Summerhouse   Sleek and chic, tiny Summerhouse is big on style: casual and party dresses, separates by Russ Berens, FLAX, and Kiko, and Tencel jeans by Signature—the best. During the holiday season the selection gets dressy and sassy, but it's a fun browse year-round. I adore the hats, accessories, easy-care clothing, and up-to-the-minute evening dresses. The high-quality T-shirts are always a cut above. The casual selection is well suited to the island lifestyle. In the Dairy Center, 395 Dairy Rd. © 808/871-1320. Also on the west side at 4405 Honoapiilani Hwy. © 808/669-6616.

EDIBLES

Down to Earth Natural Foods, 305 Dairy Rd. (© 808/877-2661), a health-food staple for many years, has fresh organic produce, a bountiful salad bar, sandwiches and smoothies, vitamins and supplements, fresh-baked goods, snacks, whole grains, and several packed aisles of vegetarian and health foods.

Maui's produce has long been a source of pride for islanders, and **Ohana Farmers Market,** in the Queen Kaahumanu Shopping Center (© 808/871-8347), on Tuesday, Wednesday, and Friday, is the place to find a fresh, inexpensive selection of Maui-grown fruit, vegetables, flowers, and plants. Crafts and gourmet foods add to the event.

WAILUKU

Located at the gateway to Iao Valley, Wailuku is the county seat, the part of Maui where people live and work. Wailuku's attractive vintage architecture, smattering of antiques shops, and mom-and-pop eateries imbue the town with a down-home charm noticeably absent in Maui's resort areas. The community spirit fuels festivals throughout the year and is slowly attracting new businesses, but Wailuku is still a work in progress. It's a mixed bag—of course, there's junk, but a stroll along Main and Market streets usually turns up a treasure or two.

Bailey House Gift Shop   For made-in-Hawaii items, Bailey House is a must-stop. It offers a thoroughly enjoyable browse through authentic Hawaiiana, in a museum that's one of the finest examples of missionary architecture, dating from 1833. Gracious gardens, rare paintings of early Maui, wonderful programs in Hawaiian arts and culture, and a restored hand-hewn koa canoe await visitors. The small shop packs a wallop with its selection of remarkable gift items, from

Hawaiian music to exquisite woods; traditional Hawaiian games to pareus and books. Prints by the legendary Hawaii artist Madge Tennent, hand-sewn pheasant hatbands, jams and jellies, Maui cookbooks, and an occasional Hawaiian quilt are some of the treasures to be found here. Bailey House Museum Shop, 2375-A Main St. ℂ 808/244-3326.

Bird of Paradise Unique Antiques Owner Joe Myhand loves furniture, old Matson liner menus, blue willow china, kimonos for children, and anything nostalgic that happens to be Hawaiian. The furniture ranges from 1940s rattan to wicker and old koa—those items tailor-made for informal island living and leisurely moments on the lanai. Myhand also collects bottles and mails his license plates all over the world. The collection ebbs and flows with his finds, keeping buyers waiting in the wings for his Depression glass, California pottery from the 1930s and 1940s, old dinnerware, perfume bottles, vintage aloha shirts, and vintage Hawaiian music on cassettes. 56 N. Market St. ℂ 808/242-7699.

Brown-Kobayashi Graceful living is the theme here. Prices range from a few dollars to the thousands in this 750-square-foot treasure-trove. The owners have added a fabulous selection of antique stone garden pieces that mingle quietly with Asian antiques and old and new French, European, and Hawaiian objects. Although the collection is eclectic, there is a strong cohesive aesthetic that sets Brown-Kobayashi apart from other Maui antiques stores. Japanese kimonos and obi, Bakelite and Peking glass beads, breathtaking Japanese lacquerware, cricket carriers, and cloisonné are among the delights here. Exotic and precious Chinese woods (purple sandalwood and huanghuali) glow discreetly from quiet corners, and an occasional monarchy-style lidded milo bowl comes in and flies out. 38 N. Market St. ℂ 808/242-0804.

Gottling Ltd. Karl Gottling's shop specializes in Asian antique furniture, but you can also find smaller carvings, precious stones, jewelry, netsuke, opium weights, and more. I saw a cabinet with 350-year-old doors, and a 17th-century Buddha lending an air of serenity next to a 150-year-old Chinese cabinet. Ming dynasty ceramics, carved wooden apples ($15), and a Persian rug ($65,000) give you an idea of the range of possibilities here. 34 N. Market St. ℂ 808/244-7779.

Sandell *(Finds* Since the early 1970s, artist, illustrator, and cartoonist David Sandell has been commenting on Maui through this artwork. Don't miss the opportunity to stop by his shop and "talk story" with this talented artist, who watched Maui go from undiscovered to discovered. His artwork—from original oils to prints to T-shirts—makes excellent souvenirs to take home. 133 Market St. ☎ 808/249-0234.

Sig Zane Designs Wailuku   Sig Zane is synonymous with the best in aloha wear. Whether it's a T-shirt, pareu, duffel bag, aloha shirt, or muumuu, a Sig Zane design has depth and sizzle. So when Hilo-based Sig Zane Designs opened in Wailuku, Maui retailers perked up. Zane and co-owner Punawai Rice have redefined Hawaiian wear by creating an inimitable style in clothing, textiles, furnishings, and bedding. The Maui store has already proven enormously successful. The staff is helpful and willing to share the background of each design, so you will learn much about the culture, botany, mythology, and beauty of the islands. 53 Market St. ☎ 808/249-8997.

EDIBLES

Located in the northern section of Wailuku, **Takamiya Market,** 359 N. Market St. (☎ **808/244-3404**), is much loved by local folks and visitors with adventurous palates. Unpretentious home-cooked foods from East and West are prepared daily. From the chilled-fish counter come fresh sashimi and poke, and in the renowned assortment of prepared foods are mounds of shoyu chicken, tender fried squid, roast pork, kalua pork, laulau, Chinese noodles, fiddlehead ferns, and Western comfort foods, such as corn bread and potato salad.

2 West Maui

LAHAINA

Lahaina's merchants and art galleries go all out from 7 to 9pm on Friday, when **Art Night** brings an extra measure of hospitality and community spirit. The Art Night openings are usually marked with live entertainment, refreshments, and a lively street scene.

If you're in Lahaina on the second or last Thursday of the month, stroll by the front lawn of the **Baldwin Home,** 120 Dickenson St. (at Front St.), for a splendid look at lei making (you can even buy the results).

What was formerly a big, belching pineapple cannery is now a maze of shops and restaurants at the northern end of Lahaina town, known as the **Lahaina Cannery Mall,** 1221 Honoapiilani Hwy. (☎ **808/661-5304**). Find your way through the T-shirt and sportswear shops to coffee at **Sir Wilfred's Coffee House,** where you can unwind with espresso and croissants, or head for **Compadres Bar & Grill,** where the margaritas flow freely. For film, water, aspirin, groceries, sunscreen, and other necessities, nothing beats **Longs Drugs** and **Safeway,** two old standbys. **Roland's** may surprise you with its selection of footwear, everything from Cole-Haan sophisticates to inexpensive sandals. At the recently expanded food court, the new **Compadres Taquería** sells Mexican food to go, while **L & L Drive-Inn** sells plate lunches.

The **Lahaina Center,** 900 Front St. (© **808/667-9216**), is still a work in progress. It's located north of Lahaina's most congested strip, where Front Street begins. Across the street from the center, the seawall is a much-sought-after front-row seat to the sunset. There's plenty of free validated parking and easy access to more than 30 shops, a salon, restaurants, a nightclub, and a four-plex movie-theater complex. **Ruth's Chris Steak House** has opened its doors in Lahaina Center, and **Maui Brews** serves lunch and dinner and offers nighttime live music on weekdays. Among the shopping stops: **Banana Republic,** the **Hilo Hattie Fashion Center** (a dizzying emporium of aloha wear), and **ABC Discount Store.**

The conversion of 10,000 square feet of parking space into the re-creation of a traditional Hawaiian village is a welcome touch of Hawaiiana at Lahaina Center. The village, called **Hale Kahiko,** features three main houses, called *hale:* a sleeping house, the men's dining house, and the crafts house, where women pounded *hala* (pandanus) strips to weave into mats and baskets. Artifacts, weapons, a canoe, and indigenous trees are among the authentic touches in this village, which can be toured privately or with a guide.

David Lee Galleries   This gallery is devoted to the works of David Lee, who uses natural powder colors to paint on silk. The pigments and technique create a luminous, ethereal quality. 712 Front St. © 808/667-7740.

Lahaina Arts Society Galleries   With its membership of more than 185 Maui artists, the nonprofit Lahaina Arts Society is an excellent community resource. Changing monthly exhibits in the Banyan Tree and Old Jail galleries offer a good look at the island's artistic well: two-dimensional art, fiber art, ceramics, sculpture, prints, jewelry, and more. In the shade of the humongous banyan tree in the square across from Pioneer Inn, "Art in the Park" fairs are offered every second and fourth weekend of the month. 648 Wharf St. © 808/661-3228.

Lei Spa Maui   Expanded to include two massage rooms and shower facilities, this day spa offers facials and other therapies. About 95% of the beauty and bath products sold here are made on Maui, and that includes Hawaiian Botanical Pikake shower gel; kukui and macadamia-nut oils; Hawaiian potpourris; mud masks with Hawaiian seaweed; and a spate of rejuvenating, cleansing, skin-soothing potions for hair and skin. Aromatherapy body oils and perfumes are popular, as are the handmade soaps and fragrances of torch ginger, plumeria, coconut, tuberose, and sandalwood. Scented candles in coconut shells, inexpensive and fragrant, make great gifts. 505 Front St. (C) **808/661-1178.**

Maggie Coulombe *(Finds)*   Imagine a high-fashion store with the unique designs of Maggie Coulombe in the midst of Lahaina. Maggie's latest couture, jersey, linen, pareo, and shoes, plus accessories, jewelry, purses, and a few surprises, are available here. 505 Front St. (C) **808/662-0696.** www.maggiecoulombe.com.

Martin Lawrence Galleries   The front is garish, with pop art, kinetic sculptures, and bright, carnivalesque glass objects. Toward the back of the gallery, however, there's a sizable inventory of two-dimensional art and some plausible choices for collectors of Keith Haring, Andy Warhol, and other pop artists. The originals, limited-edition graphics, and sculptures also include works by Marc Chagall, Pablo Picasso, Joan Miró, Roy Lichtenstein, and other noted artists. In Lahaina Market Place, 126 Lahainaluna Rd. (C) **808/661-1788.**

The Old Lahaina Book Emporium   This bookstore is a browser's dream. More than 25,000 quality used books are lovingly housed in this shop, where owner JoAnn Carroll treats books and customers well. Specialties include Hawaiiana, fiction, mystery, sci-fi, and military history, with substantial selections in cookbooks, children's books, and philosophy/religion. You could pay as little as $2 for a quality read, or a whole lot more for that rare first edition. Books on tape, videos, the classics, and old guitar magazines are among the treasures of this two-story emporium. 834 Front St. (C) **808/661-1399.**

Totally Hawaiian Gift Gallery   This gallery makes a good browse for its selection of Niihau shell jewelry, excellent Hawaiian CDs, Norfolk pine bowls, and Hawaiian quilt kits. Hawaiian quilt patterns sewn in Asia (at least they're honest about it) are labor-intensive, less expensive, and attractive, although not totally Hawaiian. Hawaiian-quilt-patterned gift wraps and tiles, perfumes and soaps, handcrafted dolls, and koa accessories are of good quality, and the artists, such as Kelly Dunn (Norfolk wood bowls), Jerry Kermode (wood), and Pat Coito (wood), are among the tops in their fields. In the Lahaina Cannery Mall, 1221 Honoapiilani Hwy. © 808/667-2558. Also in the Maui Marriott in Kaanapali. © 808/667-2171.

Village Galleries in Lahaina   The nearly 30-year-old Village Galleries is the oldest continuously running gallery on Maui, and it's highly esteemed as one of the few galleries with consistently high standards. Art collectors know this as a respectable showcase for regional artists; the selection of mostly original two- and three-dimensional art offers a good look at the quality of work originating on the island. The newer contemporary gallery offers colorful gift items and jewelry. 120 and 180 Dickenson St. © 808/661-4402 or 808/661-5559. Also at the Ritz-Carlton Kapalua, 1 Ritz-Carlton Dr. © 808/669-1800.

KAANAPALI

I am somewhat disappointed with upscale **Whalers Village,** 2435 Kaanapali Pkwy. (© 808/661-4567). Although it offers everything from whale blubber to Prada and Ferragamo, it is short on local shops, and parking at the nearby lot is expensive. The complex is home to the **Whalers Village Museum,** with its interactive exhibits, 40-foot sperm whale skeleton, and sand castles on perpetual display, but shoppers come for the designer thrills and beachfront dining. You can find most of the items featured here in the shops in Lahaina and can avoid the parking hassle and the high prices by skipping Whalers Village.

If you do decide to check it out, don't miss my favorite shoe store, **Sandal Tree** (with two other locations, one at Hyatt Regency Maui and the other at Grand Wailea Resort in Wailea). **Martin & MacArthur,** a mainstay of the village, offers a dizzying array of Hawaii crafts. The always wonderful **Lahaina Printsellers** has a selection of antique prints, maps, paintings, and engravings, including 18th- to 20th-century cartography. You can find award-winning **Kimo Bean** coffee at a kiosk, an expanded **Reyn's** for aloha wear, and **Cinnamon Girl,** a hit in Honolulu for its matching mother-daughter clothing. The return of **Waldenbooks** makes it that much easier to pick up the latest bestseller on the way to the beach. Once you've stood under the authentic whale skeleton at the **Whale Center of the Pacific** (p. 132), you can blow a bundle at **Tiffany, Prada, Chanel, Ferragamo, Vuitton, Coach, Dolphin Galleries,** the **Body Shop,** or any of the more than 60 shops and restaurants that have sprouted up in this open-air shopping center.

Other mainstays: The **Eyecatcher** has an extensive selection of sunglasses; it's located just across from the busiest **ABC** store in the state. **Pizza Paradiso** sells ice cream and smoothies in the food court. Whalers Village is open daily from 9:30am to 10pm.

Ki'i Gallery   Some of the works are large and lavish, such as the Toland Sand prisms for just under $5,000 and the John Stokes handblown glass. Those who love glass in all forms, from handblown vessels to jewelry, will love a browse through Ki'i. I found Pat Kazi's work in porcelain and found objects, such as the mermaid in a teacup, inspired by fairy tales and mythology, both fantastic and compelling. The gallery is devoted to glass and original paintings and drawings; roughly half of the artists are from Hawaii. In the Hyatt Regency Maui, 200 Nohea Kai Dr. ✆ 808/661-4456. Also at the Grand Wailea Resort (✆ 808/874-3059) and the Shops at Wailea (✆ 808/874-1181).

Sandal Tree   It's unusual for a resort shop to draw local customers on a regular basis, but the Sandal Tree attracts a flock of footwear fanatics who come here from throughout the islands for rubber thongs and Top-Siders, sandals and dressy pumps, athletic shoes and hats, designer footwear, and much more. Sandal Tree also carries a generous selection of Mephisto and Arche comfort sandals, Donald Pliner, Anne Klein, Charles Jourdan, and beachwear and casual footwear for all tastes. Accessories range from fashionable knapsacks to avant-garde geometrical handbags—for town and country, day and evening, kids, women, and men. Prices are realistic, too. In Whalers Village, 2435 Kaanapali Pkwy. ✆ 808/667-5330. Also in Grand Wailea Resort, 3850 Wailea Alanui Dr., Wailea (✆ 808/874-9006); and in the Hyatt Regency Maui, 200 Nohea Kai Dr. (✆ 808/661-3495).

KAHANA/NAPILI/HONOKOWAI

Those driving north of Kaanapali toward Kapalua will notice the **Honokowai Marketplace** on Lower Honoapiilani Road, only minutes before the Kapalua Airport. There are restaurants and coffee shops, a dry cleaner, the flagship **Star Market, Hula Scoops** for ice cream, a gas station, a copy shop, a few clothing stores, and the sprawling **Hawaiian Interiorz.**

Nearby **Kahana Gateway** is an unimpressive mall built to serve the condominium community that has sprawled along the coastline between Honokowai and Kapalua. If you need women's swimsuits, however, **Rainbow Beach Swimwear** is a find. It carries a selection of suits for all shapes, at lower-than-resort prices, slashed even further during the frequent sales. **Hutton's Fine Jewelry** offers high-end jewelry from designers around the country (lots of platinum and diamonds). Tahitian black pearls and jade are among Hutton's specialties.

KAPALUA

Honolua Store   Walk on the old wood floors peppered with holes from golf shoes and find your everyday essentials: bottled water, stationery, mailing tape, jackets, chips, wine, soft drinks, paper products, fresh fruit and produce, and aisles of notions and necessities. With picnic tables on the veranda and a takeout counter offering deli items—more than a dozen types of sandwiches, salads, and budget-friendly breakfasts—there are always long lines of customers. Golfers and surfers love to come here for the morning paper and coffee. 502 Office Rd. (next to the Ritz-Carlton Kapalua). ✆ 808/669-6128.

Village Galleries   Maui's finest exhibit their works here and in the other two Village Galleries in Lahaina. Take heart, art lovers: There's no clichéd marine art here. Translucent, delicately turned bowls of Norfolk pine gleam in the light, and George Allan, Betty Hay Freeland, Fred KenKnight, and Pamela Andelin are included in the pantheon of respected artists represented in the tiny gallery. Watercolors, oils, sculptures, handblown glass, Niihau shell leis, jewelry, and other media are represented. The Ritz-Carlton's monthly Artist-in-Residence program features gallery artists in demonstrations and special hands-on workshops that are free, including materials. In the Ritz-Carlton Kapalua, 1 Ritz-Carlton Dr. ✆ 808/669-1800.

3 South Maui

KIHEI

Kihei is one long stretch of strip malls. Most of the shopping here is concentrated in the **Azeka Place Shopping Center** on South Kihei Road. Fast foods abound at Azeka, as do tourist-oriented clothing shops like **Crazy Shirts.** Across the street **Azeka Place II** houses several prominent attractions, including **General Nutrition Center,** the **Coffee Store,** and a cluster of specialty shops with everything from children's clothes to shoes, sunglasses, beauty services, and swimwear. Also on South Kihei Road is the **Kukui Mall,** with movie theaters, **Waldenbooks,** and **Whaler's General Store.**

Hawaiian Moons Natural Foods   Hawaiian Moons is an exceptional health-food store, as well as a minisupermarket with one of the best selections of Maui products on the island. Much of the produce here, such as organic vine-ripened tomatoes and organic onions, is grown in the fertile upcountry soil of Kula. There's also locally grown organic coffee, gourmet salsas, Maui shiitake mushrooms, organic lemon grass and okra, Maui Crunch bread, free-range Big Island turkeys and chickens, and fresh Maui juices. Cosmetics are top-of-the-line: a staggering selection of sunblocks, fragrant floral oils, and Island Essence made-on-Maui mango-coconut and vanilla-papaya lotions, the ultimate in body pampering. The salad bar is very popular. 2411 S. Kihei Rd. © 808/875-4356. Also on the west side at 3636 Lower Honoapiilani Rd. © 808/665-1339.

WAILEA

CY Maui   Women who like flowing clothing in silks, rayons, and natural fibers will love this shop, formerly the popular Manikin in Kahului. If you don't find what you want on the racks of simple bias-cut designs, you can have it made from the bolts of stupendous fabrics lining the shop. Except for a few hand-painted silks, everything in the shop is washable. In The Shops at Wailea, 3750 Wailea Alanui Dr, A-30. © 808/891-0782.

Grand Wailea Shops   The sprawling Grand Wailea Resort is known for its long arcade of shops and galleries tailored to hefty pocketbooks. However, gift items in all price ranges can be found at Lahaina Printsellers (for old maps and prints), Dolphin Galleries, H. F. Wichman, Sandal Tree, and Napua Gallery, which houses the private collection of the resort owner. Ki'i Gallery is luminous with studio glass and exquisitely turned woods, and **Sandal Tree** (p. 162) raises the footwear bar. At Grand Wailea Resort, 3850 Wailea Alanui Dr. © 808/875-1234.

The Shops at Wailea   This is the big shopping boost that resort goers have been awaiting for years. Chains still rule **(Gap, Louis Vuitton, Banana Republic, Tiffany, Crazy Shirts, Honolua Surf Co.),** but there is still fertile ground for the inveterate shopper in the nearly 60 shops in the complex. **Martin & MacArthur** (furniture and gift gallery) has landed in Wailea as part of a retail mix that is similar to Whalers Village. The high-end resort shops sell expensive souvenirs, gifts, clothing, and accessories for a life of perpetual vacations. 3750 Wailea Alanui. © 808/891-6770.

4 Upcountry Maui

MAKAWAO

Besides being a shopper's paradise, Makawao is the home of the island's most prominent arts organization, the **Hui No'eau Visual Arts Center,** 2841 Baldwin Ave. (© 808/572-6560;

www.huinoeau.com). Visiting artists offer lectures, classes, and demonstrations, all at reasonable prices, in basketry, jewelry making, ceramics, painting, and other media. Classes on Hawaiian art, culture, and history are also available. Call ahead for schedules and details. The exhibits here are drawn from a wide range of disciplines and multicultural sources, and include both contemporary and traditional art from established and emerging artists. The gift shop, featuring many one-of-a-kind works by local artists and artisans, is worth a stop. Hours are Monday through Saturday from 10am to 4pm.

Altitude   This tiny shop, run by Jeannine de Roode, is a treasure-trove of interesting fashions found nowhere else on Maui, like custom jewelry by Monies (abalone shells, mother-of-pearl, and bone used to create big, big earrings, bracelets, and necklaces) and Hobo bags (Italian leather lined with contrasting fabric). She carries a range of clothing labels like Eileen Fisher, Juicy Couture, Splendid, Glima, and Sazah Arizona. 3660 Baldwin Ave. ✆ 808/573-4733.

Collections   This longtime Makawao attraction is showing renewed vigor after more than 2 decades on Baldwin Avenue. It's one of my favorite Makawao stops, full of gift items and spirited clothing reflecting the ease and color of island living. Its selection of sportswear, soaps, jewelry, candles, and tasteful, marvelous miscellany reflects good sense and style. Dresses (including up-to-the-moment Citron in cross-cultural and vintage-looking prints), separates, home and bath accessories, sweaters, and a shop full of good things make this a Makawao must. 3677 Baldwin Ave. ✆ 808/572-0781.

Gallery Maui   Follow the sign down the charming shaded pathway to a cozy gallery of top-notch art and crafts. Most of the works here are by Maui artists, and the quality is outstanding. About 30 artists are represented: Wayne Omura and his Norfolk pine bowls, Pamela Hayes's watercolors, Martha Vockrodt and her wonderful paintings, a stunning Steve Hynson dresser of curly koa and ebony. The two- and three-dimensional original works reflect the high standards of gallery owners Deborah and Robert Zaleski (a painter), who have just added to their roster the talented ceramic artist David Stabley, a two-time American Craft Council juror. 3643-A Baldwin Ave. ✆ 808/572-8092.

Gecko Trading Co. Boutique   The selection in this tiny boutique is eclectic and always changing: One day it's St. John's Wort body lotion and mesh T-shirts in a dragon motif, the next it's

Provence soaps and antique lapis jewelry. I've seen everything from hair scrunchies to handmade crocheted bags from New York, clothing from Spain and France, collectible bottles, toys, shawls, and Mexican hammered-tin candleholders. The prices are reasonable, the service is friendly, and it's more homey than glam and not as self-conscious as some of the other local boutiques. 3621 Baldwin Ave. ☏ 808/572-0249.

Holiday & Co. Attractive women's clothing in natural fibers hangs from racks, while jewelry to go with it beckons from the counter. Recent finds include elegant fiber evening bags, luxurious bath gels, easygoing dresses and separates, Dansko clogs, shawls, shoes, soaps, aloha shirts, books, picture frames, and jewelry. 3681 Baldwin Ave. ☏ **808/572-1470.**

Hot Island Glassblowing Studio & Gallery You can watch the artist transform molten glass into works of art and utility in this studio in Makawao's Courtyard, where an award-winning family of glassblowers built its own furnaces. It's fascinating to watch the shapes emerge from glass melted at 2,300°F (1,260°C). The colorful works range from small paperweights to large vessels. Four to five artists participate in the demonstrations, which begin when the furnace is heated, about half an hour before the studio opens at 9am. 3620 Baldwin Ave. ☏ **808/572-4527.**

Hurricane This boutique carries clothing, gifts, accessories, and books that are two steps ahead of the competition. Tommy Bahama aloha shirts and aloha print dresses; Sigrid Olsen's knitted shells, cardigans, and extraordinary silk tank dresses; hats; art by local artists; a notable selection of fragrances for men and women; and hard-to-find, eccentric books and home accessories are all part of the Hurricane appeal. 3639 Baldwin Ave. ☏ **808/572-5076.**

Maui Hands Maui hands have made 90% of the items in this shop/gallery. Because it's a consignment shop, you'll find Hawaii-made handicrafts and prices that aren't inflated. The selection includes paintings, prints, jewelry, glass marbles, native-wood bowls, and tchotchkes for every budget. This is an ideal stop for made-on-Maui products and crafts of good quality. The original Maui Hands is in Makawao at the Courtyard, 3620 Baldwin Ave. ☏ **808/572-5194.** Another Maui Hands can be found in Paia at 84 Hana Hwy. ☏ **808/579-9245.**

The Mercantile The jewelry, home accessories (especially the Tiffany-style glass-and-shell lamps), dinnerware, Italian linens, plantation-style furniture, and clothing here are a salute to the good life. The exquisite bedding, rugs, and furniture include hand-carved armoires, down-filled furniture and slipcovers, and a large selection of Kiehl's products. The clothing—comfortable cottons and upscale European linens—is for men and women, as are the soaps, which include Maui Herbal Soap products and some unusual finds from France. Maui-made jams, honey, soaps, and ceramics, and Jurlique organic facial and body products are among the new winners. 3673 Baldwin Ave. *©* **808/572-1407.**

Viewpoints Gallery   Maui's only fine-arts cooperative showcases the work of 20 established artists in an airy, attractive gallery located in a restored theater with a courtyard, glass-blowing studio, and restaurants. The gallery features two-dimensional art, jewelry, fiber art, stained glass, paper, sculpture, and other media. This is a fine example of what can happen in a collectively supportive artistic environment. 3620 Baldwin Ave. *©* **808/572-5979.**

EDIBLES

Working folks in Makawao pick up spaghetti, lasagna, sandwiches, salads, and wide-ranging specials from the **Rodeo General Store,** 3661 Baldwin Ave. (*©* **808/572-7841**). At the far end of the store is the oenophile's bonanza, a superior wine selection housed in its own temperature-controlled cave.

   Down to Earth Natural Foods, 1169 Makawao Ave. (*©* **808/ 572-1488**), always has fresh salads and sandwiches, a full section of organic produce (Kula onions, strawberry papayas, mangos, and litchis in season), bulk grains, beauty aids, herbs, juices, snacks, tofu, seaweed, soy products, and aisles of vegetarian and health foods. Whether it's a smoothie or a salad, Down to Earth has fresh, healthy, vegetarian offerings.

   In the more than 6 decades that the **T. Komoda Store and Bakery,** 3674 Baldwin Ave. (*©* **808/572-7261**), has spent in this spot, untold numbers have creaked over the wooden floors to pick up Komoda's famous cream puffs. Old-timers know to come early, before they're sold out. Then the cinnamon rolls, doughnuts, pies, and chocolate cake take over. Pastries are just the beginning: Poi, macadamia-nut candies and cookies, and small bunches of local fruit keep the customers coming.

FRESH FLOWERS IN KULA

Like anthuriums on the Big Island, proteas are a Maui trademark and an abundant crop on Haleakala's rich volcanic slopes. They also travel well, dry beautifully, and can be shipped with ease worldwide.

Among Maui's most prominent sources is **Sunrise Protea** (✆ 808/ 876-0200; www.sunriseprotea.com) in Kula. It offers a walk-through garden and gift shops, friendly service, and a larger-than-usual selection. Freshly cut flowers arrive from the fields on Tuesday and Friday afternoons. (Next door, the Sunrise Country Market offers fresh local fruits, snacks, and sandwiches, with picnic tables for lingering.)

Proteas of Hawaii (✆ 808/878-2533; www.proteasofhawaii. com), another reliable source, offers regular walking tours of the University of Hawaii Extension Service gardens across the street in Kula.

5 East Maui
ON THE ROAD TO HANA: PAIA

Biasa Rose Boutique   You'll find unusual gift items and clothing with a tropical flair: capri pants in bark cloth, floating plumeria candles, retro fabrics, dinnerware, handbags and accessories, and stylish vintage-inspired clothes for kids. If the aloha shirts don't get you, the candles and handbags will. You can also custom-order clothing from a selection of washable rayons. 104 Hana Hwy. ✆ 808/579-8602.

Hemp House   Clothing and accessories made of hemp, a sturdy, eco-friendly, and sensible fiber, are finally making their way into the mainstream. The Hemp House has as complete a selection as you can expect to see in Hawaii, with "denim" hemp jeans, lightweight linenlike trousers, dresses, shirts, and a full range of sensible, easy-care wear. 16 Baldwin Ave. ✆ 808/579-8880.

Maui Crafts Guild   The old wooden storefront at the gateway to Paia houses crafts of high quality and in all price ranges, from pit-fired raku to bowls of Norfolk pine and other Maui woods, fashioned by Maui hands. Artist-owned and -operated, the guild claims 25 members who live and work on Maui. Basketry, hand-painted fabrics, jewelry, beadwork, traditional Hawaiian stonework, pressed flowers, fused glass, stained glass, copper sculpture, banana bark paintings, pottery of all styles, and hundreds of items are displayed in the two-story gift gallery. Upstairs, sculptor Arthur Dennis Williams displays his breathtaking work in wood, bronze, and stone. Everything can be shipped. **Aloha Bead Co.** (✆ 808/ 579-9709), in the back of the gallery, is a treasure-trove for bead-workers. 43 Hana Hwy. ✆ 808/579-9697.

Moonbow Tropics   If you're looking for a tasteful aloha shirt, go to Moonbow. The selection consists of a few carefully culled racks of the top labels in aloha wear, in fabrics ranging from the finest silks and linens to Egyptian cotton and spun rayons. Some of the finds: aloha shirts by Tori Richard, Reyn Spooner, Kamehameha, Paradise Found, Kahala, Tommy Bahama, and other top brands. Silk pants, silk shorts, vintage-print neckwear, and an upgraded women's selection hang on neat, colorful racks. The jewelry pieces, ranging from tanzanite to topaz, rubies, and moonstones, are mounted in unique settings made on-site. 36 Baldwin Ave. ✆ 808/579-8592.

HANA

Hana Coast Gallery   This gallery is a good reason to go to Hana: Tucked away in the posh Hotel Hana-Maui, the gallery is known for its high level of curatorship and commitment to the cultural art of Hawaii. Except for a section of European and Asian masters (Renoir, Japanese woodblock prints), the 3,000-square-foot gallery is devoted entirely to Hawaii artists. Dozens of well-established local artists display their sculptures, paintings, prints, feather work, stonework, carvings, and koa-wood furniture.

Connoisseurs of hand-turned bowls will find the crème de la crème of the genre here. You won't find a better selection anywhere under one roof. The award-winning gallery has won accolades from the top travel and arts magazines in the country. In the Hotel Hana-Maui. ✆ 808/248-8636.

Hasegawa General Store   Established in 1910, immortalized in song since 1961, burned to the ground in 1990, and back in business in 1991, this legendary store is indefatigable and more colorful than ever in its fourth generation in business. The aisles are choked with merchandise: coffee specially roasted and blended for the store, Ono Farms organic dried fruit, fishing equipment, every tape and CD that mentions Hana, the best books on Hana to be found, T-shirts, beach and garden essentials, baseball caps, film, baby food, napkins, and other necessities. Hana Hwy., in Hana. ✆ 808/248-8231.

7

Maui After Dark

Centered in the $32-million **Maui Arts & Cultural Center (MACC)** in Kahului (© **808/242-7469;** www.mauiarts.org), the performing arts are alive and well on this island. The MACC remains the island's most prestigious entertainment venue, a first-class center for the visual and performing arts. The center boasts a visual-arts gallery, an outdoor amphitheater, offices, rehearsal space, a 300-seat theater for experimental performances, and a 1,200-seat main theater. The center's activities are well publicized locally, so check the *Maui News* or ask your hotel concierge what's going on during your visit.

IN SEARCH OF HAWAIIAN, JAWAIIAN & MORE

Nightlife options on this island are limited. Revelers generally head for **Casanova** in Makawao and **Maui Brews** in Lahaina. The hotels generally have lobby lounges offering Hawaiian music, soft jazz, or hula shows beginning at sunset.

HAWAIIAN MUSIC The best of Hawaiian music can be heard every Wednesday night at the indoor amphitheater at the Ritz-Carlton Kapalua with the **Masters of Hawaiian Slack Key Guitar Series** (© **808/669-3858;** www.slackkey.com). Tickets are $47.

AT THE THEATER

It's not Broadway, but Maui does have live community theater at the **Iao Theater,** 68 N. Market St., in Wailuku (© **808/244-8680** or 808/242-6969 for the box office and program information; www.mauionstage.com). Shows range from locally written productions to well-known plays to musicals.

1 West Maui: Lahaina, Kaanapali & Kapalua

Maui Brews, 900 Front St. (© **808/667-7794**), draws the late-night crowd to its corner of the Lahaina Center with swing, salsa, reggae, and jams—either live or with a DJ every night. Happy hour extends from 3 to 7pm, with $1 drafts and $1 wells. The nightclub opens at 9pm and closes at 2am. Depending on the entertainment, sometimes there's a cover charge (around $5) after 9pm. For recorded information on entertainment (which changes, so it's a good idea to check), call ℂ **808/669-2739.**

At **Longhi's** (ℂ **808/667-2288**) live music spills out into the streets from 9:30pm on weekends (with a cover charge of $5). It's usually salsa or jazz, but call ahead to confirm. Other special gigs can be expected if rock 'n' rollers or jazz musicians who are friends of the owner happen to be passing through.

You won't have to ask what's going on at **Cheeseburger in Paradise** (ℂ **808/661-4855**), the two-story green-and-white building at the corner of Front and Lahainaluna streets. Just go outside and you'll hear it. Loud, live tropical rock blasts into the streets and out to sea nightly from 4:30 to 11pm (no cover charge).

Other venues for music in west Maui include the following:

- **B.J.'s Chicago Pizzeria,** 730 Front St. (ℂ **808/661-0700**), offers live music from 7:30 to 10pm every night.
- **Cool Cat Café,** 658 Front St. (ℂ **808/667-0908**), features live music every night from 7:30 to 10pm.
- **Maui Brewing Co.,** Kahana Gateway Center (ℂ **808/ 669-3474**), has live music every night from 6:30 to 8:30pm (6–9pm in summer).
- **Hula Grill,** Whalers Village (ℂ **808/667-6636**), has live music (usually Hawaiian) from 3 to 5pm and again from 7 to 9pm nightly.
- **Kimo's,** 845 Front St. (ℂ **808/661-4811**), has live musicians Friday to Monday nights and Wednesday nights; call for details.
- **Leilani's on the Beach,** Whalers Village (ℂ **808/661-4495**), has live music from 2:30 to 5pm Friday through Sunday; the styles range from contemporary Hawaiian to rock.
- **Moose McGillycuddy's,** 844 Front St. (ℂ **808/667-7758**), offers a DJ most nights (the schedule varies; call for details) from 5:30 to 9pm.
- **Pacific'O,** 505 Front St. (ℂ **808/667-4341**), offers live jazz Friday and Saturday from 9pm to midnight.
- **Paradise Blue,** 744 Front St. (ℂ **808/667-5299**), features live music or a DJ every night from 9pm to 2am.
- **Pineapple Grill,** 200 Kapalua Dr. (ℂ **808/669-9600**), features Hawaiian on Friday and jazz on Saturday, from 7 to 10pm.

- **Pioneer Inn,** 658 Wharf St. (© **808/661-3636**), offers a variety of live music Tuesday, Wednesday, and Thursday nights starting at 6pm.
- **Sea House Restaurant,** Napili Kai Beach Resort (© **808/ 669-1500**), has live music from 7 to 9pm Wednesday through Monday and a Polynesian dinner show on Tuesday.

A NIGHT TO REMEMBER: LUAU, MAUI STYLE

Most of the larger hotels in Maui's major resorts offer luau on a regular basis. You'll pay about $75 to attend one. Don't expect it to be a homegrown affair prepared in the traditional Hawaiian way. There are, however, commercial luau that capture the romance and spirit of the luau with quality food and entertainment in outdoor settings.

Maui's best luau is indisputably the nightly **Old Lahaina Luau** (© **800/248-5828** or 808/667-1998; www.oldlahainaluau.com). On its 1-acre site just ocean side of the Lahaina Cannery at 1251 Front St., the Old Lahaina Luau maintains its high standards in food and entertainment in a peerless setting. There's no fire dancing in the program, but you won't miss it (for that, go to **The Feast at Lele;** p. 79). This luau offers a healthy balance of entertainment, showmanship, authentic high-quality food, educational value, and sheer romantic beauty. The cost is $89 for adults, $59 for children 12 and under.

'ULALENA: HULA, MYTH & MODERN DANCE

The highly polished **'Ulalena,** staged in the Maui Myth and Magic Theatre, 878 Front St. (© **877/688-4800** or 808/661-9913; www.ulalena.com), is a riveting production that weaves Hawaiian mythology with drama, dance, and state-of-the-art multimedia capabilities in a brand-new, multimillion-dollar theater. A local and international cast performs Polynesian dance, original music, acrobatics, and chant to create an experience that often leaves the audience speechless. It's interactive, with dancers coming down the aisles, drummers and musicians in surprising corners, and mind-boggling stage and lighting effects that draw the audience in. The effects of the modern choreography and traditional hula are surprisingly evocative. Performances are Tuesday through Saturday at 6:30pm. Tickets are $50 to $70 for adults and $30 to $50 for children ages 12 and under.

MAGIC—MAUI STYLE

A very different type of live entertainment is **Warren & Annabelle's,** 900 Front St., Lahaina (© **808/667-6244;** www.

warrenandannabelles.com), a magic/comedy cocktail show with illusionist Warren Gibson and "Annabelle," a ghost from the 1800s who plays the grand piano (even taking requests from the audience) as Warren dazzles you with his sleight-of-hand magic.

The **Kaanapali Beach Hotel** has a wonderful show called *Kupanaha* that is perfect for the entire family. It features the renowned magicians Jody and Kathleen Baran and their entire family, including child prodigy magicians Katrina and Crystal. The dinner show features magic, illusions, and the story of the Hawaii fire goddess, Pele, presented through hula and chant performed by the children of the Kano'eau Dance Academy. For tickets, call ✆ **808/661-0011** (www.kbhmaui.com).

2 Kihei-Wailea

The Kihei area in south Maui also features music in a variety of locations:

- **Blue Marlin Harbor Front Bar & Grill,** Maalaea Harbor. (✆ **808/244-8844**), has a variety of music Thursday to Saturday from 6:30 to 9pm.
- **Capische,** Diamond Resort, 555 Kaukahi St., Wailea (✆ **808/879-2224**), has live music Friday to Sunday from 7 to 10pm.
- **Henry's Bar and Grill,** 41 E. Lipoa (✆ **808/879-2849**), offers live music Thursday through Sunday from 9pm to midnight.
- **Kahale's Beach Club,** 36 Keala Place (✆ **808/875-7711**), offers a potpourri of live music nightly; call for details.
- **Life's a Beach,** 1913 S. Kihei Rd. (✆ **808/891-8010**), has nightly live music; call for times.
- **Lobby Lounge,** Four Seasons Wailea (✆ **808/874-8000**), features nightly live music from 5:30 to 11:30pm.
- **Lulu's,** 1945 S. Kihei Rd. (✆ **808/879-9944**), offers entertainment starting at 9pm; karaoke on Wednesday, live music Thursday through Saturday.
- **Maalaea Grill,** Maalaea Village Shops (✆ **808/243-2206**), features live music Thursday to Saturday from 6:30 to 9pm.
- **Mulligan's on the Blue,** 100 Kaukahi St., Wailea (✆ **808/874-1131**), has live music nightly (times vary). Friday night is a dinner show; reservations required.
- **South Shore Tiki Lounge,** 1913 S. Kihei Rd. (✆ **808/874-6444**), has live Hawaiian music daily from 4 to 6pm, entertainment and dance from 10pm to 2am.

- **Sports Page Bar,** 2411 S. Kihei Rd. (© **808/879-0602**), has live music Wednesday through Saturday starting at 10pm.
- **Tip Up Tavern,** 1279 S. Kihei Rd. (© **808/874-9299**), has live music Tuesday through Sunday starting at 10pm.
- **Yorman's by the Sea,** 760 Kihei Rd. (© **808/874-8385**), generally features jazz every night from 6:30pm onward.

3 Upcountry Maui

Upcountry in Makawao, the party never ends at **Casanova,** 1188 Makawao Ave. (© **808/572-0220**), the popular Italian ristorante where the good times roll. DJs take over on Wednesday (ladies' night), and on most Friday and Saturday nights, live entertainment draws fun-lovers from even the most remote reaches of the island. Entertainment starts at 9:45pm and continues to 1:30am. The cover is usually $5 to $20. Come every other Sunday afternoon from 3 to 6pm for excellent live jazz.

Another place for live music in the upcountry area is the **Stopwatch Sports Bar,** 1127 Makawao Ave. (© **808/572-1380**), which has live music from 9pm on Friday and Saturday.

4 Paia & Central Maui

In the unlikely location of Paia, **Moanai Bakery & Café,** at 71 Baldwin Ave. (© **808/579-9999**), not only has some of the best and most innovative cuisine around, but recently it added live jazz on Friday nights from 6:30 to 9pm. There's no cover; just come and enjoy. Also in Paia, **Charley's Restaurant,** 142 Hana Hwy. (© **808/ 579-8085**), features an eclectic selection of music from country and western (Willie Nelson has been seen sitting in) to fusion/reggae to rip-roaring rock 'n' roll; call for details.

In central Maui the **Kahului Ale House,** 355 E. Kamehameha Ave. (© **808/877-9001**), features live music on Monday, Wednesday, Friday, and sometimes Saturday nights (call for times), from 10pm until close.

Other locations for live music include **Mañana Garage,** 33 Lono Ave., in Kahului (© **808/873-0220**), which has live music Monday and Saturday nights from 6:30pm on and DJs Wednesday and Friday. There's a cover of $10 for DJ nights. **Sushi Go,** in the Queen Kaahumanu Shopping Center, 275 Kaahumanu Ave., in Kahului (© **808/877-8744**), features live music on Thursday, Friday, and Saturday.

Index

See also Accommodations and Restaurant indexes below.

RESTAURANTS

FROMMER'S® CRUISE GUIDES

Alaska Cruises & Ports of Call | Cruises & Ports of Call | European Cruises & Ports of Call

FROMMER'S® NATIONAL PARK GUIDES

Algonquin Provincial Park | National Parks of the American West | Yosemite and Sequoia & Kings
Banff & Jasper | Rocky Mountain | Canyon
Grand Canyon | Yellowstone & Grand Teton | Zion & Bryce Canyon

FROMMER'S® MEMORABLE WALKS

London | Paris | San Francisco
New York | Rome

FROMMER'S® WITH KIDS GUIDES

Chicago | National Parks | Toronto
Hawaii | New York City | Walt Disney World® & Orlando
Las Vegas | San Francisco | Washington, D.C.
London

SUZY GERSHMAN'S BORN TO SHOP GUIDES

France | London | Paris
Hong Kong, Shanghai & Beijing | New York | San Francisco
Italy

FROMMER'S® IRREVERENT GUIDES

Amsterdam | London | Rome
Boston | Los Angeles | San Francisco
Chicago | Manhattan | Walt Disney World®
Las Vegas | Paris | Washington, D.C.

FROMMER'S® BEST-LOVED DRIVING TOURS

Austria | Germany | Northern Italy
Britain | Ireland | Scotland
California | Italy | Spain
France | New England | Tuscany & Umbria

THE UNOFFICIAL GUIDES®

Adventure Travel in Alaska | Hawaii | Paris
Beyond Disney | Ireland | San Francisco
California with Kids | Las Vegas | South Florida including Miami &
Central Italy | London | the Keys
Chicago | Maui | Walt Disney World®
Cruises | Mexico's Best Beach Resorts | Walt Disney World® for
Disneyland® | Mini Mickey | Grown-ups
England | New Orleans | Walt Disney World® with Kids
Florida | New York City | Washington, D.C.
Florida with Kids

SPECIAL-INTEREST TITLES

Athens Past & Present | Frommer's Exploring America by RV
Best Places to Raise Your Family | Frommer's NYC Free & Dirt Cheap
Cities Ranked & Rated | Frommer's Road Atlas Europe
500 Places to Take Your Kids Before They Grow Up | Frommer's Road Atlas Ireland
Frommer's Best Day Trips from London | Great Escapes From NYC Without Wheels
Frommer's Best RV & Tent Campgrounds | Retirement Places Rated
   in the U.S.A.

FROMMER'S® PHRASEFINDER DICTIONARY GUIDES

French | Italian | Spanish

CLOSED
due to
accidental demolition

WEGEN BISSIGEN
EICHHÖRNCHEN GESCHLOSSEN

Κλειστό
Μετεωρίτες

POOL CLOSED

ELECTRIC EELS

プールも 閉鎖中

CERRADO
CABRAS

Hotel
closed for
facelifting

FERMÉ POUR
RAISON
DE GRÈVE
DES BONNES

FECHADO!
POR CAUSA DE
ATAQUES DOS CROCODILOS

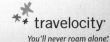

There's a parking lot where my ocean view should be.

 À la place de la vue sur l'océan, me voilà avec une vue sur un parking.

 Anstatt Meerblick habe ich Sicht auf einen Parkplatz.

 Al posto della vista sull'oceano c'è un parcheggio.

 No tengo vista al mar porque hay un parque de estacionamiento.

 Há um parque de estacionamento onde deveria estar a minha vista do oce

 Ett parkeringsområde har byggts på den plats där min utsikt över oceane
borde vara.

 Er ligt een parkeerterrein waar mijn zee-uitzicht zou moeten zijn.

 هناك موقف للسيارات مكان ما وجب ان يكون المنظر الخلاب المطل على المحيط .

 眼前に広がる紺碧の海・・・じゃない。窓の外は駐車場

 停车场的位置应该是我的海景所在。

— I'm fluent in
pig latin.

Hotel mishaps aren't bound by geography.

Neither is our Guarantee. It covers your entire travel experience,
including the price. So if you don't get the ocean view you
booked, we'll work with our travel partners to make it right,
right away. See Travelocity.com/guarantee for details.

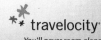 travelocity
You'll never roam alone.